Open Access and the Library

Open Access and the Library

Special Issue Editors

Anja Oberländer
Torsten Reimer

MDPI • Basel • Beijing • Wuhan • Barcelona • Belgrade

Special Issue Editors

Anja Oberländer
University of Konstanz
Germany

Torsten Reimer
British Library
UK

Editorial Office
MDPI
St. Alban-Anlage 66
4052 Basel, Switzerland

This is a reprint of articles from the Special Issue published online in the open access journal *Publications* (ISSN 2304-6775) from 2018 to 2019 (available at: https://www.mdpi.com/journal/publications/special_issues/open_access_university_library)

For citation purposes, cite each article independently as indicated on the article page online and as indicated below:

LastName, A.A.; LastName, B.B.; LastName, C.C. Article Title. *Journal Name* **Year**, *Article Number*, Page Range.

ISBN 978-3-03897-740-7 (Pbk)
ISBN 978-3-03897-741-4 (PDF)

Cover image courtesy of Torsten Reimer.

Contents

About the Special Issue Editors

Anja Oberländer, Dr., is Head of Open Science at the Communication, Information, Media Centre at the University of Konstanz in Germany. In this role, she is responsible for all services, activities, and projects regarding Open Access and Research Data at the University of Konstanz. Since 2007, she coordinates open-access.net, the central German-speaking information platform on open access, and is also leading the program committee of the main German-speaking open access conference "Open-Access-Tage". She is a very active member of the German and European open access community and a member of several working groups at state (OA-Baden-Württemberg), national (DINI-AG-Epub) and European levels (YERUN Working group on open science). At the University of Konstanz, she is responsible for several third party-funded projects like OpenAIRE (EU), OJS.de (DFG), OA-FWM, and OLH-DE (BMBF), as well as for the publication fund by the DFG. She is also very active in supporting alternative open access models and initiatives like FAIR OA and the Open Library of Humanities. Anja holds a PhD in Economics from the University of Wuppertal.

Torsten Reimer, Dr., is Head of Research Services at the British Library and the lead for 'Everything Available', one of the Library's five strategic change management portfolios. In this role, Torsten is responsible for developing the Library's contemporary collections and services for research. This includes both online and onsite services, as well as those aimed at other research and knowledge organizations. A key element of Torsten's work is to formulate the UK's national library's response to the ongoing changes in the scholarly communications environment, in particular open access and open research. This remit builds on previous work experience, for example at Imperial College London, where Torsten was responsible for developing open science services and strategy, working with international stakeholders. He is a member of relevant sector groups, such as the Universities UK Open Access Coordination Group, and the founder of the London Open Access Network. Previously, Torsten managed national research infrastructure programs for Jisc, the UK's digital service provider for higher and further education, and worked at King's College London, the University of Munich, and the Bavarian State Library in roles relating to digital scholarship and scholarly communications. Torsten holds a PhD in modern history from the University of Munich and is a fellow of SSI, the UK's Software Sustainability Institute."

Editorial

Open Access and the Library

Anja Oberländer [1] and **Torsten Reimer** [2,*]

[1] Head of Open Science at the University of Konstanz, Universitaetsstrasse 10, 78457 Konstanz, Germany; Anja.Oberlaender@uni-konstanz.de
[2] Head of Research Services at the British Library, 96 Euston Road, London NW1 2DB, UK
* Correspondence: Torsten.Reimer@bl.uk

Received: 24 December 2018; Accepted: 7 January 2019; Published: 9 January 2019

Libraries are places of learning and knowledge creation. While this mission has been the same for centuries, the way it is delivered is constantly evolving. Over the last two decades, digital technology—and the changes that came with it—have accelerated this transformation to a point where evolution starts to become a revolution.

The wider Open Science movement, and Open Access in particular, is one of these changes, and it is already having a profound impact. Under the subscription model, the role of libraries was to buy or license content on behalf of their users and then act as gatekeepers to regulate access on behalf of rights holders. In a world where all research is open, the role of the library is shifting from licensing and disseminating to facilitating and supporting the publishing process itself.

This requires a fundamental shift in terms of structures, tasks and skills. It also changes the idea of a library's collection. Under the subscription model, contemporary collections largely equal content bought from publishers. Under an open model, the collection is more likely to be the content created by the users of the library (researchers, staff, students etc.), content that is now curated by the library. Instead of selecting external content, libraries have to understand the content created by their own users and help them to make it publicly available— be it through a local repository, payment of article processing charges or through advice and guidance. Arguably this is an overly simplified model and it leaves aside special collections and other areas. Even so, it highlights the changes that research libraries are undergoing, changes that are likely to accelerate due to initiatives like Plan S.

This special issue investigates some of the changes in today's library services that relate to open access.

The shift of focus from procuring scholarly content to becoming a partner in creation and dissemination is shown in an article by Taylor and Jensen. They show how the University of Huddersfield has developed an open University Press to meet the increasing demand for demonstrating research impact [1]. Dealing with the problem that many researchers are in favor of open access but do not deposit in repositories due to various reasons, Daoutis and Montserrat Rodriguez-Marquez discuss the benefits of a mediated deposit approach, such as the one used by the University of Surrey [2]. An article by Walters and Daley shows how data from open science services can be used to enhance publication records [3].

New services require new structures and put new demands on library staff. The article by Bass and Slowe shows how new roles are implemented at the University of Kent through a hybrid matrix working model [4]. The University of Göttingen goes a different way of implementing and fostering open science—through a collaboration with several campus units and a wide range of activities and projects [5].

Two articles in the special issue deal with the financial side of Open Access. Colleagues from the research library in Jülich present a data-driven approach to budget control for both subscription and publication expenditure as an opportunity to enable the shift from one to the other, alongside the establishment of an Open Access Monitor [6,7]. Kohls and Mele describe the conversion of a whole scientific field (High Energy Physics) to open access via an international consortium of supporting institutions [8]. A different perspective is given by authors from the Federal Institute for Vocational Education and Training, who analyze the technical, structural and policy-related conditions of academic research in the context of open access use [9]. Finally, Revez' review article argues that through enhanced research support services, libraries can play a role to sustain an open path for knowledge production [10].

Together, these contributions highlight several facets of the changes research libraries are undergoing, and they set the scene for an ongoing transformation of library services. With growing international support for Plan S, a transition to a full open access publishing model (at least for articles) now looks closer than ever before. Research libraries should not just follow this process but closely shape it, as well—this requires ongoing reflection of and research into our own role.

Author Contributions: Conceptualization, A.O. and T.R.; Writing—Original Draft Preparation, A.O. and T.R.; Writing—Review & Editing, A.O. and T.R.

Funding: This research received no external funding.

Conflicts of Interest: The authors declare no conflict of interest.

References

1. Taylor, M.; Jensen, K.S.H. Engaging and Supporting a University Press Scholarly Community. *Publications* **2018**, *6*, 13. [CrossRef]
2. Daoutis, C.A.; Rodriguez-Marquez, M.M. Library-Mediated Deposit: A Gift to Researchers or a Curse on Open Access? Reflections from the Case of Surrey. *Publications* **2018**, *6*, 20. [CrossRef]
3. Walters, D.; Daley, C. Enhancing Institutional Publication Data Using Emergent Open Science Services. *Publications* **2018**, *6*, 23. [CrossRef]
4. Bass, R.; Slowe, S. Supporting Open Access at Kent—New Staff Roles. *Publications* **2018**, *6*, 17. [CrossRef]
5. Schmidt, B.; Bertino, A.; Beucke, D.; Brinken, H.; Jahn, N.; Matthias, L.; Mimkes, J.; Müller, K.; Orth, A.; Bargheer, M. Open Science Support as a Portfolio of Services and Projects: From Awareness to Engagement. *Publications* **2018**, *6*, 27. [CrossRef]
6. Barbers, I.; Kalinna, N.; Mittermaier, B. Data-Driven Transition: Joint Reporting of Subscription Expenditure and Publication Costs. *Publications* **2018**, *6*, 19. [CrossRef]
7. Arndt, T.; Frick, C. Getting Scientists Ready for Open Access: The Approaches of Forschungszentrum Jülich. *Publications* **2018**, *6*, 24. [CrossRef]
8. Kohls, A.; Mele, S. Converting the Literature of a Scientific Field to Open Access through Global Collaboration: The Experience of SCOAP3 in Particle Physics. *Publications* **2018**, *6*, 15. [CrossRef]
9. Langenkamp, K.; Rödel, B.; Taufenbach, K.; Weiland, M. Open Access in Vocational Education and Training Research. *Publications* **2018**, *6*, 29. [CrossRef]
10. Revez, J. Opening the Heart of Science: A Review of the Changing Roles of Research Libraries. *Publications* **2018**, *6*, 9. [CrossRef]

Article

Engaging and Supporting a University Press Scholarly Community

Megan Taylor [1,*] and Kathrine S. H. Jensen [2]

1   University of Huddersfield Press, Huddersfield HD1 3DH, UK
2   Independent Research Consultant, Huddersfield HD1 3DH, UK, kathrineshjensen@gmail.com
*   Correspondence: m.taylor2@hud.ac.uk

Received: 17 January 2018; Accepted: 22 March 2018; Published: 27 March 2018

Abstract: In this paper we explore how the development of The University of Huddersfield Press, a publisher of open access scholarly journals and monographs, has enabled the sharing of research with a wider online audience. We situate the development of the Press within a wider research environment and growing community of New University Presses (NUPs) where there is an increasing demand for demonstrating research impact, which drives the need for improved analysis and reporting of impact data, a task that often falls within the remit of library and academic support services. We detail the benefits of the University Press Manager role in terms of ensuring professional service that delivers consistency and sustainability. We go on to outline the experiences of engaging with different online spaces and detail the extensive support for student authors. We argue that in order for the Press to support building a strong and engaged scholarly community and provide new spaces for emerging research, continued investment in both platform development and infrastructure is required.

Keywords: open access; publishing; library; journals; monographs; scholarly communications; social media

1. Introduction

New University Presses (NUPs) are on the rise, with at least 17 now in existence just in the UK [1]. The majority of these are publishing open access research via journals and monographs [2], including the University of Huddersfield Press (the Press). Established in 2007, the Press has grown to become a primarily open access publisher of high quality research. Our authors and editorial boards bring international research expertise and a strong orientation to practice and real-world application to their publications. The Press is keen to support emerging researchers and foster research communities by providing a platform for developing or niche academic areas. The Press activities are aligned with the key tenets and identified strategic priorities of the *University of Huddersfield Research Strategy* [3] and all publications undergo a rigorous review process by our Press Editorial Board, in addition to individual journal editorial boards. We publish scholarly journals and monographs across a broad range of subject areas including Music, History, Art, Theatre, Pharmacy, Education, Politics and Literature, and our portfolio currently includes a pioneering student research journal, *Fields: Journal of Huddersfield Student Research* (Fields) [4]. The Press operates a not for profit business model, whereby any potential profits that could be made from monograph sales would be reinvested into the Press to fund the publication of further research.

As an open access publisher, a key function of the Press is to provide support to the scholarly community to aid dissemination of research and to promote the knowledge and skills needed for researchers to successfully engage with open access publishing. Through continually assessing and developing our approach to the publishing process and surrounding community support, we have found that a two-fold approach, encompassing systems development and resource infrastructure, is needed in order to create, support and curate these community spaces. This paper looks at how investing in systems and infrastructure together can help to build a strong and engaged scholarly community. For the scope of this paper, we have focused on five key areas of activity within the outlined approach:

- Developing resources for our community
- Publication workflow
- Support infrastructure
- Online community spaces
- Supporting student authors

2. Developing Resources for Our Community

Whilst the Press is meeting its aims and objectives of providing a platform for research and a support service for authors, the journey is not without its challenges, past and present. Limited resources and an organic growth rate, which can fluctuate unpredictably [5], has made consistency of procedures, documentation and services difficult to maintain. After internal research carried out with a selection of editors and authors, the Press has developed an online resource centre for authors and editors to help improve our levels of support and streamline the work involved in the production process. A space was created on the Press website to house a range of newly developed documents, including the House Style Guide, author license to publish, editor agreement and article template.

One of the main pieces of documentation to come out of this project was the House Style Guide [6]. A scoping project was carried out looking at existing style guides including those from Manchester University Press, University College London (UCL), and Liverpool University Press. From this project key areas were identified which were believed to be of importance to authors and editors, including fomatting, reference styles and copyright guidelines. Once an initial draft was ready it was shared with our journal editors and previous monograph editors and authors for their feedback and suggestions. Community input at this stage was integral to developing a guide which would be able to address the needs of those using it. Following the implementation of this guide we have already seen a reduction in the number of style queries and the level of alterations needed at the production stage.

In addition to the style guide the resource centre also houses article templates, proposal forms, editor contracts and licensing agreements for journal and monograph authors. The legal documents (licensing agreements and editor contracts) have been checked and approved by the University solicitor to ensure that all terms are appropriate and legally sound, giving a reassuring level of protection for authors and editors, and the Press.

Anecdotal feedback from current authors and editors has been overwhelmingly positive, with emphasis on the ease of access of these documents, and the practicality of having them all in one place to download whenever they need them. Having the documents in this online resource centre also ensures that authors and editors are always issued with the most up to date version.

3. Publication Workflow

The organic development of the Press has meant that, whilst the publishing and production workflow systems the Press had in place at the beginning were fit for purpose at the time, they have struggled to keep up with the relatively rapid pace of expansion in recent years. We now have 10 active journals and publish around two monographs a year. With a staff total of 0.6, which is below the NUP average of 1 FTE [1], it is important to have systems in place that enable a professional, efficient and effective publishing process that suits our journal and monograph portfolio.

Developments across the wider research environment, including OA requirements of research assessment exercises and an increasing emphasis on impact, alongside the above mentioned internal resource pressures, have directed the need for change. With academic staff under increasing pressure to demonstrate research impact, not just in terms of scholarly impact but also impact on communities and end users, the need for improved analysis and reporting is continually growing. This increase in demand for demonstration of research impact and environment highlights the importance of properly funded and resourced support within the Library to deliver this across universities and ensure academic staff are well prepared and supported in these needs.

Pre-empting the requirement for this kind of data ahead of the Research Excellence Framework in 2021 [7] has led the Press to carry out a large scoping project looking at the relevant publishing requirements and the range of platforms available that might be best suited to meet these needs. A full analysis of the publishing platform project is out of scope for this paper, but for information the basic requirements identified are listed below:

- Full journal publication platform from submission to publication
- Pre-production checklist
- Integrated copyediting stage
- COUNTER compliant
- Crossref compatible
- Linked with ORCID
- PDF proof production
- High level statistics analysis
- Administration dashboard
- Front end monograph section
- Chapter level metadata for monographs

At the time of writing the Press has identified a platform to address these requirements and details will follow in a second paper later this year.

4. Support Infrastructure

The Press was launched in 2007 as a result of the personal interest in open access of the Repository Manager at the time. Slowly the Press grew in both reputation and number of publications, but it was still being managed as a side project to the Repository Manager's main role responsibilities. The Press Manager role was established by the Library in 2016 in a move to recognise and meet the need for a higher level of dedicated professional resource for the Press. The aim was to create a separate post to the Repository Manager, one which could focus solely on the Press and improve levels of service in addition to expanding operations. This post is funded by the Library budget as a permanent post, and there is a small budget also funded by the Library to spend on book production, marketing and platforms. Currently a 0.6 FTE, the Press Manager has an internal and an external focus in terms of raising the awareness of and developing the Press' portfolio. Acting as first point of contact for researchers who are interested in starting a new journal, transferring an existing journal or publishing a monograph, the Press Manager also has responsibility for active commissioning, raising awareness of open access publishing and developing and evaluating publishing processes, platforms and resources. A large part of this role is managing community relationships with authors, editors, reviewers and researchers.

By investing in this role, the Library and the University are recognising the need for support infrastructure in library publishing and the importance of supporting a professional and informed approach to open access publishing. The role has been strategically created within the Information Resources Team, as part of Academic Services in Computing and Library Services. As a result of this role the Press has been able to establish a wide range of best practice activities that are enhancing the publishing experience for our scholarly community, including:

- Annual review meetings for each journal
- A move to an improved publishing platform

- Tailored marketing plans for each title
- Streamlined sales and distribution processes for monographs
- Social media management and analysis
- A standardised publishing production workflow
- Legal documentation to ensure the rights of authors and editors

5. Online Community Spaces

Through a range of platforms and channels including the Press website, Twitter, Facebook and WordPress sites, opportunities have been created for authors to come together and form a community to support each other, find information they need, and raise awareness of publications. Much of this work has been focused on four key platforms: Twitter, Facebook, WordPress and Jiscmail.

Twitter was the first platform to be utilised as it was identified as a popular social media channel for researchers across a wide range of subject areas. The Press Twitter account is used to raise awareness at Press and publication level via a structured marketing plan [6] which ties in the wider scholarly community by linking to relevant author and organisation accounts. This platform also allows the Press to get involved in national and international scholarly events such as Open Access Week and Peer Review Week, creating opportunities to share resources with our community in these key areas.

Facebook has proved less immediately popular than twitter for the Press, but nevertheless our community is growing steadily and the platform has some particular features that we would otherwise miss out on. In particular, it allows the Press to link closely with the social media marketing campaigns directed at our student research community, by linking posts to our Students Union, Student Alumni and School-specific groups. This proves especially useful in the case of our student research journal *Fields*, for helping to raise awareness across a diverse range of student groups.

The WordPress blog [8] functions as a content hub that other social media platforms can signpost back to. The blog features interviews with authors, excerpts from publications, reviews of relevant events, and posts written by editors. This platform has proved ideal for creating a space where researchers can tell our readers more about their research in an informal discussion style, whilst always linking back to the original underpinning publication to help drive downloads and, ultimately, citations. The Press has followed the model demonstrated by Professor of Digital Humanities at University College London, Melissa Terras [9], in terms of providing enhanced content based around a publication to increase readership and make the work more accessible to a wider audience. In 2017 the Press blog received over 1500 views from across a wide range of countries with the majority of views coming from the UK, US, India and Germany (see Figure 1). The in-built analytics show that the majority of traffic coming to the blog is from social media platforms (see Figure 2), and this has been reflected in the analytics from the Press Facebook and Twitter accounts, which show posts highlighting the blog are highly shared and retweeted.

The new platform mentioned in the previous *publication workflow* section will provide us with further opportunities to analyse how our activity across the above online platforms is translating into downloads and citations. At the time of writing the Press has seen a recent rise in citations to some journals, with *Fields* in particular attracting an impressive three citations to its first ever issue [10]. Future research using improved analytics will enable the Press to look at links between the different communication and dissemination activities and the peaks and troughs in citation levels.

In addition to working to create and curate spaces for author communities to come together, the Press also works with other presses to share best practice in an effort to continually improve our resources and support for authors. Following discussions between the Press and colleagues working across the library and publishing sector, it was found that many NUPs were undergoing similar processes and facing similar challenges, and yet don't always find it easy to share resources or access advice. The Press set up the University Press and Publishing Jiscmail list [11] to provide a space for collaboration and best practice sharing, and to foster a sense of community around university presses. In the 18 months since it has been set up there have been over 60 separate discussions involving over 100 subscribers on subjects ranging from publishing platform companies to ways to manage information and ideas for event management.

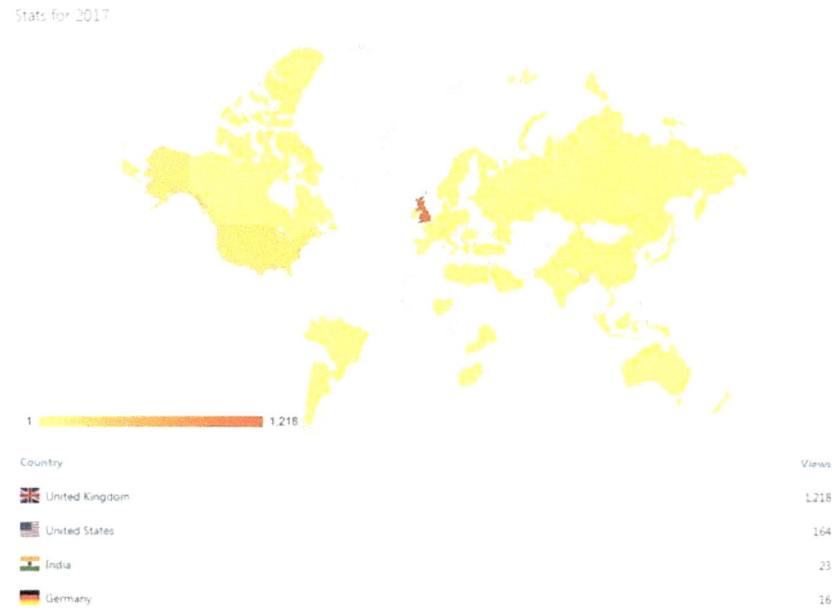

Figure 1. Blog views by geographical location 2017.

Figure 2. Blog referrers for 2017.

6. Supporting Student Authors

In addition to developing author support across the journal and monograph portfolio, the Press also carries out activities specifically designed for student author support as part of our journal of undergraduate research, *Fields*. Most of the students published in *Fields* did not have any previous experience of the academic publishing process so we developed a number of resources and activities in order to support them. This support ranged from bursaries to ensure students could afford the time to edit and rewrite their work, a writing retreat, written resources explaining the process of copy editing and writing an abstract to drop in sessions. After each volume of *Fields*, students were asked to give feedback on their experience and evaluate the activities on offer and we used this to enhance the activities and edit the journal guidance. In addition, all of the students were also encouraged to submit a poster or a presentation to the British Conference for Undergraduate Research [12] and if they did attend they wrote up their experiences as a blog post for the Teaching and Learning Institute (TALI) blog. Whilst *Fields* was launched out of a project run by TALI, the Institute has since closed and future issue of *Fields* are being organised solely by the Press. As a result of this, future reflections from student authors will be published via the Press blog, and promoted over the Press social media channels.

6.1. Publishing as Skills Development

Fields was set up not only as a way to make excellent undergraduate research available but also as to give students an opportunity to develop and hone their writing for publication skills. Activities at the writing retreat focused on what makes a good abstract, how to choose keywords, writing jargon free and more. Additional drop in sessions were set up to offer a second support point and to include the students who were unable to attend the writing retreat so they could raise any queries about the journal requirements.

The main aim of the writing retreat was to get the students familiar with the journal requirements and get them started on writing in an environment where they could ask questions as facilitators were present throughout the day. At the writing retreat the students also had the opportunity to share their research and paper ideas with other students and student feedback indicated that talking to and getting to know student work from other disciplines was really appreciated. In fact, feedback from the 2016 writing retreat included a request for the students to be enabled to form a support community by finding a way to actively share their contact details. This is something that the Press is planning to include in the publication workflow for our next *Fields* issue.

Another feature of the writing retreat is the Editorial Panel. This aspect was included to give the students the opportunity to ask questions about the publishing process from experienced academics. The colleagues on the editorial panel was briefed to talk about typical issues that first time authors might encounter and to offer their editorial perspective so that the students could get a better understanding of the full publishing process.

It is clear from the student feedback collected as part of the evaluation process, and analysed in a previous article published on *Fields* [4], that *Fields* has been very successful in developing academic writing skills. Students had to consider their audience, explain subject jargon and take on board critical feedback from their supervisors, the editorial board as well as the copy editor.

> My journal was based on my final year project report which was a considerably larger body of work; this experience therefore provided experience in extracting key information and creating a more concise article. It also meant I was able to identify what information from my report would be suited to an academic style paper, adapting certain sections to explain terminology and provide context. Writing for a wider audience, with the aim to interest and educate the reader, was a challenge I enjoyed throughout the process.
>
> Nick Horne, engineering student

> I feel my ongoing studies have vastly improved due to the new level of scrutiny I can impose on my own writing and content after working with the *Fields* team so closely to re-draft and improve my work throughout the past year. Attention to detail was never a strength of mine, but this experience demanded a high level of this skill and so I can now apply this both academically and professionally to my other projects.
>
> Katie McAdam, history student

All of the students were proud to be published. For at least one student being published increased their confidence in their own abilities and made a really positive difference to their professional lives.

Having my research published in *Fields* has been the pinnacle of my achievements, particularly as I am working full-time with a young family. It has enabled me to finally believe in my own abilities as a writer and researcher, as well as raising my professional status in my workplace.

Student author

Lessons so far from having students attend a writing retreat have included the importance of icebreaker activities, activities that actively allow the students to apply new knowledge about the journal requirements, space for students to work independently as well as in groups and keeping the environment as informal as possible. It can sometimes be difficult to achieve an informal feel if the event takes place on campus. It is also important to realise that not all students are comfortable writing in a space with other people and this needs to be taken into account.

6.2. Open Access: Making Student Research Available

At the writing retreat we made it clear to the students that the journal was open access and that this meant the content was freely available online and this was further emphasised by the copyright permission that all students signed. It is difficult to say to what extent the explanation of open access meant at this point as students were more concerned with the writing itself. However, a growing understanding of open access in our student authors can be seen in part of a series of Author Spotlight blog posts on the University Press blog [13]:

Open access not only allows fellow researchers, potential collaborators or interested and curious individuals from anywhere in the world to gain free access to essential information and insight but it also provides the researcher with a breadth of demonstrable tools, experiences and skills when seeking further employment, applying for funding or when building a portfolio of work. Allowing free access to research may actually be essential as the arts typically suffer from funding cuts, with some secondary schools recently appearing in the mainstream news for removing music and arts education from their curriculum altogether. Open access publishing not only provides students and researchers with viable methods to disseminate their work but it also expands the opportunity for anyone, anywhere, to gain access to essential inspirational and educational material.

7. Conclusions

The University of Huddersfield Press is part of a growing collection of NUPs within the UK library and publishing sector. There are increasing demands from the wider research environment for scholarly research to be available and accessible to public, private and professional audiences as well as the traditional academic sector [14,15]. Huddersfield, like many other NUPs, focuses on addressing the requirements of the research environment by providing an open access platform that is enriched by a high level of scholarly community activity and support. It is important to recognise that high quality community support requires both investment in systems/platforms, as well as investment in infrastructure. This paper has explored five of the key areas the Press recommends focusing on when providing support for authors: developing resources, publication workflow, support infrastructure, online community spaces and supporting student authors. Further research remains to be done in terms of the processes of implementing a new publication workflow system, and looking at ways in which analytics can help to identify relationships between online communication activities and article and monograph downloads.

Author Contributions: Both authors worked on this research and carried out the analysis and discussion jointly.

Conflicts of Interest: The authors declare no conflict of interest.

References

1. Adema, J.; Stone, G. *Changing Publishing Ecologies: A Landscape Study of New University Presses and Academic-Led Publishing*; Jisc: London, UK, 2017.
2. Lockett, A.; Speicher, L. New university presses in the UK: Accessing a mission. *Learn. Publ.* **2016**, *29*, 320–329. [CrossRef]
3. University of Huddersfield. Research Strategy and Governance. 2018. Available online: https://research.hud.ac.uk/strategy/ (accessed on 17 January 2018).
4. Stone, G.; Jensen, K.; Beech, M. Publishing undergraduate research: Linking teaching and research through a dedicated peer-reviewed open access journal. *J. Sch. Publ.* **2016**, *47*, 147–170. [CrossRef]
5. Stone, G. Developing a Sustainable Publishing Model for a University Press: A Case Study of the University of Huddersfield, 2011–2015. Ph.D. Thesis, University of Huddersfield, Huddersfield, UK, 2017.
6. Taylor, M. *Forms for Authors*; University of Huddersfield: Huddersfield, UK, 2017.
7. HEFCE. The Second Research Excellence Framework. 2017. Available online: http://www.hefce.ac.uk/rsrch/ref2021/ (accessed on 17 January 2018).
8. Taylor, M. About University of Huddersfield Press. 2017. Available online: https://hudunipress.wordpress.com/about/ (accessed on 17 January 2018).
9. Terras, M. Melissa Terras' Blog. 2012. Available online: http://melissaterras.blogspot.co.uk/2012/04/is-blogging-and-tweeting-about-research.html (accessed on 17 January 2018).
10. Jensen, K.; Research by Huddersfield Students is Accessible and Citeable. Teaching and Learning Institute. 2017. Available online: https://theinstituteblog.co.uk/2017/05/24/research-by-huddersfield-students-is-accessible-and-citeable/ (accessed on 17 January 2018).
11. Jisc. JiscMail—Universitypress Home Page. 2017. Available online: https://www.jiscmail.ac.uk/cgi-bin/webadmin?A0=UNIVERSITYPRESS (accessed on 17 January 2018).
12. BCUR. British Conference of Undergraduate Research. Available online: http://www.bcur.org/ (accessed on 17 January 2018).
13. Fox, J.; Author Spotlight: Open Access Publishing and Video Art. University of Huddersfield Press. 2017. Available online: https://hudunipress.wordpress.com/2017/03/23/author-spotlight-open-access-publishing-and-video-art/ (accessed on 17 January 2018).
14. Mudditt, A. The past, present, and future of American university presses: A view from the left coast. *Learn. Publ.* **2016**, *29*, 330–334. [CrossRef]
15. Mrva-Montoya, A. Open Access Strategy for a 'New' University Press: A View through the Stakeholder Lens. *J. Sch. Publ.* **2017**, *48*, 221–242. [CrossRef]

 *publications*

Case Report

Library-Mediated Deposit: A Gift to Researchers or a Curse on Open Access? Reflections from the Case of Surrey

Christine Antiope Daoutis * and Maria de Montserrat Rodriguez-Marquez

Library and Learning Support Services, University of Surrey, Guildford, Surrey GU2 7XH, UK;
M.Rodriguez-Marquez@surrey.ac.uk
* Correspondence: c.daoutis@surrey.ac.uk; Tel.: +44-1483-686-823

Received: 20 February 2018; Accepted: 7 April 2018; Published: 23 April 2018

Abstract: The University of Surrey was one of the first universities to set up an open access repository. The Library was the natural stakeholder to lead this project. Over the years, the service has been influenced by external and internal factors, and consequently the Library's role in developing the OA agenda has changed. Here, we present the development and implementation of a fully mediated open access service at Surrey. The mediated workflow was introduced following an operational review, to ensure higher compliance and engagement from researchers. The size and responsibilities of the open access team in the Library increased to comply with internal and external policies and to implement the fully mediated workflow. As a result, there has been a growth in deposit rates and overall compliance. We discuss the benefits and shortcomings of Library mediation; its effects on the relationship between the Library, senior management and researchers, and the increasing necessity for the Library to lead towards a culture of openness beyond policy compliance.

Keywords: open access; repositories; library-mediated deposit; researcher engagement

1. Introduction

Attitudes and responses towards open access have changed dramatically in the last decade, both among scholarly communications professionals and within the research community. While several initiatives as we know them today stretch back to the early nineties (e.g., the launch of ArxiV in 1991 [1], the CERN preprint server in 1993 [2], and CogPrints in 1997 [3]; the setup of the first open access journals; and Harnad's seminal subversive proposal [4], which influenced significantly the early discourse on open practices), it is only from the mid-2000s onwards, with the emergence of institutional and funder policies, that we start seeing a shift of focus from open access as 'a nice to have' or 'best practice' to a 'must-have' practice, framed by specific guidelines and requirements. This shift is accompanied by changes in the—both perceived and actual—role of the Library in promoting and supporting open access specifically and open research at large.

In this paper, we present a case study showing how recent mandates and reporting requirements have led to the setting up of services designed to take the burden off academics, with the aim of increasing compliance and ensuring efficient monitoring and reporting. We discuss the implications of running a fully mediated service: what are the short- and long-term benefits and drawbacks? Can a fully mediated model co-exist with the evolving role of the Library as the centre of expertise and a major agent of change in scholarly communication? And how does the shifting of responsibility from the academic to the Library affect engagement with open access; does it facilitate or impede culture change?

2. Background in the UK: The Shift from Good Practice to Compliance

In the UK, several developments have driven open access into the mainstream, formally embedding it in research practice. The 2004 House of Commons Science and Technology Committee report on scientific publications [5] was instrumental in making institutions take notice. Central to the report's recommendations was the formal endorsement of institutional repositories as a means to provide free access to scholarly publications. Within a few years, UK institutions responded to both the report and the growing awareness of the open access movement by setting up and populating repositories, raising awareness among academics and drafting local policies or mandates [6]. Surrey was among the first to respond, with a growing repository and open access policy in place by 2005. The responsibility for this sat largely with the Library, resulting in whole new roles or new responsibilities added to existing roles.

These changes opened new opportunities for Library practitioners: roles moving from the mere provision of resources to not only building new, public-facing resources, but—importantly—working with the creators of knowledge to curate, showcase, and publicly share this knowledge. The challenges for the librarian were—and still are—cultural, as well as operational; education and advocacy of open access call for communication, negotiation and influencing skills on one hand, and setting up systems and services requiring technical knowledge and management experience on the other. The goal was to ensure researchers embrace and adopt open practices as part of their research activities; and in this goal, the messages from the Library were key.

Indeed, what is widely called 'open access advocacy' was the main tool for informing researchers about open access, encouraging open practices and populating the newly established repositories. Institutional policies/mandates were also helpful to varying degrees, depending on how strongly they were implemented or enforced [7].

In 2005, the Wellcome Trust introduced the first major funder mandate [8], followed by the publication of the RCUK policy on open access in 2006 [9]. Institutions began to build their policies around these mandates; the open access messages were tightened. However, it was only following the Finch report and the subsequently updated RCUK and HEFCE policies [9–11], effective from 2013 and 2016, respectively, that open access became a widespread requirement; deadlines, rules and exceptions, and proposed processes require that institutions and their researchers comply in specified ways and expect to see evidence of compliance.

From that point onwards, it became necessary for research institutions, particularly their libraries and research offices, to review their policies, platforms and workflows on open access. In the next section we discuss how Surrey responded to the newly introduced mandates.

3. The Case Study: University of Surrey and Open Access

As mentioned earlier, Surrey was one of the first Universities to respond to the House of Commons report [5], by initially carrying out a pilot study in the first half of 2005. This resulted in setting up the institutional repository by the end of 2005, implementing the University's open access policy, and creating a full-time position for a repository manager/open access advocate within the Library. The policy required academics to deposit their published journal articles upon publication and encouraged them to deposit any other research outputs as well; local Faculty policies were also set up to reflect disciplinary priorities. If the policy was not enforced in the first few years, at least it increased awareness and led to a moderate growth of the repository and the service. The policy itself was reviewed and more strongly enforced from 2011, and its messages aligned further with those of HEFCE's in 2016.

3.1. HEFCE's OA Policy: A New Workflow for Surrey

Up to 2016, the Library offered a partly mediated service. Academics logged into the University's publications database (Symplectic Elements) to approve or—more rarely—manually add their publication records and to upload full text for open access. The Library would then check/update the metadata, check the version uploaded, check copyright/seek publishers' permissions, apply any necessary embargoes and make the paper public in the SRI Open Access repository (Eprints).

A significant part of the Library's role in open access was advocacy. At that point in time, this was led by the repository managers, through presenting at Faculty meetings, reporting/highlighting key recommendations to senior management, disseminating newsletters, information packs and online materials, organising/participating in relevant events (OA week, scheduled help desks, festivals of research) and running workshops. It is worth noting that a large part of the advocacy typically reverted to systems and other operational issues, rather than promoting open practices. What staff and senior management were most interested in, for example, was to be shown how to add a record, resolve a technical issue or comply with a policy. This led to the Library being perceived almost solely as a systems/problem-solving service rather than as the focus of expertise in scholarly communications.

In 2016, an operational review on the University's open access implementation took place. The review was led jointly by the Library, the Research & Innovation office and a working group including academics and research support staff from all Faculties. Associate Deans Research and individual academics took part in the consultations. In addition, the Library carried out a functionality review of the systems available. The aim was to assess whether the existing processes would ensure that the HEFCE requirements would be met, and to identify factors that might increase the risk of non-compliance.

The review, which considered a range of possible scenarios, from a fully unmediated workflow to a fully mediated one, concluded the following:

- The setup of Symplectic, which harvested published papers after they had been indexed in databases, did not ensure timely compliance with the Research Excellence Framework (REF). It was deemed essential that outputs would be deposited at the point of acceptance, and it was desirable, for the institution's reporting purposes, that the acceptance date would also be captured.
- Both the consultation with the academics and the review of the systems concluded that the academics engaging with the systems to upload their papers directly involved a high risk of non-compliance.
- Comments from the Faculties strongly suggested that the Library taking over as much of the workload as possible was very desirable.
- A scoping exercise was conducted to develop a business case. Library staff taking over the uploading of the publications was deemed feasible in the short term: at least for the duration of the REF reporting period.

As a result of this joint review, the following steps were taken:

1. From 1 April 2016, academics are required to forward the acceptance notification email, attaching their accepted manuscript, to the Library.
2. The Library is fully responsible for every step of the process, from manually creating records to applying embargoes to updating metadata on publication. This applies to both outputs in scope and out of scope of the REF.
3. The Library, along with the Research & Innovation office, is responsible for raising awareness of the policy and its implications for the next REF.
4. In May 2017, the Symplectic Elements publications database was decommissioned because the institution could not rely on auto-harvesting to comply with HEFCE's open access requirement.
5. As a result, the University's repository changed from a full-text repository to a hybrid publications database/open access repository, i.e., it holds both full-text records and metadata-only records. This led to a steep increase in the size of the repository and an overall increase in the visibility of Surrey outputs; publication records are now public, regardless of whether they hold full text or not. Research dataset records are also public; they are assigned a DOI, but the actual datasets are currently held in other locations that vary by discipline.

6. To meet the resource demands of the new workflow, the Open Access team grew from 1.35 full-time equivalent (FTE) repository manager and 1.5 FTE assistants, to 1.35 FTE repository manager, 1 FTE supervisor, and 3 FTE assistants.

3.2. Effects of the Fully Mediated Workflow

Full mediation was one of several changes introduced in April 2016; the new workflow was part of an implementation package that also included raising awareness of the policy and its implications for the next REF, and strengthening the messages to the Faculties. While, for this reason, the effects of the workflow in terms of deposit activity cannot be assessed in isolation, looking at deposits over a wider range of years allows us to draw certain conclusions.

Table 1 shows the timeline of changes to the service since the set-up of the repository up to now.

Table 1. Changes to the service from 2005 to date.

Year	New Developments (Internal and External)	Repository Staffing	Workflow
2005	• Repository setup • Institutional OA policy • Wellcome Trust OA policy	1 FTE repository manager	Pilot phase. No established workflow, but papers solicited from early adopters.
2007	• Formal launch of repository service. • Local Faculty mandates.	1 FTE	Academic uploads paper in the repository.Library checks copyright and makes the record OA.
2010	Service is divided into advocacy and copyright checking	1 FTE repository manager (shared role)1 FTE assistant	Same as above.
2011	• New CRIS and new deposit workflow introduced at the beginning of the year. • University-wide OA mandate (replacing local faculty mandates) • University deposit mandate strengthened in November 2011.	1 FTE repository manager (shared role)1 FTE assistant	Academic approves and uploads full text in Symplectic.Library checks copyright and makes the record OA.
2012	The Finch report [10] is published.	1 FTE repository manager (shared role)2 FTE assistant[1] plus additional staffing when needed.	
2013	University receives RCUK OA block fund.	1 FTE repository manager (shared role)0.5 FTE supervisor role2 FTE assistants	APC workflow introduced.
2014	• University mandates e-theses deposit. • The HEFCE policy on OA [11] is published.	1.35 FTE repository manager[2] (shared role)0.5 FTE supervisor role2 FTE assistants	E-theses workflow introduced.
2016	HEFCE policy on OA comes into effect.		
2017	• Symplectic is withdrawn; the repository doubles as the University's publications database. • New, fully mediated workflow is introduced.	1.35 FTE repository manager (shared role).1 FTE supervisor role.3 FTE assistants.	• Academic e-mails publications to the Library. Library checks copyright, creates and posts the record. • Library monitors compliance.

In response to these changes, both the deposit rate of new publications and the size of the Open Access team increased in parallel. This increase is shown in Figure 1.

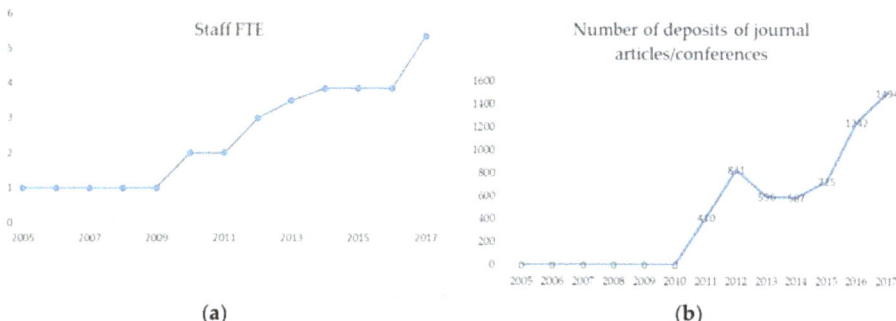

(a)   **(b)**

Figure 1. (**a**) Increase in the number of staff from 2005 to 2017; (**b**) increase in the number of deposits of journal and conference papers with full text.

There were two parallel increases over the years: an increase in staffing (Figure 1a) to meet the increasing demand for Library resources as the open access messages tightened and expectations from academics to deposit their papers became more pressing; and an increase in the deposit of full texts (Figure 1b).

In particular, there were two steep increases in the deposit rate of new publications (Figure 1b). The first one was in 2012, which immediately followed a strong message from senior management to deposit publications. The other was in 2016, which followed both communications from senior management and the provision of the fully mediated service. It can be argued that it is the policy, rather than the workflow, that triggers stronger engagement from researchers.

A compliance exercise, based on publication information from Scopus, estimated that about 45% of Surrey journal articles and conference papers were available on open access in 2014. The same exercise carried out in 2017 suggests a much higher estimate of 73%.

In short, implementation of the HEFCE policy, which included a fully mediated service, has resulted, on one hand, in increased deposit rates and higher compliance and, on the other, in increased staffing within the Library. In the next section, we further discuss the implications of these changes for both researcher engagement with open practices and the role of the Library in promoting and supporting those practices.

3.3. Discussion of the Fully Mediated Workflow: Benefits and Shortcomings

The increased deposit rates are not surprising. There is evidence that the strength of an open access mandate does have an effect both on deposit rates and the latency of depositing [12]. The HEFCE policy is strong both in its timing of deposit requirement and in its use/opt-out conditions, measures that correlate highly with compliance [13]. It can be argued, therefore, that it is the strength of the requirements, rather than the workflow itself, that increases deposits.

However, this does not imply that full mediation itself has no benefits. The mediated workflow has removed a number of barriers (actual or perceived) that affect deposit rates: namely workload, difficulties in engaging with the platforms, lack of confidence regarding publishers' policies,

---

[1] The increase in the number of assistants was a direct result of the push from senior management to deposit full text in the University CRIS.

[2] The increase in staffing was as a result of managing the RCUK OA fund, but also to cope with the volume of deposits and copyright checking.

and an overall perception of any workflow as 'too time-consuming or complicated'. These are the very barriers documented as affecting researchers' engagement [14,15]. Further, the mediated service has helped establish a relationship of trust with the Library which, in turn, facilitates outreach and increases engagement further, in line with previous findings [16]. Consistent feedback from all Faculties also supports this: academics respond very positively to the Library taking over the administrative burden and providing fast levels of service.

At the same time, a fully mediated model increases resource demand within the Library, as reflected in the increase of staffing, especially at assistant level (see Figure 1a above). While this is, at present, supported by senior management, as it ensures compliance, its long-term sustainability needs to be addressed. The number of members of staff is not the only issue here: the roles undertaken at every level of the team are also changing. While, at assistant level, new areas of expertise emerge—in understanding and reconciling various policies, interpreting publishers' conditions, and communicating with authors, to name but a few—additional administrative tasks are also required at manager level, often at the expense of advocacy. Monitoring and reporting compliance, leading technical improvements and liaising with IT and suppliers, as well as managing additional staff, are the most important among them.

Thus, a service led and mediated by the Library, endorsed by senior managers and welcomed by researchers, should be successful at many levels. First, paired with a strong mandate, it does increase compliance and engagement, at least insofar as researchers send the correct versions of their papers on acceptance. Second, by moving administrative tasks from the hands of the researchers to the Library, it helps forge a relationship that could, at least in theory, lead to a more fruitful and interesting discussion on scholarly communication. Third, it places the Library in a position to lead this discussion to foster an open research culture, beyond compliance.

At the same time, this model is proving to be too resource-intensive to allow these opportunities to develop. Institutional priorities seem, at least at the moment, too concerned with compliance issues to place importance on developing and supporting open researchers in the longer term. It is increasingly challenging to plan and run advocacy activities, especially if these are mainly the responsibility of the repository managers whose time is still taken up by managerial and operational activities. With more management responsibility, increasing reporting requirements and technical/operational issues to resolve, the role of the repository manager risks being side-tracked from education and advocacy. The general discussion below addresses how these issues can affect the progress of open research itself, and how they can be overcome.

4. Discussion

In this case report, we presented the implementation of a workflow that ensures open access compliance for the REF and also increases overall deposit rates independently from the REF. We discussed how this workflow, which relies almost solely on Library resources, minimises effort on the part of the researcher while being very resource-intensive for the Library, and how this shift of responsibility leads to the perception of the Library as the main facilitator of open access.

4.1. Sustainability Concerns

As already discussed, a fully mediated service calls for an increase in staffing. While, in the shorter term, this is necessary for ensuring timely deposits for compliance, in the longer term, this is problematic; the larger and more research-intensive the institution, the less sustainable this model is expected to be. One solution to this can be to offer a mixed service, where researchers can opt for direct or mediated deposit; at the University of Edinburgh, some Schools/Departments also have local support [17,18]. Some US institutions also employ students to solicit and deposit content [19]. While these approaches may free up resources in the Library, overall, the model remains resource-intensive and potentially financially unviable.

Sustainability concerns are not limited to financial and operational issues. It can be argued that such an approach runs the risk of narrowing the skill sets of both Librarystaff and academic/research staff. Moreover, this concern extends beyond mere skills; the whole concept of open research risks being reduced to (mediated) data entry, deposit and copyright checking, leaving little room for developing an open culture and engaging with scholarly communication in a meaningful way.

It is therefore advisable, even at universities where mediated services are embedded and well received, to keep reviewing existing processes with a view to a longer-term transition to a more researcher-led model. For this to happen, it is necessary to continue engaging researchers with open practices.

4.2. Advocates or Compliance Checkers? Evolving Perceptions of the Library, Open Research and Scholarly Communication

With regard to institutional priorities, mediated services can be seen as successful, as they support the box-ticking, compliance aspect of open access. Indeed, it can be argued that developing a fully or heavily mediated service is the inevitable outcome of the requirements of HEFCE and other funders. However, there is a concern around what the policies—and workflows that support them—mean for the way open research is perceived and addressed.

Since the launch of the open access policy for REF 2021, open access as a concept started being associated more closely with issues of monitoring and assessment. As a result, the relevant educational messages were also simplified, moving from a discourse aiming at cultural change to more pragmatic 'how-to' guidance[3]. Institutions stand to risk too much by not complying; while, in the long term, researchers actively engaging with open practices is still the desirable outcome, in the shorter term, certain requirements must be met, regardless of how much researchers really understand, or care about, open access. And so it is that the day-to-day responsibility for compliance sits with the Library and the Research office, with the Library becoming, at least for the purposes of the REF, less of an advocate and more of a guardian.

Fortunately, this does not have to be the case. HEFCE itself offers us the opportunity to engage researchers at a deeper level. In its circular letter dated September 2017 [20] in response to the Stern report [21], HEFCE states that "The revised template will also include a section on 'open research', detailing the submitting unit's open access strategy, including where this goes above and beyond the REF open access policy requirements, and wider activity to encourage the effective sharing and management of research data. The panels will set out further guidance on this in the panel criteria". Considering that HEFCE's policy on open access has already contributed to engaging academics with the Library, this new requirement may well further opportunities to change the culture.

For this to be achievable, we need to rethink the way in which advocacy is done. As mentioned earlier, at Surrey this role has so far resided with the repository managers. However, given the already increased responsibilities of repository managers and the heavy workloads of researchers, it is reasonable to question how many advocacy activities can be carried out and, indeed, whether they can be successful in engaging researchers. It is increasingly the case that opportunities to meet face to face are limited and events are not well attended; communicating via email or the website is limited to information sharing rather than dialogue and engagement.

There are at least two ways round this challenge. One involves moving away from 'advocacy' to dialogue, and even debate. Having gained the researchers' trust in offering efficient services, it is time for libraries to offer engagement opportunities, not simply by advocating, but also by giving researchers a voice in matters that affect their own day to day research practices: not only opportunities to champion, endorse, and adopt open practices, but also question and debate them if necessary.

---

[3] An interesting study, beyond the scope of the current one, would be to examine how the online advocacy/information on open access has changed over the years, and how the language used to describe and advocate open access has evolved in response to mandate pressures.

While the sector has been leading the debate for years, e.g., through negotiations with publishers, setting up open presses, open data and, more recently, through the launch of the UK Scholarly Communications Licence, these initiatives, and their relevance to researchers' lives, need to become more visible and accessible to researchers.

The second suggestion, which draws on the principles of embedded librarianship [22,23], involves engaging different parties, within and across institutions, for a more collaborative approach. Although this is already done to varying degrees at different institutions, including Surrey, here we suggest a more integrated, strategic approach that brings together cultures and skills from different areas: open access managers, copyright consultants and subject/liaison librarians in the Library; academics, researchers and support staff from different Faculties; researcher development experts; and key parties in the research office and press office. This not only distributes responsibilities across different parties, but also allows the messages to be shaped more flexibly and innovatively for different audiences and disciplines within the University; multiple voices rather than a single one enrich and facilitate the discussion. Library staff, including subject/liaison librarians and repository managers, continue being the source of expertise, especially to dispel common myths or highlight new developments in open initiatives, but the issues are open for discussion across the University.

Finally, a collaborative approach across the sector ensures consistency of messages while allowing a fruitful exchange of ideas and approaches. An example of this is the JISC open access pathfinder project [24], which has produced workflows, advocacy packs and best practice guidelines that can be used and built on by other institutions.

5. Conclusions

The case report presented here highlights challenges that most institutions and their Libraries are facing at this point in time. Regardless of the deposit model adopted, the tensions around scholarly communication and open access are universal: the mixed perceptions of librarians as gatekeepers, service providers, advocates and experts; the perception of open access as a compliance exercise or as one aspect of a wider culture of openness and transparency with political implications; and the way libraries perceive and reinvent themselves. These are all issues to consider, both collectively and within the context of a particular institutional culture. We would like to conclude with a few general remarks that should hopefully be helpful to other institutions facing similar issues.

First, the feasibility and sustainability of a particular workflow or policy need to be evaluated, not only in financial and operational terms, but also in a wider context. A mediated service will almost certainly become increasingly resource-intensive; however, the additional question we need to ask is whether it will facilitate or impede the advancement of the open research agenda within an institution. At Surrey, mediation has helped embed the Library and plant the seeds for further dialogue. This, in turn, may facilitate a transition to a model that relies on researcher engagement in the future.

Second, while ensuring open access compliance will remain a central priority, it is now up to the Library to build on existing relationships with senior management and researchers and work together towards an open culture: to adopt practices that ensure transparency at every step of the research lifecycle, to recognise and respond to publishing trends and even to engage with the political agenda of open research. Again, the best way to do this depends on local cultures and practices, but sharing and building on these practices is essential.

To achieve this, libraries and their staff must take a central advisory and facilitating role that enables researchers to contribute to the conversation and hopefully shape the scholarly communications agenda. A culture of dialogue rather than one-way advocacy should ensure that engagement addresses numerous aspects of open research and extends beyond deposit activities and compliance.

Conflicts of Interest: The authors declare no conflict of interest.

References

1. arXiv.org e-Print archive. Available online: https://arxiv.org/ (accessed on 18 February 2018).
2. CERN. Available online: https://home.cern/ (accessed on 18 February 2018).
3. Cogprints. Available online: http://cogprints.org/ (accessed on 18 February 2018).
4. Harnad, S. A subversive proposal. In *Scholarly Journals at the Crossroads: A Subversive Proposal for Electronic Publishing*; Okerson, A., O'Donnell, J., Eds.; Association of Research Libraries: Washington, DC, USA, 1995; ISBN 0-918006-26-0.
5. House of Commons Science and Technology Committee. *Scientific Publications: Free for All?* Tenth Report of Session 2003–2004. Available online: https://publications.parliament.uk/pa/cm200304/cmselect/cmsctech/399/399.pdf (accessed on 18 February 2018).
6. Registry of Open Access Repository Mandates and Policies. Available online: http://roarmap.eprints.org/ (accessed on 18 February 2018).
7. Xia, J.; Gilchrist, S.B.; Smith, N.X.P.; Kingery, J.A.; Radecki, J.R.; Wilhelm, M.L.; Harrison, K.C.; Ashby, M.L.; Mahn, A.J. A review of open access self-archiving mandate policies. *Portal Libr. Acad.* **2012**, *12*, 85–102. [CrossRef]
8. Wellcome Trust Open Access Policy. Available online: https://wellcome.ac.uk/funding/managing-grant/open-access-policy (accessed on 18 February 2018).
9. RCUK Policy on Open Access. Available online: http://www.rcuk.ac.uk/research/openaccess/ (accessed on 18 February 2018).
10. Finch, J. Accessibility, Sustainability, Excellence: How to Expand Access to Research Publications; Report of the Working Group on Expanding Access to Published Research Findings. Available online: https://www.acu.ac.uk/research-information-network/finch-report-final (accessed on 18 February 2018).
11. HEFCE Policy on Open Access. Available online: http://www.hefce.ac.uk/rsrch/oa/Policy/ (accessed on 18 February 2018).
12. Vincent-Lamarre, P.; Boivin, J.; Gargouri, Y.; Larivière, V.; Harnad, S. Estimating open access mandate effectiveness: The MELIBEA score. *J. Assoc. Inf. Sci. Technol.* **2016**, *67*, 2815–2828. [CrossRef]
13. Swan, A.; Gargouri, Y.; Hunt, M.; Harnad, S. Open Access Policy: Numbers, Analysis, Effectiveness. *Pasteur4OA Work Package 3 Report: Open Access Policies*. 2015. Available online: https://eprints.soton.ac.uk/375854/ (accessed on 18 February 2018).
14. Kim, J. Faculty self-archiving: Motivations and barriers. *J. Assoc. Inf. Sci. Technol.* **2010**, *61*, 1909–1922. [CrossRef]
15. Troll Covey, D. Recruiting content for the institutional repository: The barriers exceed the benefits. *J. Digit. Inf.* **2011**, *12*, 1–18.
16. Zhang, H.; Boock, M.; Wirth, A.A. It takes more than a mandate: Factors that contribute to increased rates of article deposit to an institutional repository. *J. Librariansh. Sch. Commun.* **2015**, *3*, eP1208. [CrossRef]
17. University of Nottingham's Deposit Policy. Available online: https://www.nottingham.ac.uk/library/research/open-access/depositing-article.aspx (accessed on 26 March 2018).
18. University of Edinburgh's Deposit Policy. Available online: https://www.ed.ac.uk/information-services/research-support/publish-research/open-access/deposit (accessed on 26 March 2018).
19. Confederation of Open Access Repositories (COAR). *Incentives, Integration, and Mediation: Sustainable Practices for Populating Repositories*, 2013. Available online: https://www.coar-repositories.org/files/Sustainable-best-practices_final.pdf (accessed on 26 March 2018).
20. HEFCE. Circular Letter 33/2017. Initial Decisions on REF 2021. Available online: http://www.hefce.ac.uk/pubs/year/2017/CL,332017/ (accessed on 19 February 2018).
21. Stern, N. Research Excellence Framework (REF) Review: Building on Success and Learning from Experience. 2016. Available online: https://www.gov.uk/government/uploads/system/uploads/attachment_data/file/541338/ind-16-9-ref-stern-review.pdf (accessed on 19 February 2018).
22. Dewey, B.I. The embedded librarian. Strategic campus collaborations. *Resour. Shar. Inf. Netw.* **2004**, *17*, 5–17. [CrossRef]

23. Delaney, G.; Bates, J. Envisioning the academic library: A reflection on roles, relevancy and relationships. *New Rev. Acad. Librariansh.* **2015**, *21*, 30–51. [CrossRef]

24. JISC Open Access Pathfinder Project. Available online: https://openaccess.jiscinvolve.org/wp/pathfinder-project-finalised-outputs/ (accessed on 26 March 2018).

Article

Enhancing Institutional Publication Data Using Emergent Open Science Services

David Walters [1] and **Christopher Daley [2,*]**

[1] Open Access Officer, Information Services, Brunel University London, London UB8 3PH, UK; david.walters@brunel.ac.uk

[2] Research Development Officer, Research Support and Development Office, Brunel University London, London UB8 3PH, UK

* Correspondence: christopher.daley@brunel.ac.uk; Tel.: +1-895-265-314

Received: 5 March 2018; Accepted: 14 May 2018; Published: 16 May 2018

Abstract: The UK open access (OA) policy landscape simultaneously preferences Gold publishing models (Finch Report, RCUK, COAF) and Green OA through repository usage (HEFCE), creating the possibility of confusion and duplication of effort for academics and support staff. Alongside these policy developments, there has been an increase in open science services that aim to provide global data on OA. These services often exist separately to locally managed institutional systems for recording OA engagement and policy compliance. The aim of this study is to enhance Brunel University London's local publication data using software which retrieves and processes information from the global open science services of Sherpa REF, CORE, and Unpaywall. The study draws on two classification schemes; a 'best location' hierarchy, which enables us to measure publishing trends and whether open access dissemination has taken place, and a relational 'all locations' dataset to examine whether individual publications appear across multiple OA dissemination models. Sherpa REF data is also used to indicate possible OA locations from serial policies. Our results find that there is an average of 4.767 permissible open access options available to the authors in our sample each time they publish and that Gold OA publications are replicated, on average, in 3 separate locations. A total of 40% of OA works in the sample are available in both Gold and Green locations. The study considers whether this tendency for duplication is a result of localised manual workflows which are necessarily focused on institutional compliance to meet the Research Excellence Framework 2021 requirements, and suggests that greater interoperability between OA systems and services would facilitate a more efficient transformation to open scholarship.

Keywords: open access; scholarly communication; repositories; compliance; REF 2021; Research Excellence Framework; research information systems; UK funder policies

1. Introduction

Described within Suber's seminal monograph on open access [1], the history of open scholarly communication can be traced back almost two decades. The most succinct articulation of the open access movement was found through the 2002 Budapest Open Access Initiative [1,2]. The clear message delivered by this declaration led to the adoption of OA policies at an institutional and funder level, with OA becoming, in recent years, a notable area of focus for librarians, research offices, and funding bodies. Such enthusiasm has resulted in an increasingly complex policy terrain whereby institutional policies exist alongside those of various funding bodies. At the time of writing, the Registry of Open Access Repository Mandates and Policies (ROARMAP) lists 928 distinct policies by research organisations and funding bodies [3]. Most recently, UK institutions have been required to implement the Higher Education Funding Council England's (HEFCE) OA policy for the 2021 Research Excellence

Framework (REF) [4] (from 1 April 2018, HEFCE has been replaced by a new body named Research England). This policy requires all journal articles and published conference papers to be deposited into an institutional or disciplinary repository within three months of acceptance for publication. The policy contains a series of exceptions, which include those papers which have been made OA via the Gold route—a preference for researchers in receipt of the Research Councils UK (RCUK, from 1 April 2018 now named UK Research and Innovation) grant funding [5]. Failure to comply may see research papers ineligible for submission to REF 2021 or researchers denied future funding opportunities.

HEFCE's policy has positively embedded OA firmly within the minds of researchers and ensured that practical steps have been taken to make publications openly available. Some library professionals, notably Kingsley [6], have nonetheless commented on the difficulties in providing local services to researchers within a complex UK policy terrain and the international, collaborative research environment. However, so far, there has been little analysis of institutional repository (IR) workflow interactions with existing channels for open dissemination.

Alongside recent policy developments, there has also been a growth in online services that we refer to as emergent open science services. These are typically global services or platforms, used by researchers and university staff around the world to support research processes, collaboration and dissemination. The '101 Innovations in Scholarly Communication' project [7] documented many of these and demonstrated the proliferation and application of tools and services within various research lifecycles and workflows. Publishers and other private entities have developed some of these innovations while others are publicly maintained and led by research communities and libraries. A number of services enable programmatic access to data, particularly where this concerns scholarly outputs. Typically, REST interfaces enable access to resources, maximising the potential re-use and application of data. Data from these services can be used to provide insights into OA publishing and scholarship.

Commercial products that provide data on OA works include 1findr (1science) and the freemium Lantern service (Cottage Labs) [8]. Non-commercial products include CORE (Jisc/The Open University), the Bielefeld Academic Search Engine (Bielefeld University Library), Dissemin (CAPSH), and the Open Access Button (SPARC). These organisations are based in the US, UK, Germany, and France. OA information is of intense and growing interest to many stakeholders in the global research community.

Three such services were selected to provide data for this study: Sherpa REF, Unpaywall, and CORE. Sherpa REF resources indicate possible OA locations from serial policies. Unpaywall and CORE services aggregate information on OA content and location, for example, of outputs hosted by institutional repository systems. These services were selected because of the size and type of data holdings (for example, OA/publications/serials), confidence in data quality (for example, use in mainstream research and information system tools), and the reputation of the service or organisation provider. The data they hold also aligns with the aims and objectives of the study, described towards the end of this section.

One complexity of the modern scholarly communication landscape is that individual works may be available to be accessed from several 'OA locations' on the internet. Unpaywall describes an OA location as 'the particular location where a given OA article is found. The same article is often available from multiple locations. There may be differences in format, version, and licence from one location to another, even if it is the same article in all cases' [9]. An instance of an OA location may be where it is hosted on a publisher platform or in an institutional or disciplinary repository.

Sherpa REF [10] holds data on specific REF compliance information taking account of REF Panel requirements. The service also holds data about the number of possible OA locations that authors have available when publishing in a scholarly journal or conference proceeding, exclusive of REF policy requirements. Therefore, Sherpa REF data indicates the potential availability of multiple OA locations for a single publication.

Sherpa REF builds on the functionality of its sister SHERPA RoMEO service (Jisc). SHERPA RoMEO is a reputable and heavily used service by the scholarly community, holding data on self-archiving policies for individual journal titles [11]. Sherpa REF is still in Beta, but its data model quantifies machine-readable OA permissions data. This contrasts to the SHERPA RoMEO service, which provides qualitative insights through free-text fields that must be interpreted by humans during a typical permissions assessment process.

CORE is an aggregation service that harvests full-text repository content and makes metadata and outputs available via their API [12]. CORE's repository connector, developed for the OpenMinTeD project [13], means they currently hold the most extensive datasets for text mining Open Access content. CORE data include geolocation fields such as country codes and physical coordinates. In 2016, the authors of this study conducted a 10 years analysis of global OA activity relating to Brunel University, London, using CORE [14]. At the time, this resource indicated growth in Gold and Green OA beyond the visibility of local institutional systems.

Unpaywall was released in 2017 and has been quickly adopted, in part due to the popularity of the related browser extension that provides users with seamless access to OA works, but also because the reuse of the data is not restricted. The Unpaywall service independently monitors content host locations, including Gold OA journals, Hybrid journals, institutional and disciplinary repositories. A study by Bosman [15] applied the availability of Unpaywall data in the Web of Science database to provide a detailed breakdown of OA by type for universities in the Netherlands. Piwowar and Priem (et al.) recently conducted research using Unpaywall to reveal a global 'state of OA' whereby 45% of recent scholarly works were found to be legally available through Gold or Green publishing models [16]. Additionally, a similar study conducted by Universities UK found 37% of UK publications were open access in 2016 [17]. Piwowar and Priem (et al.) comment on the fluidity of OA definitions and different subtypes identified by researchers, and the challenges this presents in delivering acceptable data to the sector [16]. At the highest level, Piwowar and Priem (et al.) define OA as 'free to read online, either on the publisher website or in an OA repository' and 'all articles not meeting this definition were defined as Closed' [16]. Nonetheless, Piwowar and Priem (et al.) also define several OA subtypes to classify data from Unpaywall. These classifications correspond with the terminology used by institutions and funding bodies. These are:

- Gold: Published in an open-access journal that is indexed by the DOAJ (Directory of Open Access Journals—a directory indexing open access peer-reviewed journals).
- Green: Toll-access on the publisher page, but there is a free copy in an OA repository.
- Hybrid: Free under an open licence in a toll-access journal.
- Bronze: Free to read on the publisher page, but without a clearly identifiable licence.
- Closed: All other articles, including those shared only on an Academic Social Network or in Sci-Hub [16].

Bronze is a new classification singled out by Piwowar and Priem (et al.) to highlight the emerging trend for publishers to release 'free-to-read' content while retaining copyrights, which corresponds with Suber's well-known 'Gratis' definition [1]. Piwowar and Priem (et al.) describe Bronze as 'articles made free-to-read on the publisher website, without an explicit Open licence' [16]. This type increases access to outputs by researchers, but paradoxically contravenes reusability benefits advocated by RCUK, HEFCE, and the Charity Open Access Fund (COAF) which drive the UK agenda. The Bronze classification holds properties of the Gold and Hybrid models, in the sense that it is a comparative form of publisher hosted OA. For example, at the time of writing 403 journal titles listed in the DOAJ publish under a 'free-to-read' licence. These serials specify the 'journal licence' as 'Publisher's own licence.' Piwowar and Priem (et al.) discovered that half of 'Bronze' serials were 'hosted on journals that published 100% of content as free-to-read but were not listed on the DOAJ and did not formally licence content', which they refer to as 'Dark Gold' [16].

Piwowar and Priem's (et al.) study was acknowledged by Himmelstein (et al.) [18], where they imply that the universal adoption of a Bronze model by publishers for 'closed' works may remedy the dangers to the ecosystem posed by piracy sites. This landscape presents challenges for automated tools, which can check the access 'state' of papers at the article level, particularly regarding Hybrid publications. For example, works might become freely accessible when subscription journals release content on their platform after an embargo period ('Delayed OA' according to Piwowar and Priem), or promotional access, where subscription publishers enable access to content for a limited period to increase subscriber levels—a current example of this practice is the American Dental Association, who are presently offering time-limited 'free access' to the *Journal of Prosthodontists* [19]. Piwowar and Priem's (et al.) results may suggest that the monitoring of OA data should be continuous to track publisher activities and ensure perpetual access to research where reuse rights are restricted. We applaud the authors for bringing great attention to this issue and agree that longitudinal research should be undertaken on a global scale to assess these trends. The availability of the Unpaywall dataset through a REST API and other mechanisms [20] enables this level of scrutiny without manual effort, at different levels of scale.

A recent study by Martín-Martín (et al.) [21] utilised Google Scholar (GS) as a source of data to analyse OA levels across all countries and fields of research. Data from GS is extracted with difficulty because GS does not maintain a public API. Martín-Martín (et al.) discovered OA levels comparable with other recent studies in the field, but they also provide new insights on the open availability of research through other routes—mainly due to the academic social network ResearchGate, but also personal websites and harvesters. They discovered 23.1% available as Gold, Hybrid, Delayed, or Bronze OA, 17.6% available as Green OA and 40.6% available from other sources. The study is a further indication of the multiple host locations available to researchers when disseminating their work. This study aims to enhance Brunel University London's publication data by using software to retrieve and process data from open science services. The data produced develops from previous studies by exploring the complexities in OA choice for authors wishing to submit papers and also investigates OA volume and multiplicity. This encompasses the following objectives:

- Create OA classification schemes to interpret the data; a 'best location' hierarchy to measure publishing trends and whether open access dissemination has taken place, and a relational 'all locations' dataset to examine whether individual publications appear across multiple OA dissemination models.
- Investigate possible OA locations from serial policies described in Sherpa REF resources.
- Investigate OA locations from CORE resources and plot the geolocation of works.
- Investigate OA locations and volume from related Unpaywall and CORE resources.

From the data and classifications, this paper explores if local institutional systems capture the full range of OA publishing activity made visible by these new services and considers whether a more vibrant picture of OA activity may be recorded. HEFCE's policy emphasises the importance of on-acceptance deposit for manuscripts and metadata for discoverability. We, therefore, apply the data capture methodology and classifications to published and accepted research outputs in the sample to provide a comparative view of OA dissemination by Brunel researchers at the point of acceptance in addition to publication.

This research is important because UK higher education institutions (HEI) are currently seeking to accurately report on both Green and Gold OA activities by their researchers. Additionally, a comprehensive understanding of OA behaviours amongst researchers is crucial for institutions as they seek to provide tailored scholarly communication training and services to their academic staff. Localised and manual processes, which are detailed and resource intensive, are currently necessary to provide an institutional picture of OA compliance. This study explores how the adoption of emerging open science services that hold OA metadata and manifestations may streamline processes and reduce the administrative burden for academics and support staff.

The data generated highlights wide-ranging engagement with OA across a variety of models. However, it also indicates potential duplication of effort in OA workflows with single publications appearing in multiple locations. From the data, we consider whether current workflows—and particularly those surrounding HEFCE's OA Policy—may assume such heavy focus on local IRs that they do not entirely register other methods for compliance such as deposits within disciplinary repositories, the IRs of co-authors, or Gold routes. From an institutional perspective, the intense focus on IRs is understandable as this currently provides the most robust and controllable mechanism for reporting on compliance levels at a given institution. This paper does not, therefore, criticise UK institutions for their responses to the current policy environment, but instead investigates how new open science services can be applied to increase the accuracy of institutional reporting on OA compliance, especially in helping to validate existing manual work undertaken by library staff.

2. Materials and Methods

Brunel University London manages a Symplectic Elements Current Research Information System (CRIS) to record all publication and research activity by the organisation. The system links data from authority sources including ORCID, CrossREF, Scopus, and Web of Science. Records may also be input manually, thereby increasing the local visibility of research activity for disciplines where coverage in authority sources is incomplete. For the study, the institution provided a data sample from their Elements system; the complete set of journals articles and conference proceedings from the period January 2014 to December 2017. This comprised outputs of 5570 published and 403 accepted works. There is more data available for the on-publication view as the organisation began collecting on-acceptance metadata in 2016 to coincide with the activation of HEFCE's OA policy. Works are defined as published when they have an early-online or publication issue date in the metadata. Works are defined as accepted, when they have no publication date, but have included a date of acceptance. Data were retrieved from the open science services using attributes from the Brunel sample by a small software program customised by the authors.

The Elements dataset contains some OA data attributes used in the analysis. These are:

- DOAJ; matched on ISSN
- SHERPA RoMEO; identifies publisher policy 'banding', matched on ISSN
- Records and file locations from some large repositories; Europe PMC, ArXiv
- Deposits in local IR (Brunel University Research Archive)

Sherpa REF service data provides possible OA locations from journals in the sample. We investigate only possible locations that enable OA and ignore embargo, cost, or funder policy restrictions. We omit 'submitted' article version types from the results due to the community focus on accepted/published versions. CORE service data identifies OA locations and provides additional location information such as the names of host resources where Brunel content is held and geolocation data.

Unpaywall service data identify a 'best' OA location hierarchy. Unpaywall qualifies a 'best' OA location for an OA work by prioritising publisher-hosted content first (for example, Hybrid or Gold), and then versions closest to the version of record [9]. A 'best location' can help libraries answer the typical compliance question of 'is it Gold or Green?' All location objects that relate to works are retrieved from the service to ascertain the total OA volume. 'Closed' access publications are inferred where there is no discoverable OA location from any data source.

Using a small Java SE software program [22], attributes from the data sample (DOIs and serial ISSNs) provided the inputs to retrieve resources from the Unpaywall, CORE, and Sherpa REF REST APIs and return OA data at the article or serial level. The software manages data in the publication and open access domain. The software replicates data from adjacent systems (that is, business systems like Symplectic Elements) and uses data attributes to make HTTP requests and access the resources of

OA RESTful web services. This data is persisted in a MySQL relational database using the Hibernate framework [23]. Entities and relationships are described in the data model in Figure 1.

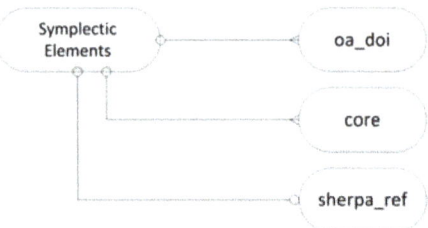

Figure 1. The conceptual data model, showing all entities and relationships used in the data analysis. Unpaywall stopped using the OaDOI brand in January 2018, after the data for this study was collected.

All software [24] and related data outputs [25] produced during the study are published online and described in the Supplementary Data Section. Data analyses are the product of SQL relational queries on the MySQL database. For example, one SQL query produced an enhanced OA publication dataset by joining the Elements, CORE, and Unpaywall entities together in a relational query [26]. Logical conditions test attribute values and this identifies the type of OA according to the classifications defined in the methodology outlined below. As mentioned in the Introduction, the study uses two classification schemes; 'best location', which highlights publishing trends and whether OA dissemination has taken place, and 'all locations', indicating the multiplicity of works across OA dissemination models.

The 'best location' classification extends Unpaywall's definitions but with some fundamental differences between the Gold, Green, and Closed access subtypes (see Table 1). The types enable us to measure publishing trends and open access dissemination.

Table 1. The open access classification (1) by 'best' available location.

Hierarchy	Classification (1): "Best Location"	Description
1	Gold	A publisher hosted 'Gold' OA location
2	Hybrid	A publisher hosted 'Hybrid' OA location
3	Green (External)	A repository hosted OA location (external system)
4	Green (Brunel IR)	A repository hosted OA location (Brunel IR)
5	Closed (Green option)	The paper is not OA, but a Green OA option is available
6	Closed (publisher)	The paper is not OA, and no Green OA option is available

Like Unpaywall, we monitored the OA publisher content first (Gold OA and Hybrid), followed by external disciplinary and institutional repository locations and, finally, Brunel's institutional repository.

Unpaywall data does not explicitly distinguish Bronze OA from Gold and Hybrid classifications in its API. Rather, it attributes it in its data model (including host location descriptors, publication licences, and Gold journal indicators) and enables these types to be derived. For example, the service matches Gold locations by ISSN entries in the DOAJ. The API documentation says that this indicator for Gold OA journals is 'useful for most definitions of Gold OA. Currently this is based entirely on the inclusion in the DOAJ but eventually may use additional ways of identifying all-OA journals' [9]. In our method, we subsume Piwowar and Priem's (et al.) Bronze classification within the Gold and Hybrid types because Bronze characteristics are prevalent within both publishing models, that is, documents that are free-to-read from the publisher, but do not have an explicit OA licence. As discussed in the introduction, we do not wish to conflate Bronze with Gold or Hybrid OA. Therefore, in this study, we examine the licence data retrieved by the Unpaywall service to inform our discussions on any Bronze OA characteristics displayed by publications in the sample.

SHERPA RoMEO data, sourced within Elements, use a Yellow and Green banding scheme for serial titles, which is used to indicate whether an archival option for peer-reviewed content is available. Otherwise, we consider no compliant archival option as available. In this way, RoMEO data distinguishes closed access works between 'publisher' and 'author,' that is, where a journal policy prohibits archiving and where an author has apparently failed to take up a possible Green OA location. This distinction can help libraries target researchers to achieve OA where this is possible and highlight publisher stakeholders who are not engaged in the movement. The 'best location' classification is derived from the dataset by comparing the values of OA attributes from the various data sources. Supplementary Data [27] describes the tests performed against the attributes to derive the classification.

Unpaywall data describes unique publisher host locations and the multiplicity of repository hosts as location objects. The total number of location objects enable an OA 'count' of published works. To distinguish disciplinary repositories and IR locations, we excluded outputs found by Unpaywall that have an oai:bura identifier (of Brunel's local IR—the Brunel University Research Archive). We instead use internal records via Elements to measure engagement with Brunel's IR. This is due to embargoed works not being returned by Unpaywall and because the aim of this study is to maximise the identification of OA locations.

By establishing a comprehensive, relational dataset on all OA publishing activity discovered by the services, we can describe an 'all location' classification to explore the possible effects of UK's Gold and Green policies (see Table 2):

Table 2. The open access classification (2) by all available locations.

Classification (2): "All Locations"	Description
Gold	A publisher hosted OA location ('Gold'/'hybrid') and no repository OA locations
Gold and Green	A publisher hosted OA location ('Gold'/'hybrid') and 1 or more repository OA locations ('External'/'Brunel IR')
Green	No publisher hosted OA location and 1 or more repository OA locations ('External'/'Brunel IR')

From this data and the classification schema, we may infer whether duplication is evident in OA dissemination for Brunel University London. UK funder policies may encourage this outcome because in combination they preference both publisher (RCUK) and IR (HEFCE) OA locations and this effect may be exacerbated by research collaborations across institutions and territories. The variance in publisher archival policies may also increase the likelihood of multiple OA locations for a single work.

3. Results

This section is partitioned by the data and analyses of the specific open science services used in the study.

3.1. Sherpa REF Data

The Sherpa REF data highlights the scale of possible OA locations available to authors when making dissemination decisions for their research. The Brunel data sample comprised of 5570 published journal articles and conference proceedings; 4475 records had ISSN or ESSN attributes. Of these, there were 2154 distinct serial ISSN or ESSNs. Sherpa REF returned 1808 records. The service covered 84% of serials in the sample.

The possible locations derive from the 'route', 'version', and 'type' attributes within the data. Combining these values reveals the count and description of possible locations that may be selected by authors and that are described by publisher policies:

- Open access 'route': 'Publish', 'Hybrid', and 'Archive', which refer to 'Gold', 'Hybrid', and 'Green' OA publishing models respectively
- Article 'version': Accepted or Published

- Repository 'type': Disciplinary, Institutional, Other.

From the serials in the sample, the most common OA location is the archiving of an accepted manuscript into an institutional repository. The results demonstrate that many publisher policies align with the requirements of UK funding bodies. However, the data shows 34 total OA scenarios for authors [28]. There is an average of 4.767 permissible open access options in the publications selected by our authors. A total of 6% of titles had 8 or more possible OA locations available to authors. Additionally, 99% of journals in the sample had at least two possible OA locations. As shown in Table 3, a small number of publications had as many as 13 possible OA locations, such as the *Journal of Applied Physics* (0021-8979).

Table 3. The Sherpa REF results: open access dissemination options for the *Journal of Applied Physics* (AIP Publishing).

Count	Sherpa REF Results
1	Archive, Accepted Version, Author Website
2	Archive, Accepted Version, Department website
3	Archive, Accepted Version, Institutional Repository
4	Archive, Accepted Version, Other
5	Archive, Accepted Version, Disciplinary repository
6	Archive, Published Version, Author Website
7	Archive, Published Version, Department website
8	Archive, Published Version, Institutional Repository
9	Archive, Published Version, Other
10	Archive, Published Version, Disciplinary repository
11	Hybrid, Published Version, Author Website
12	Hybrid, Published Version, Institutional Repository
13	Hybrid, Published Version, Disciplinary repository

The results may indicate that authors are engaged in many OA workflows, given the availability of options per publishing policy. The number of institutions and authors involved in collaborations may increase this possibility. We conclude that the complexities and range of publisher policies, combined with funder and institutional policies, may create opportunities for duplication in OA locations.

3.2. CORE Data

CORE data finds multiple OA locations hosting content affiliated to Brunel University London. The data shows 131 hosts with Brunel research holdings [29]. The service found 1894 OA locations for 1073 distinct publications. CORE records contain additional geolocation data, enabling physical host locations to be plotted on a map.

Figure 2a plots data from repository hosts, which tend to include coordinates specifying the physical location of the institution or repository. Readers of this study may wish to access the interactive online publication of this map, which plots the coordinates along with the names of OA works and host locations—see Supplementary Data 'Collection B: Artefacts'.

Figure 2b,c plots data from publisher hosts, which tend to include country code data, assumed to reflect their general base of operations. This data is available here and published online [29–31]. The visualisations provide some insight into the global distribution of Brunel's research.

The highest concentration of OA locations is in European territories. The results show collaboration in OA dissemination, likely reflecting the international research process and author networks. The results discovered 370 distinct works in multiple OA locations. CORE found one publication, 'Improving the experience of dementia and enhancing active life-living well with dementia: Study protocol for the IDEAL study' (2014), available in 9 OA locations. This data may be incomplete because the service harvests only full-text PDF content from hosts and no other document formats. For example, a Google Scholar search for this paper finds 24 OA locations.

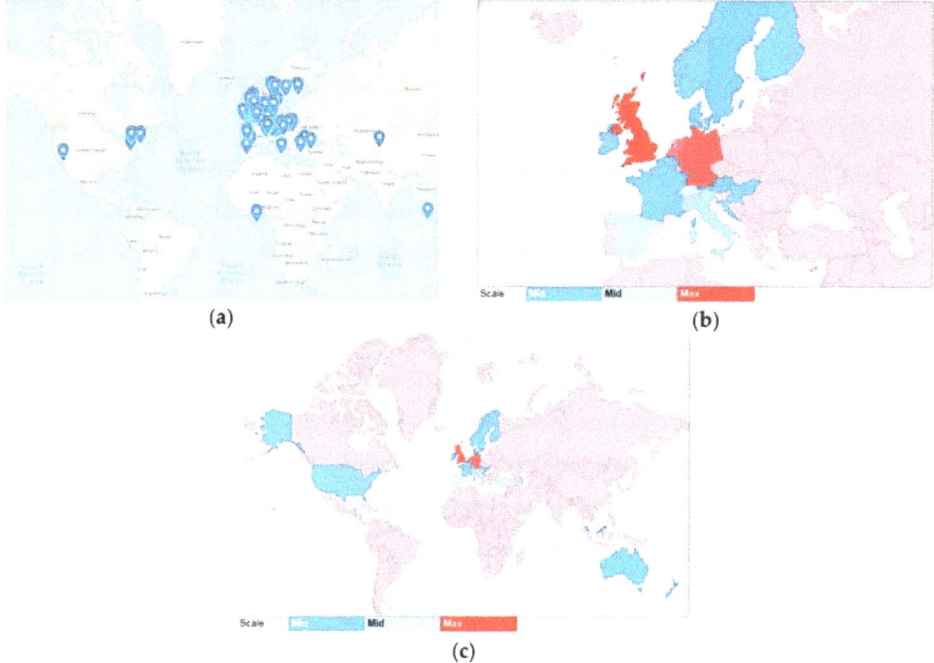

Figure 2. The geolocation data for Brunel publications found within CORE (**a**) Brunel publications by repository host locations (latitude and longitude coordinates); (**b**) Brunel publications by repository host locations in Europe (country code); (**c**) Brunel publications by repository host locations globally (country code).

3.3. Enhanced Publications Dataset and Unpaywall Data

The results in this section describe Brunel's institutional sample enhanced by open science services [32]. This combined Unpaywall, CORE and Elements data to investigate complete OA locations for the institution's research.

Unpaywall found 1589 publisher hosts with OA locations and 1563 repository hosts [33]. The results also show collaboration in OA dissemination. A total of 821 publications were discoverable in multiple OA locations. In this data, the most highly replicated paper was from the CMS collaboration entitled 'Search for pair production of excited top quarks in the lepton+ jets final state', which was available in 9 OA locations. Like CORE, we found that this data may also be incomplete. A comparison with search results from Google Scholar for this paper finds 57 OA locations.

3.3.1. 'Best Location' Classification Data

Using the 'best available' OA classification scheme, we produced a data set of 5973 institutional publication records enhanced using Unpaywall data [32]. An 'on-publication' view shows increasing trends of Gold, Hybrid, and Green. Figure 3a shows an increase mainly in the IR deposit and Hybrid publications in 2017. Gold levels appear stable across time.

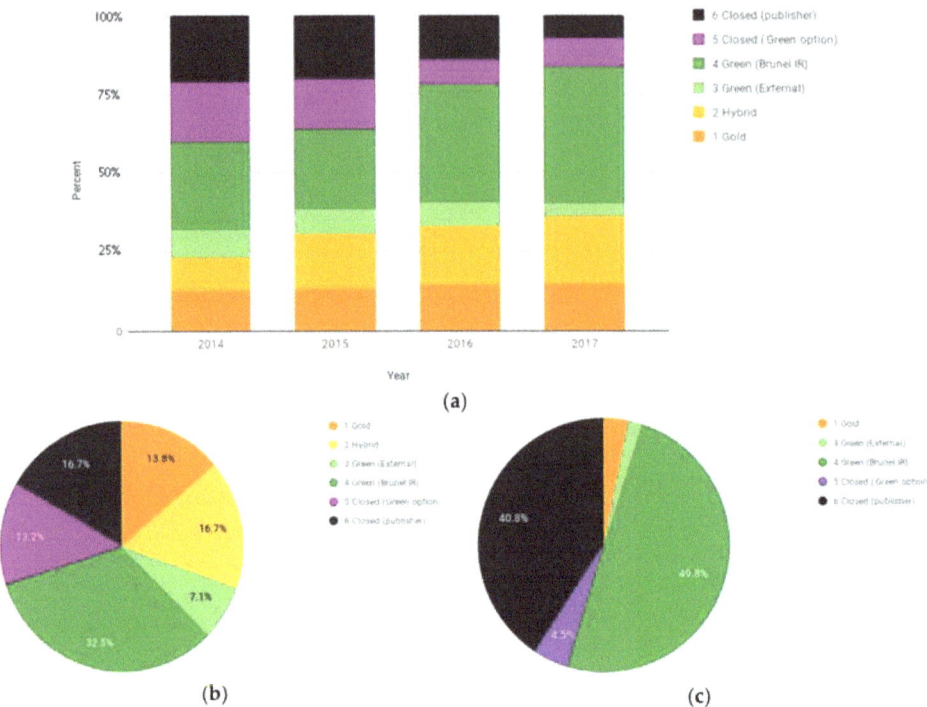

Figure 3. The enhanced publication dataset ("Best available" classification) 2014–2017, (**a**) Brunel OA dissemination by year (percentages on publication); (**b**) Brunel OA dissemination 2014–2017 (percentages on publication); (**c**) Brunel OA dissemination 2014–2017 (percentages on acceptance).

Figure 3a,b show that the institution has levels of OA consistently higher than Piwowar and Priem's (et al.) global baseline of 45% OA for recent works [16]. A small subset of publications require action to be made Green open access—that is where Sherpa RoMEO indicates a compliant archival option and where an OA location has not been established.

Figure 3b,c show the comparative view of OA for published and accepted works, respectively, from the sample of enhanced records. The 'on publication' view shows 13% with a possible Green OA location apparently not taken by the authors—in 2016 (when HEFCE's policy became active), this was just 7.7%. Comparatively, the 'on acceptance' view indicates a much-reduced volume and diversity of OA dissemination. This may be because manual entries made by authors, to meet institutional compliance workflows, lack the critical attributes that enable the automated, hierarchical checks that are possible on publication, such as DOIs and ISSNs.

Unpaywall data include OA publishing licences across publisher and repository hosts. Figure 4a shows the 'Creative Commons with Attribution' (CC-BY) as the dominant licence selected for Gold and Hybrid works, which may indicate the impact of UK and European funder policies. Nonetheless, many demonstrate Bronze OA properties with some publishers clearly retaining rights [32] (see 'Elsevier specific: OA user licence'), and others where licences cannot be established (see 'Implied-OA'). We found that 28% of Gold or Hybrid works in the sample are available with Bronze OA characteristics, as described by Piwowar and Priem (et al.) [16].

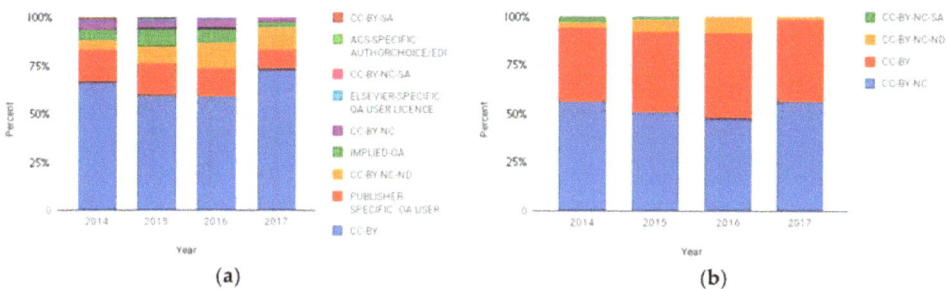

Figure 4. Unpaywall: Licence adoption by publisher and repository host locations: (**a**) publisher licences; (**b**) repository licences.

Of the 1563 repository host locations returned by the Unpaywall service, 1122 did not return any licence data [33]. This accounts for 71% of repository hosted OA locations found by Unpaywall. Figure 4b shows that where this data was identifiable by the service, non-commercial licences are the most widely adopted. The lack of Green repository licences suggests there may be difficulties in Unpaywall identifying these or it may indicate that repositories adopt stricter licences on reuse than the RCUK and COAF standards. Where copyright allows, the Brunel University Research Archive applies a CC-BY licence to deposits.

3.3.2. 'All Location' Classification Data

The 'all location' OA classification scheme [32] demonstrates the effect of Gold and Green policies on access workflows. Total OA locations for individual published works are also extracted from the data.

Figure 5 shows that 40% of OA outputs are available in Gold and Green host locations. Most Gold published outputs are available in other Green locations.

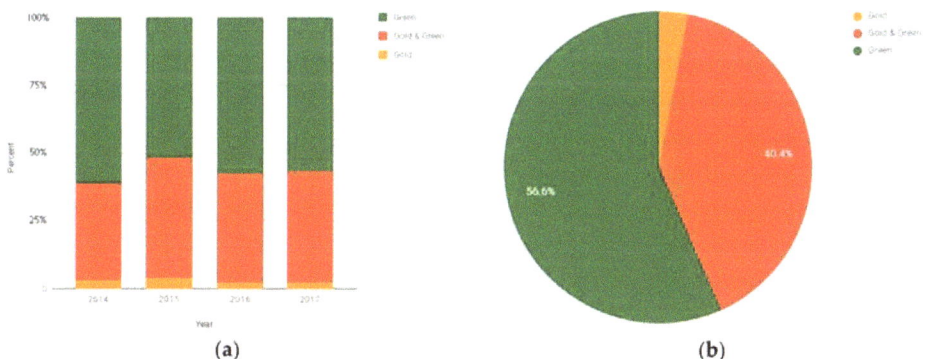

Figure 5. The enhanced publication dataset ('All location' classification) 2014–2017, (**a**) Brunel OA dissemination by year (percentages on publication); (**b**) Brunel OA dissemination 2014–2017 (percentages on publication).

Figure 6a shows a comparison of the total OA locations against the count of distinct publications. There appears to be a significant volume of OA locations where Gold and Green hosts are available. In this scenario there is an average replication of OA works in 2.78 locations.

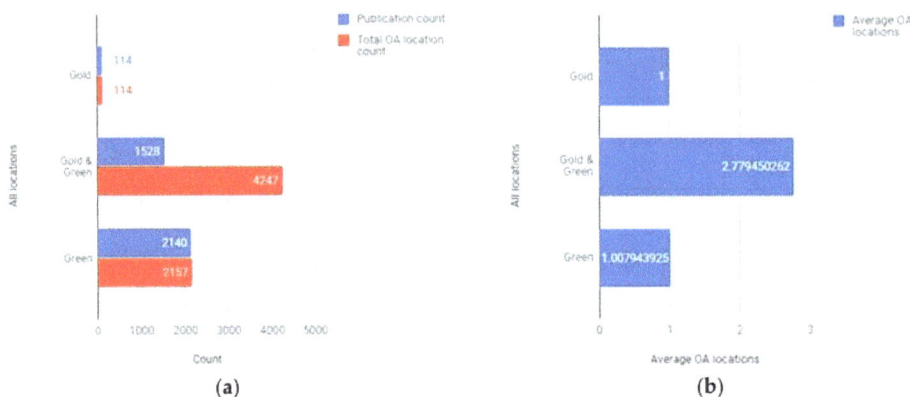

Figure 6. The total OA locations ('All location' classification) 2014–2017, (**a**) total OA locations; (**b**) average OA locations.

Figure 7 repeats this approach using the 'best location' classification. This shows Gold publications with the highest levels of replication, with an average availability of 3.08 locations. Hybrid has an average availability of 2.3 locations. The data on exclusive Green publications does not indicate any duplication.

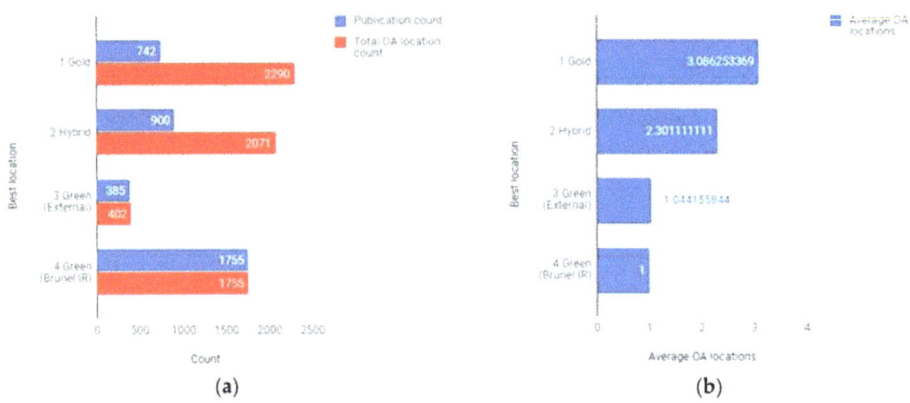

Figure 7. The total OA locations ('Best available' classification) 2014–2017, (**a**) total OA locations; (**b**) average OA locations.

In combination, the figures show a significant proportion of outputs singularly available via Green locations—which underlines the importance of the HEFCE OA policy and the repository networks—and a significant replication where a Gold publication has taken place.

4. Discussion

This study aimed to enhance Brunel University London's publication records using data from open science services. The results show high levels of OA for the institution. The results also reveal OA activity external to institutional systems. This study resultantly contributes to two broad discussions for UK university staff involved in OA compliance reporting and service delivery.

Firstly, dialogue may focus on localised systems and whether they can be wholly relied upon to provide an accurate picture of OA behaviours amongst academic staff. Secondly, this study's ability to use emergent open science services to enhance institutional data suggests that there may be the opportunity for greater interoperability between emerging services such as Unpaywall, CORE and Sherpa REF and established providers of IRs and research information systems.

An objective of the study was to investigate possible OA locations from serial policies described in related Sherpa REF resources. This provided insight into the complexities of OA choice prior to OA dissemination. The data in Section 3.1 demonstrates that authors have multiple OA options available to them, which can be attributed to the success of the OA movement in producing a range of platforms for the open dissemination of research. The variety of dissemination channels available may increase the likelihood of duplication, with multiple versions of any given paper potentially existing on a mixture of disciplinary repositories, IRs, social platforms and publisher websites. Some publications in the sample offer as many as 13 possible OA locations for peer-reviewed works.

This study also generated a 'best location' hierarchy to measure publishing trends and to determine whether open access dissemination had taken place, and a relational 'all locations' dataset to examine whether individual publications appear across multiple OA dissemination models. As set out in the introduction, there are challenges when classifying OA works, particularly in light of Piwowar and Priem's (et al.) Bronze OA definition. In Section 3.3.1 we used licence data to investigate reuse trends across Gold and Hybrid types. The results may indicate a positive, cultural impact of RCUK policy as CC-BY is the dominant licence selected for Gold and Hybrid works.

However, as with Piwowar and Priem's (et al.) discoveries, we found that 28% of Gold or Hybrid works in the sample display Bronze OA characteristics. Access by authors to other funding sources and the collaborative research environment may leave little recourse for intervention by institutional services. It may also be the case that in some circumstances researchers may not be granted any form of open licence by their journal. Such reuse limitations may prevent replication of the final published version in repository hosts. However, the evidence provided in this study suggests this may not be the case as we found that almost all Gold and Hybrid works in our sample are available in other OA locations, irrespective of Bronze publication indicators. It may be that, in practice, reuse is not prevented by rightsholders. The reasoning behind Gold OA publishers retaining copyrights to works is not fully understood by the sector and requires further study.

Although providing the greatest levels of access, the reusability of repository content is much less clear from the data. Section 3.3.1 shows that 71% of repository hosts discovered by Unpaywall do not return any licence information and that non-commercial licences were the most common of the remaining set. HEFCE's policy advises a CC-BY-NC-ND license to satisfy minimum reuse requirements [4]. Concerning repository hosts, RCUK's policy does not require a specific licence for green OA, only that there are no publisher restrictions on non-commercial re-use. This can be met by a Creative Commons Attribution Non-commercial (CC-BY-NC) licence. Further research may be useful to explore the effects of stricter restrictions on the use of repository contents. Such investigations may inform future policy direction.

Described in the methodology, the 'best location' classification is inclusive of closed OA works, distinguishing author and publisher. This is an important consideration often overlooked by OA research. In Section 3.3.1, the 'Closed (Green option)' category indicates the 'gap' to 100% legal Green OA, accounting for just 7.7% of Brunel publications in 2016. By targeting support towards the authors of these works, institutional services may have the greatest opportunity to improve compliance figures and boost the OA agenda.

In contemplating how we may drive greater levels of access for the 'Closed (publisher)' category (that is, where no legal Green archival option was found to exist), we must also consider the lack of parity in access to Gold and Hybrid funding by researchers that is exacerbated by rising APC and subscription costs [17]. Additionally, there is a specific challenge presented by small society publications, who may argue that they require subscription models to sustain their activities. Initiatives like SCOAP3, the Open Library of the Humanities, and offsetting deals like the 'Springer Consortium agreement' may begin to redress this imbalance by shifting costs from authors to institutions. However, financial difficulties may continue to prevent the transformation of the remaining literature to 'open'. Advocacy activities by libraries may help authors to consider these issues when selecting their publisher.

The 'all location' classification examined OA location multiplicity and possibly highlights the impact of mandatory policies at an institutional level. Section 3.3.2 found that 40% of OA publications have taken Gold and Green routes. Whilst this duplication is not problematic *per se*, it does raise questions about the extent to which local institutional workflows fully capture the diversity of OA activity. The data in Sections 3.2 and 3.3 show that aggregation services may help to increase institutional compliance figures by increasing the visibility of OA dissemination. Indeed, emerging open science services may run concurrent to localised workflows necessarily imposed by UK institutions to ensure compliance. CORE data shows 131 hosts that have Brunel research holdings [29].

Section 3.3.2 found Gold works to have the highest number of OA locations, on average, followed by Hybrid. This may be due to publisher-driven archival policies. Gold models increase the likelihood that the journal will share content directly with disciplinary repositories. For example, Biomed Central mirrors all content into the PubMed platform [34]. However, significant replication of Gold and Hybrid publications may also indicate that the policy terrain is driving a duplication of effort in access workflows. Further study may explore whether the most affected are funded authors in the UK, who have specific mandatory requirements. We found no evidence of duplication within exclusively Green works. This indicates that HEFCE's policy may be successfully driving OA access to works that might otherwise be closed.

Presently, certain aspects of policy and the effectiveness of internal procedures are only measurable by engagement with local IRs/research information systems. This is partly because certain administrative data are not defined within global bibliographic and metadata standards. For example, the 'date of deposit' is not part of the RIOXX standard, and has only become important recently for UK institutions due to HEFCE's policy and audit requirements. At the time of writing, there are no indicators that this data will be adopted within global metadata standards, as it regards system administration and has yet to become a mainstream descriptor of a scholarly work. New, existing, and growing OA cultures in disciplinary repositories and other researcher-led communities may now be disregarded by UK institutions because only internal workflows that engage with local IRs/research information systems can capture the necessary administrative data to mitigate the perceived risk to the institution.

Section 3.3.1 highlights the lack of OA information available for accepted works. This lack of information may drive a sense of risk within institutions and possibly inform manual and localised workflows and strategies. Tools like Unpaywall currently only accept DOI identifiers that are maintained by DOI providers and these correspond to published works. This particular finding may, therefore, strengthen calls for publisher engagement with the Jisc Publications Router, a service to transfer on-acceptance metadata and manuscripts between publishers and research systems. However, at the time of writing, just five publishers are listed on the website as content providers and three of these are Gold OA publishers [35].

A further challenge facing institutions is that authors frequently change employers and import publications and records into local systems as they change jobs. Further studies could look at the impact of author mobility on OA compliance, and will probably add further weight to a need for global OA solutions. CORE data [29,30] show the majority of external host OA locations are spread across external IR systems in the UK/EU such as 'Spiral' (Imperial College London) and King's College London's Research Portal.

Sections 3.2 and 3.3 describe a spot check comparison with Google Scholar. This indicated many more OA locations available than shown within the CORE and Unpaywall data. Martín-Martín's (et al.) research [21] has highlighted the extent to which these OA locations are funder assured, such as disciplinary and institutional repositories, and not social networking repositories, such as ResearchGate, or uploads to project websites. Further study may explore the extent to which 'other' OA locations benefit the discovery of research. Large-scale and reproducible data in this area may also inform UK and other funder policies, such as ongoing reviews by Research England and the Wellcome Trust [36,37].

At the broadest level, this paper has highlighted a tension between the reality of research as a highly collaborative enterprise, with partnerships that cross institutional and territorial boundaries, and the requirements of nationally focused policies. This makes monitoring OA activity for compliance difficult as institutions tend to rely on local IRs and research information systems to report back to national funders. Approaches by institutions—in the UK at least—are therefore understandably driven by reactions to RCUK (now named UKRI) and HEFCE (now named Research England), with the former displaying a preference for Gold OA and the latter favouring repository usage. This study acknowledges the significance of these policies, which have been crucial in embedding OA within the minds of authors. However, the OA landscape comprises of a vast network of repositories, social systems, and open initiatives by new and longstanding publishers, which is not easily captured within local systems. The results of this paper, therefore, point to the need for interoperability between local systems and emergent open science services which are attempting to aggregate OA activity. Such two-way communication has the potential to enhance data for compliance reporting, limit the possibility of manual duplication, and free up library staff to target effort on those who have not yet engaged with OA.

Supplementary Materials: The data listed below is available online within the following collections:

Collection A

- Walters, D.; Daley, C. Exploring researcher engagement with open access using emergent open science services: Software Artefacts, 2018, *figshare*. doi:10.6084/m9.figshare.c.3966030

Collection B

- Walters, D.; Daley, C. Exploring researcher engagement with open access using emergent open science services: Data Artefacts, 2018, *figshare*. doi:10.6084/m9.figshare.c.3966027

Collection A: Artefacts

- Walters, D. Open access publishing data: File conversion and retrieval software, 2018, *figshare*. doi:10.6084/m9.figshare.5774244
- Walters, D. 'Enhanced' OA publications data SQL query, 2018, *figshare*. DOI: 10.6084/m9.figshare.5808375
- Walters, D. 'Best location' OA classification tests, 2018, *figshare*. doi:10.6084/m9.figshare.5892748
- Walters, D. Sherpa REF: SQL query and data sample, 2018, *figshare*. doi:10.6084/m9.figshare.5799339
- Walters, D. CORE: SQL query and data sample, 2018, *figshare*. doi:10.6084/m9.figshare.5799336
- Walters, D. Elements: SQL query and data sample, 2018, *figshare*. doi:10.6084/m9.figshare.5799222
- Walters, D. Unpaywall: location SQL query and data sample, 2018, *figshare*. doi:10.6084/m9.figshare.5799303
- Walters, D. OA database MySQL dump-table structure, 2018, *figshare*. doi:10.6084/m9.figshare.5765499
- Walters, D. Report: A Java application to create and persist objects from XML data, and interact with 'open access' RESTful web services, 2018, *figshare*. doi:10.6084/m9.figshare.4887011

Collection B: Artefacts

- Walters, D. Live google map plotting co-ordinates of repository outputs for Brunel University (2014–2017), 2018. figshare. doi:10.6084/m9.figlarge.5947855
- Walters, D. Google sheets: CORE location data and figures, 2018, *figshare*. doi:10.6084/m9.figshare.5820753
- Walters, D. Google sheets: 'Enhanced' OA publications data and figures, 2018, *figshare*. doi:10.6084/m9.figshare.5799342

Author Contributions: Conceptualisation: D.W. and C.D. Methodology: D.W. Software: D.W. Formal Analysis: D.W. and C.D. Data Curation: D.W. Visualisation: D.W. Writing-Original Draft Preparation: D.W. and C.D. Writing-Review and Editing: D.W. and C.D. Project Administration: C.D.

Acknowledgments: The study received no sources of funding. The authors wish to thank Monique Ritchie and Margaret Weaver for their diligent feedback and copyediting of the draft.

Conflicts of Interest: The authors declare no conflict of interest.

References

1. Suber, P. *Open Access*; MIT Press: Cambridge, MA, USA, 2012.
2. Budapest Open Access Initiative, 2002. Available online: http://www.budapestopenaccessinitiative.org/read (accessed on 15 May 2018).
3. ROARMAP. Available online: http://roarmap.eprints.org/ (accessed on 1 February 2018).
4. Higher Education Funding Council England. Policy for Open Access in Research Excellence Framework 2021, November 2016. Available online: http://www.hefce.ac.uk/media/HEFCE,2014/Content/Pubs/2016/201635/HEFCE2016_35.pdf (accessed on 19 February 2018).
5. Research Councils UK. RCUK Policy on Open Access and Supporting Guidance, 12 September 2017. Available online: https://www.ukri.org/files/legacy/documents/rcukopenaccesspolicy-pdf/ (accessed on 9 May 2018).
6. Kingsley, D. Could the HEFCE Policy Be a Trojan Horse for Gold OA? *Unlocking Research Blog*, 2016. Available online: https://unlockingresearch.blog.lib.cam.ac.uk/?p=488 (accessed on 19 February 2018).
7. Kramer, B.; Bosman, J. 101 Innovations in Scholarly Communication—The Changing Research Workflow. *Figshare* **2015**. [CrossRef]
8. Walters, D.; Daley, C. Brunel's 10 Year Journey towards Open Scholarship: Measuring 'Openness' over Managing Mandates. *Hindawi Opinion Blog*, 2016. Available online: https://about.hindawi.com/opinion/brunels-10-year-journey-towards-open-scholarship-measuring-openness-over-managing-mandates/ (accessed on 19 February 2018).
9. Unpaywall API Documentation Version 2. Available online: http://unpaywall.org/api/v2 (accessed on 19 February 2018).
10. JISC Sherpa REF. Available online: https://www.jisc.ac.uk/rd/projects/sherpa-ref (accessed on 19 February 2018).
11. Tennant, J.; Mounce, R. Open Research Glossary. *Figshare* **2015**. [CrossRef]
12. Knoth, P.; Zdrahal, Z. CORE: Connecting Repositories in the Open Access Domain. CERN workshop on Innovations in Scholarly Communication (OAI7): Geneva, Switzerland, 2017. Available online: http://oro.open.ac.uk/32560 (accessed on 19 February 2018).
13. Knoth, P.; Anastasiou, L.; Basile, G.; Pearce, S.; Pontika, N. Machine Accessibility of Open Access Scientific Publications from Publisher Systems via ResourceSync. *OAI10*, 2017. Available online: http://oro.open.ac.uk/50181 (accessed on 19 February 2018).
14. Walters, D.; Daley, C. 'Measuring' and Managing Mandates. *CORE Blog*, 2016. Available online: https://blog.core.ac.uk/2016/07/07/measuring-and-managing-mandates/ (accessed on 19 February 2018).
15. Bosman, J.; Kramer, B. Open Access Levels: A Quantitative Exploration Using Web of Science and oaDOI data. *PeerJ Preprints* **2018**, *6*, e3520v1. [CrossRef]
16. Piwowar, H.; Priem, J.; Larivière, V.; Alperin, J.P.; Matthias, L.; Norlander, B.; Farley, A.; West, J.; Haustein, S. The state of OA: A large-scale analysis of the prevalence and impact of Open Access articles. *PeerJ* **2018**, *6*, e4375. [CrossRef] [PubMed]
17. Jubb, M.; Plume, A.; Oeben, S.; Brammer, L.; Johnson, R.; Butun, C.; Pinfield, S. Universities UK. *Monitoring the Transition to Open Access*, 2017. Available online: http://www.universitiesuk.ac.uk/policy-and-analysis/reports/Documents/2017/monitoring-transition-open-access-2017.pdf (accessed on 9 April 2018).
18. Himmelstein, D.; Romero, A.R.; Levernier, J.G.; Munro, T.A.; McLaughlin, S.R.; Tzovaras, B.G.; Greene, C.S. Sci-Hub provides access to nearly all scholarly literature. *eLife* **2018**, *7*, e32822. [CrossRef] [PubMed]
19. ADA News. Open Access to Select Articles in Prosthodontic Journal until May 31, 2018. Available online: https://web.archive.org/web/20180416110028/https://www.ada.org/en/publications/ada-news/2018-archive/april/open-access-to-select-articles-in-prosthodontic-journal-until-may-31 (accessed on 12 April 2018).
20. Priem, J.; Piwowar, H. The Unpaywall Dataset. *Figshare* **2018**. [CrossRef]
21. Martín-Martín, A.; Rodrigo Costas, T.; Emilio, D. Evidence of Open Access of Scientific Publications in Google Scholar: A Large-scale Analysis. *ArXiv* **2018**. [CrossRef]
22. Walters, D. Open access publishing data: File conversion and retrieval software. *Figshare* **2018**. [CrossRef]
23. Hibernate. Hibernate ORM. Available online: http://hibernate.org/ (accessed on 8 May 2018).
24. Walters, D. Analysing the 'State of Open Access' at Brunel University London (2018): Software Artefacts. *Figshare* **2018**. [CrossRef]

25. Walters, D. Analysing the 'State of Open Access' at Brunel University London (2018): Data Artefacts. *Figshare* **2018**. [CrossRef]
26. Walters, D. 'Enhanced' OA publications data SQL query. *Figshare* **2018**. [CrossRef]
27. Walters, D. 'Best location' OA classification tests. *Figshare* **2018**. [CrossRef]
28. Walters, D. Sherpa REF: SQL query and data sample. *Figshare* **2018**. [CrossRef]
29. Walters, D. CORE: SQL query and data sample. *Figshare* **2018**. [CrossRef]
30. Walters, D. Live google map plotting co-ordinates of repository outputs for Brunel University (2014–2017). *Figshare* **2018**. [CrossRef]
31. Walters, D. Google sheets: CORE location data and figures. *Figshare* **2018**. [CrossRef]
32. Walters, D. Google sheets: 'Enhanced' OA publications data and figures. *Figshare* **2018**. [CrossRef]
33. Walters, D. Unpaywall: Location SQL query and data sample. *Figshare* **2018**. [CrossRef]
34. Biomed Central. What Is the Relationship between BioMed Central, PubMed Central and PubMed? Available online: https://web.archive.org/web/20160708212906/https://old.biomedcentral.com/about/faq/pubmed (accessed on 19 February 2018).
35. Jisc Router. Current Content Providers. Available online: https://pubrouter.jisc.ac.uk/about/providerlist/ (accessed on 19 February 2018).
36. Research England. Research England Launches Real-Time REF Review, 11 April 2018. Available online: https://re.ukri.org/news-events-publications/news/research-england-launches-real-time-ref-review/ (accessed on 13 April 2018).
37. Wellcome Trust. Wellcome Is Going to Review Its Open Access Policy, 5 March 2018. Available online: https://wellcome.ac.uk/news/wellcome-going-review-its-open-access-policy (accessed on 13 April 2018).

 *publications*

Article

Supporting Open Access at Kent—New Staff Roles

Rosalyn Bass and Sarah Slowe *

University of Kent, Canterbury, Kent CT2 7NS, UK; R.Bass-583@kent.ac.uk
* Correspondence: S.E.Slowe@kent.ac.uk

Received: 31 January 2018; Accepted: 10 April 2018; Published: 17 April 2018

Abstract: Open Access has been supported at the University of Kent from an early stage with the establishment of the Kent Academic Repository in 2007. Initially, this work was accommodated within the existing library staff structure, but the pace of change, funder requirements, and a new university plan meant that support for Open Access needed to become explicit. Therefore, a research support team was established using a matrix working system [1]. This article details this new structure and reflects on the benefits and challenges it brings.

Keywords: open access; staff; library; research support; scholarly communication

1. Introduction, Historical Position, and the UK Open Access Policy Framework

Historically, Open Access support at the University of Kent was ad hoc; we look at this position, then outline the changing Open Access Policy in the UK and the pressure this placed on our structure. We then summarise the changes we made, outlining the details of our current staff roles and establish whether this can be compared with the situation in other University libraries. We end with reflections on both the benefits and challenges that the new structure provides.

1.1. The Historical Position of Open Access Support at Kent

While Open Access has been supported at the University of Kent from an early stage with the establishment of the Kent Academic Repository in 2007, this work was accommodated within the existing library staff structure. This was a fairly traditional structure for an academic library, with an Academic Liaison Services team (ALS) selecting and recommending resources, monitoring library budgets, and helping staff and students to make the best use of library material. In addition, a Collections Management team was responsible for cataloguing, content description, and the discovery and acquisition of print and online resources. Liaison Librarians in ALS supported individual faculties and, within those, specific schools or academic departments. The Collections Management team was team was not aligned with specific faculties or schools.

The Kent Academic Repository (KAR) was established by a member of the ALS Science Faculty team working with EPrints and the dedicated IT Learning and Resource Development team within the Information Services Department, of which the Library is a part. The fact that this initiative came from within the ALS Sciences Faculty team was more closely linked to personal interest than planned development; nevertheless, responsibility for the KAR remained within the Sciences team. The ALS Sciences team undertook training, answered queries, and produced guidance while the Collections Management metadata team checked and reviewed entries in the KAR. No additional posts were created and no additional staff resources were allocated.

---

[1] Matrix management is a technique of managing an organisation through a series of dual-reporting relationships instead of a single linear management structure. At Kent, within the library, this is achieve through roles having both a faculty (Sciences, Humanities, Social Sciences) and thematic (Education, Engagement, Research) responsibility.

Initially the KAR's function was as a register of University outputs because no such central register existed. The deposit of full text was encouraged but there was no specific advocacy for Open Access. Until 2012, an ad hoc approach to Open Access was taken; use of the repository was down to the preferences of individual researchers or schools.

1.2. The Changing Open Access Policies in the UK

Open Access policy in the UK has been changing at a considerable rate. This stemmed the Finch report [1] published in June 2012 recommending a policy to support Open Access publishing, which was then outlined in a government policy paper published in July 2012 [2]. The policy paper highlighted the government's intention to increase the number of taxpayer-funded research papers freely available to the public. The policy has been encouraged through both HEFCE (Higher Education Funding Council for England, superseded by the Office for Students and Research England on 1 April 2018) [3] (assessed through the REF (Research Excellence Framework)[2]) and major funders such as RCUK (Research Councils UK, superseded by UK Research and Innovation, 1 April 2018) [4] and Wellcome [5].

The effect of these policies was for the University of Kent to publish its "Open Access Policy" [6] which was ratified in its original form in 2013. This policy stated that:

"The University requires that all research publications produced by its staff as part of their employment by the University are registered in the KAR (the Kent Academic Repository: http://kar.kent.ac.uk/) and, where allowed by the publisher, that a 'full text' be deposited at the same time or as soon as permitted."

This change in policy, with enforced compliance for REF inclusion and research funding eligibility, alongside an increasingly complex administrative burden, as publisher and funder policies differed on licensing, embargos, method, place of archiving and availability, and technical intricacies on the version that could be made available placed an unsustainable burden on an already overstretched team.

1.3. The Problem

This pace of change and new funder requirements led to Open Access becoming increasingly important to business objectives at Kent. Although the library was already supporting Open Access, this was not always clear to researchers or senior management. It was necessary to raise awareness of the ways in which the library and other professional services departments could assist. The University Plan 2015–2020 (https://www.kent.ac.uk/about/plan/) later set out its key objectives within three specific areas: research, education, and engagement. With the institutional objectives specified, clarifying the library contribution to each strand was key. Running alongside this was a desire to provide specialist support, so that researchers could concentrate on original research and the administrative burden for academics would be reduced.

This pace of change and new funder requirements led to Open Access becoming increasingly important to business objectives at Kent. Although the library was already supporting Open Access, this was not always clear to researchers or senior management. It was necessary to raise awareness of the ways in which the library and other professional services departments could assist. The University Plan 2015–2020 (https://www.kent.ac.uk/about/plan/) later set out its key objectives within three specific areas: research, education, and engagement. With the institutional objectives specified, clarifying the library contribution to each strand was key. Running alongside this was a desire to provide specialist support, so that researchers could concentrate on original research and the administrative burden for academics would be reduced.

---

[2]   The REF is a process of expert review undertaken by the UK higher education funding bodies, which assesses the quality of research outputs, their impact beyond academia, and the environment that supports research at each institution. The previous cycle was REF2014; the next will be REF2021.

The KAR and the work that a limited engagement with Open Access entailed had been added into the ALS Sciences team's and the metadata team's duties. No additional staff resources were available and other work was not diverted elsewhere. As Open Access grew more critical to business objectives, the work demands increased. For example, deposits into the KAR increased from 2037 in 2010 to 5606 in 2015, to the extent that the metadata team were no longer able to keep up with the volume of entries requiring checking in the "Under Review" section of the KAR. With the need to demonstrate compliance to national bodies, there were requests to organise and participate in major University-wide high profile Open Access events and a need to provide web guidance and training sessions to equip researchers with the knowledge and skills to adapt to the new agenda. In order to incentivise open access to research outputs for individual researchers, in 2014 it became mandatory for staff applying for promotion at the University of Kent to ensure that all publications they wished to use in support of their application were in the KAR. This meant that the ALS Science team needed to participate in the promotions exercise and the metadata team had to manage the spike in deposits that the annual promotions exercise caused, accommodating this within their usual workload.

The University of Kent is a recipient of funds from RCUK, allowing articles arising from their funded projects to be openly accessible through the payment of Article Processing Charges (APC). This again increased the need for provision of guidance, as well as support to administer applications to use the funds and to report back to RCUK each year. The University of Kent also arranged for supplementary funds to pay for APCs for non-RCUK articles, creating a further need to establish and publish criteria for institutional APC funding. Increasingly, publishers had individual platforms to manage APCs, from dashboards to bundles, and expertise was needed to navigate the variety of systems in use.

These additional demands put undue pressure on the ALS Sciences team, and detracted from their core liaison roles, such as selecting and helping students to use library resources. It was becoming increasingly difficult to meet the Open Access research support demands and the traditional liaison role within the team of four people. There was increasing evidence that the structure was not capable of supporting Open Access adequately, as, for example, APC funds were underspent each year, indicating that awareness of the funds' existence and purpose was low. Also, the changes made to institutional requirements meant that the team was unable to respond to demand from the research community. In 2015, this resulted in a backlog of KAR entries where the metadata had not been checked or improved. There was no time for proactive development work, and four months before HEFCE's Open Access requirements for the Research Excellence Framework began, guidance had not been created for University of Kent staff nor had a mechanism for checking and reporting upon compliance been established. While there was much enthusiasm for Open Access to research outputs, the structure of support was plainly unsustainable.

2. The changes Made

Adjustments to the staff structure within the library, and to the way the library and other professional services departments related to each other and to researchers, were necessary to meet Open Access needs in a positive and dynamic way. These included:

- The creation of a new Research Support Post in ALS;
- Aligning staff members in ALS to the University's strategic themes;
- Use of matrix team working [7];
- The creation of two new REF-Assisted Deposit posts;
- The establishment of an Office for Scholarly Communication (OSC) with two posts.

The new structure created a sustainable environment where the support for Open Access, and open scholarship more widely, is embedded in the Library Collections team. We are confident that this has equipped us to be in the best place possible to support Open Access as organisations such as

Jisc review the ongoing transition to openly accessible research [8]. Below we set out the roles now involved in Open Access support at Kent and the benefits and challenges of such an approach.

3. The New Structure in Detail

The University of Kent Library Collections team sits within the Information Services department, which is comprised of four sections: Customer Support, Library Collections, IT Development and Planning, and Administration. Library Collections manages the planning, acquisition, and provision of physical and digital learning and research resources. It is, in turn, made up of three separate teams: Academic Liaison Services, Collections Management, and the Office for Scholarly Communication (see Appendix A).

In addition to their primary team roles, many members of library collections now also have a strategic theme (Research, Education, or Engagement) within which they work.

Academic Liaison Services (ALS) manage and develop the physical and electronic content of library collections in line with the learning, teaching, and research priorities of the University. ALS works with the Academic Schools to select, provide, and maintain library resources for the University community, as well as to enable users to get the best from these resources. Key areas of service delivery are: information and digital literacy; library services for research; liaison with academic schools; collection engagement and development; the management of subject-based library budgets; and user support for all student and staff group. The provision of library services for research within ALS is outlined in more detail below.

Collections Management are responsible for acquisitions, digital resource management, and metadata management and stock processing. Within the metadata team, one senior library assistant and two library assistants are part of the research support provided within Library Collections.

The Office for Scholarly Communication is a new team within Library Collections, launched in September 2017. The Office showcases all of the research support provided across Kent to deliver a researcher-focussed service that offers support and advice across the research lifecycle. Building on the existing expertise at Kent, both within and beyond information services, the office provides support for researchers in maximising the dissemination, in the widest sense, of their work. The office supports innovative dissemination of research, identifies issues, and finds solutions for sharing the research outputs of the University more effectively, to both academic and non-academic audiences globally.

3.1. Academic Liaison Services

The 16.5 FTE (full time equivalent) posts within Academic Liaison Services consist of Liaison Librarians, Senior Library Assistants, and Library Assistants working in three teams. Each team supports one faculty (Sciences, Humanities, and Social Sciences) and is managed by a Faculty Librarian who also leads one of the University's strategic themes, which are Education, Engagement, and Research.

3.1.1. Faculty Librarian for Sciences and Research Support

The Faculty Librarian for Sciences and Research Support line manages the four roles outlined below and provides strategic leadership for research within Library Collections, coordinating work on Open Access across all the teams by means of a research support strategy, team meetings, planning, and setting and prioritising objectives. This role also pulls library and IT support together by chairing a Research Technologies Development Group in which technological development and fixes are captured, discussed, and scheduled. The Faculty Librarian is responsible for Open Access guidance, web pages, training, enquiries, and reporting. They also ensure that colleagues within ALS are equipped with basic Open Access knowledge and feel confident when and where to refer students and staff.

This strategic role is combined with overseeing the management and development of library collections and the support for students and staff within the Faculty of Sciences.

3.1.2. Liaison Librarian (Sciences)

This librarian works with the five schools in the faculty in a more traditional academic library liaison role. They do not play a specific part in supporting Open Access.

3.1.3. Research Support Librarian

This post enabled the Liaison Librarian for Sciences to focus on the faculty and provided a clear point of contact and source of advice for the Liaison Librarians. The post leads on research data management, bibliometrics, and Open Access advocacy. The roles of the post include monitoring and evaluating changing Open Access needs and opportunities.

3.1.4. Senior Library Assistant (Sciences)

The Senior Library Assistant (Sciences) role is split 50/50 between support for the Sciences Faculty and support for research. The post requires a detailed knowledge of Open Access, and is responsible for answering enquiries and taking a lead on Kent Academic Repository training.

3.1.5. Library Assistant (Sciences)

The Library Assistant primarily supports the Liaison Librarian (Sciences) in collection development, stock management, ordering, and user support, but also has a working knowledge of the Kent Academic Repository and assists with full text requests, training, and triaging of enquiries.

3.2. Collections Management

3.2.1. Metadata Team

Within the Collections Management section, a Curation and Discovery Manager is responsible for ensuring that metadata schemas comply with industry standards, the interoperability of research support systems, and the prioritisation of non-technical development work, while a Senior Library Assistant (Digital Curation) runs daily and scheduled quality control work on the repository and supervises staff to do so. This post is also responsible for testing metadata following development; producing data for Open Access reporting; and administering the Research Technologies Development Group.

3.2.2. Content and Purchasing Team—Article Processing Charge Support

The administration of Article Processing Charges and the processing of applications to use University funds for APCs is undertaken by a Library Assistant and Senior Library Assistant in the Content Purchasing team.

3.2.3. REF-Assisted Deposit—Two Library Assistants

We developed the REF-Assisted Deposit Service in response to the changes to requirements for the Research Excellence Framework (REF) relating to publications and Open Access, which have brought increasing levels of complexity to this area of academic activity. The launch of an assisted service model provided reassurance to researchers, and the University as a whole, that outputs are eligible for the REF and reduced the administrative burden on researchers that compliance introduced. We expanded the Metadata team within Collections Management to include two posts that were specifically focussed on delivering assisted deposits into the Kent Academic Repository.

The increased capacity created by these appointments also enabled us to monitor databases and social networks for new, potentially REF-eligible research outputs that had not been included in the repository or submitted through the REF-Assisted Deposit service. This increased our compliance rates.

3.3. Office for Scholarly Communication

3.3.1. Head of the Office for Scholarly Communication

The Head of Scholarly Communication contributes to the delivery of Kent's research strategy by maximising the impact of our research outputs to build our research profile and our reputation for research excellence. Working with the Assistant Director, Library Collections, and Director of Research Services in setting the strategic direction of scholarly communication across the University, the Head of the office leads the creation of a cohesive research support service at Kent by implementing best practice in Open Access and piloting innovative processes and technologies.

3.3.2. Scholarly Communications Coordinator

The initial focus of the role was the design, introduction, development, and management of the mediated deposit service for the university's institutional repository (KAR), which now forms part of the Curation and Metadata team. Following the successful launch of this service, the role broadened out to include dedicated support to scholarly communications to ensure the smooth running of the office of Scholarly Communication's service. The OSC coordinator works closely with the Research Support Team to continue to improve the current provision for Open Access and Research Data Management as well as to provide information, guidance, and support for dissemination through academic and non-academic outlets, social media, alternative publishing platforms, specialist output, and other related activities.

4. How does This Compare to Elsewhere?

A systematic review of emerging roles for librarians illustrates that support for Open Access was not a role under consideration in articles written between 2000 and 2014 [9]. Moreover, while there are plenty of later surveys that indicate a need to address how libraries support researchers [10,11], few of these link roles specifically to Open Access. Lara's survey of librarians' opinions of the role they should play in the management of Open Access found that there was agreement that education and advocacy of Open Access should be a vital role for librarians [12]. RLUK's survey into the role and skills of librarians required to support the needs of researchers [13] revealed that 22% of the respondents believed that it was essential for their Subject Librarians to have the "ability to advise on current trends, best practice, and available options in research publication and dissemination methods and models nationally and internationally, including scholarly communication and open access publishing" [13] (p. 101). Sixty percent stated that this knowledge would be essential by 2017 [13] (p. 101). Knowledge to support researchers in complying with the various mandates of funders, including Open Access requirements, was identified as one of the most significant skills gaps [13] (p. 43). However, these attitude surveys do not compare specific approaches or staff structures in libraries in relation to Open Access. DeGroff provided examples of Open Access good practice across institutions in the UK [14], but this pre-dated the start of HEFCE's Open Access requirements for the REF. Blatchford et al. [15] summarised the different approaches to addressing research support: some libraries have completely restructured to create dedicated research support teams, while some have a more dispersed model. However, again Open Access roles were not explicitly discussed. It is therefore difficult to evaluate the approach at the University of Kent against those adopted elsewhere in the UK since 2016. The Open Access survey commissioned by HEFCE, JISC, the Wellcome Trust, and RCUK, due to be published in spring 2018, addresses staff costs associated with Open Access and so may provide some of this missing information [16].

5. Benefits of the New Structure

5.1. Specialist Expertise in Open Access

A key benefit of this way of working with research support spread across a wide range of teams is that each individual brings a specialist perspective to an issue. The role holders involved in Open Access support within Library Collections each have a primary area of expertise, which they bring to their support for Open Access. An example of the benefits of this is that, in our recently established data repository, we have both expertise on the sector-wide standards for research data storage from the Research Support Librarian and on the underlying metadata needs from the Curation and Discovery Manager. The current role holders are from a wide variety of backgrounds, including administration, publishing, academic libraries, archives, and research support. This variety of perspectives and knowledge means that new development and processes in supporting Open Access are applicable beyond the immediate requirements of the REF and funder compliance.

5.2. Resilience Across the Support for Open Access

Whilst each role holder brings a specialist knowledge to the support for Open Access, the range of people involved also ensures that Open Access support is embedded across all relevant teams in Library Collections. Whilst there are key leads for research support within the teams, the research leads also ensure that other members of their primary team are aware of key information and where to access support on issues such as funder compliance or the REF deposit. This means that, without having to know the specific requirements of licensing or embargos for a particular funder, any liaison librarian would be confident in providing basic information or referring researchers to the ways of accessing this specialist support. This resilience is also shown in the lack of backlog for KAR entries—the peaks in demand for support, for example, around promotions time, are less onerous. This is due to both the higher proactive rate of the inclusion of publications and the wider team of people able to respond to queries at busy times.

5.3. Making Open Access Easy for Researchers

With such a large and diverse team, it is easy for researchers to access the Open Access support that they need—it is very rare that no one in the team would be available to answer queries, and members of the research support team are all confident in answering most of the queries that researchers have.

It has been a key aim to make Open Access compliance as administratively simple as possible for researchers, and the large team has been essential to this—with one contact email for all research support and a team that is nearly always available within office hours, this has been very successful. In particular, feedback on the REF-assisted deposit has been overwhelmingly positive:

> "In my view, the REF-assisted deposit service has been extremely useful for colleagues in the school. The service is efficiently operated and the KAR staff are quick to answer queries. Because the service is provided centrally, it provides peace of mind that the item has been uploaded accurately and in accordance with REF requirements."

> "It was a very helpful and reassuring service!"

> "I personally have found the REF-assisted deposit service extremely useful in my role. It certainly speeds up the process when having to deposit multiple papers on the KAR, and I believe the service is used by many researchers in our school."

As these changes have been introduced, we have seen our APC funds move from a substantial annual underspend to spending our allocation (£95,000 from RCUK; £85,000 from the University). A single point of contact by email has meant that enquiries are now handled efficiently and effectively, and we have seen an increasing interaction with researchers. The team answered 3400 enquiries in 2016 and over 5000 in 2017.

The additional expertise and capacity afforded by this revised structure has also meant that we are able to offer proactive support. The REF-assisted deposit team check Scopus, Springer, Ebsco, ProQuest, Wiley, T&F, and Sage for Kent researchers outputs to ensure that they are also appearing in the KAR and are REF-compliant. Since June 2017, they have contacted researchers regarding 257 publications. This marks a change in support for Open Access, where the support is approaching researchers, rather than responding to approaches from researchers.

Focus on Open Access to date has been on articles (following the REF and funder requirements), but our increased specialism and capacity has enabled us to look at supporting other forms of outputs to be openly accessible. Examples of this include making funding available for openly accessible books, support for data sharing with a new data repository, and a project to look at supporting non-textual or non-digital outputs.

6. Challenges of the New Structure

6.1. Competing Time Demands

One of the drawbacks of matrix working with roles aligned to Academic Schools and strategic themes is the potential for staff to feel pulled in several different directions. There is a risk that priorities become unclear and that people grow anxious that they are devoting too much time and weight to one aspect of their job and not enough to another. This can lead to a perpetual feeling of guilt and dissatisfaction. This risk has been minimised through careful planning, and the setting and reviewing of short- and long-term objectives, alongside annual appraisals and regular one-to-one meetings with line managers.

6.2. Ownership, Decisions, and Reaction Time

Because many staff roles play a part in Open Access, "ownership" of particular issues is not always immediately clear. Problems and development suggestions sometimes need unpicking in order to define responsibility for taking forward actions. For example, we do not have a designated Repository Manager for the Kent Academic Repository. This can increase the time it takes to react to situations. A departmental Research Technologies Development Group helps with this and allows for the escalation of issues. The structure also means that issues are always assessed from multiple angles. This prevents one viewpoint from becoming dominant.

6.3. Communication

The involvement of many people in supporting Open Access means that good communication is vital. However, the need to discuss items and ideas with multiple people could start feel like an impediment and may not suit all personalities. Decisions and actions taken without reference to other members of the team who support Open Access can lead to misunderstanding and duplication of effort. Given that the Open Access environment is a complex one, shared understanding is essential. Regular team meetings, Sharepoint, wikis, and online notices have helped with this.

7. Conclusions

It is interesting that thoughts and predictions expressed in RLUK's 2012 survey Re-Skilling for research reflect the changes we have seen [17]:

"We will need teamwork to cover all these new roles". [17] (p. 108)

"All of this is a big change and very important for the whole library—it is not just about Subject Librarians—it is really about whole structures, a library wide approach". [17] (p. 108)

"Subject Librarians cannot be expert in themselves in each new capability, but knowing when to call in a colleague . . . will be key to the new liaison role. Just as researchers are often working in teams to leverage compatible expertise, liaison librarians will need to be team builders among library experts where this advances client research". [17] (p. 109)

Response from our researchers has been positive. The volume of items deposited (1627 deposits in 2007 increasing to 4440 in 2017), the number of enquiries received and dealt with, the take up of APC funds, our levels of Open Access compliance, and the security of the shared specialist knowledge and "trust" approach among our librarians indicate that our approach is successful. We have been able to develop our support model and respond in a timely and effective manner to internal needs. The new model also engages professional services departments across the institution, embedding Open Access as an agenda beyond the library.

Additionally, the new structure has given us the ability to respond proactively to changes in the open scholarship environment globally, moving beyond a compliance agenda to support for openly accessible research outputs more broadly.

On the whole, the benefits of our hybrid matrix working model to support Open Access outweigh the challenges, but time and care is being dedicated to planning and managing the model to keep it this way. However, a more thorough and periodic evaluation with agreed benchmarks would be beneficial.

Acknowledgments: We acknowledge the very helpful feedback received through the peer review process, and would like to thank the reviewers for their time and suggestions. We would also like to thank Justine Rush and Trudy Turner for their ongoing support and specifically for feedback given on this article.

Author Contributions: Both authors co-wrote this article. We prepared the original draft, and reviewed & edited it in line with feedback.

Conflicts of Interest: The authors declare no conflict of interest.

Appendix

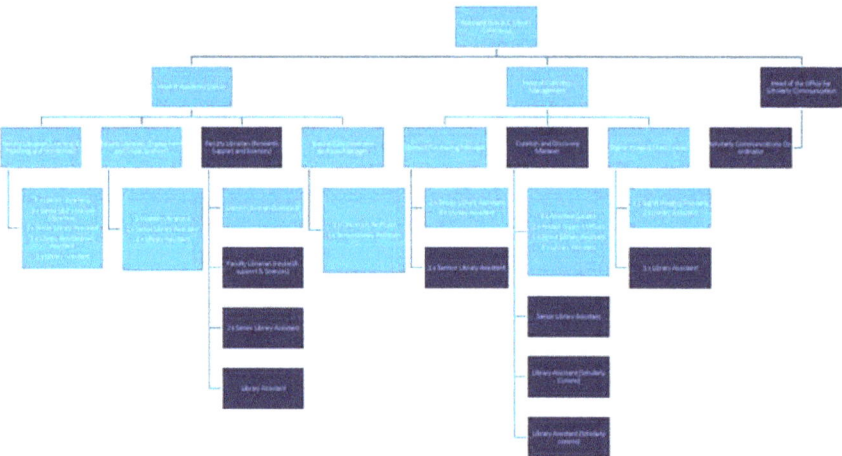

Figure A1. Library Collections—Organisational chart highlighting those involved in Open Access (dark blue).

References

1.   Finch, J. Accessibility, Sustainability, Excellence: How to Expand Access to Research Publications Report of the Working Group on Expanding Access to Published Research Findings. 2012. Available online: https://www.acu.ac.uk/research-information-network/finch-report-final (accessed on 26 March 2018).

2. Department for Business, Innovation and Skills. Accessibility, Sustainability, Excellence: How to Expand Access to Research Publications' Finch Group Report: Government Response on Open Access. 2013. Available online: https://www.gov.uk/government/publications/letter-to-dame-janet-finch-on-the-government-response-to-the-finch-group-report-accessibility-sustainability-excellence-how-to-expand-access-to-research-publications (accessed on 26 March 2018).
3. Higher Education Funding Council for England. Policy for Open Access in the next Research Excellence Framework: Updated November 2016. 2016. Available online: http://www.hefce.ac.uk/pubs/year/2016/201635/ (accessed on 26 March 2018).
4. Research Councils UK. RCUK Policy on Open Access. 2013. Available online: http://www.rcuk.ac.uk/documents/documents/rcukopenaccesspolicy-pdf/ (accessed on 26 March 2018).
5. Wellcome. Open Access Policy. Available online: https://wellcome.ac.uk/funding/managing-grant/open-access-policy (accessed on 26 March 2018).
6. University of Kent. Open Access Policy. 2013. Available online: Https://www.kent.ac.uk/library/research/docs/Kent%20Open%20Access%20policy.pdf (accessed on 26 March 2018).
7. Galbraith, J. Matrix Organization Designs: How to combine functional and project forms. *Bus. Horiz.* **1971**, *14*, 29–40. [CrossRef]
8. Japanese Industrial Standards Committee (JISC). Supporting the Transition to Open Access. Available online: https://www.jisc-collections.ac.uk/About-JISC-Collections/Supporting-transition-to-Open-Access/ (accessed on 26 March 2018).
9. Vassilakaki, E.; Moniarou-Papaconstantinou, V. A systematic literature review informing library and information professionals' emerging roles. *New Libr. World* **2015**, *116*, 37–66. [CrossRef]
10. Kennan, M.; Corrall, S.; Afzal, W. "Making space" in practice and education: Research support services in academic libraries. *Libr. Manag.* **2014**, *35*, 666–683. [CrossRef]
11. Saunders, L. Academic libraries' strategic plans: Top trends and under-recognized areas. *J. Acad. Libr.* **2015**, *41*, 285–291. [CrossRef]
12. Lara, K. The library's role in the management and funding of open access publishing. *Learn. Publ.* **2015**, *28*, 4–8. [CrossRef]
13. Auckland, M. Re-skilling for Research: An Investigation into the Role and Skills of Subject and Liaison Librarians Required to Effectively Support the Evolving Information Needs of Researchers. Research Libraries UK. 2012. Available online: http://www.rluk.ac.uk/wp-content/uploads/2014/02/RLUK-Re-skilling.pdf (accessed on 26 March 2018).
14. DeGroff, H. Preparing for the Research Excellence Framework: Examples of Open Access Good Practice across the United Kingdom. *Ser. Libr.* **2016**, *71*, 96–111. [CrossRef]
15. Blatchford, B.; Borwick, C.; Glen, S.; Hall, B.; Harding, A.; Hilliar, M.A.; Oakley, S. Librarians supporting research in Wales: Collaborative staff development and capacity building. *Sconul Focus* **2016**, *67*, 37–42.
16. Higher Education Funding Council for England. Open Access Survey. 2018. Available online: http://www.hefce.ac.uk/rsrch/oa/survey/ (accessed on 26 March 2018).
17. Brewerton, A. Re-skilling for research: Investigating the needs of researchers and how library staff can best support them. *New Rev. Acad. Libr.* **2012**, *18*, 96–110. [CrossRef]

 *publications*

Case Report

Open Science Support as a Portfolio of Services and Projects: From Awareness to Engagement

Birgit Schmidt *,† , Andrea Bertino , Daniel Beucke , Helene Brinken , Najko Jahn,
Lisa Matthias , Julika Mimkes , Katharina Müller, Astrid Orth  and Margo Bargheer †

State and University Library, University of Göttingen, 37073 Göttingen, Germany;
bertino@sub.uni-goettingen.de (A.B.); beucke@sub.uni-goettingen.de (D.B.);
brinken@sub.uni-goettingen.de (H.B.); najko.jahn@sub.uni-goettingen.de (N.J.);
matthias@sub.uni-goettingen.de (L.M.); mimkes@sub.uni-goettingen.de (J.M.);
katharina.mueller@sub.uni-goettingen.de (K.M.); orth@sub.uni-goettingen.de (A.O.);
bargheer@sub.uni-goettingen.de (M.B.)
* Correspondence: bschmidt@sub.uni-goettingen.de; Tel.: +49-551-39-33181
† These authors contributed equally to this work.

Received: 20 February 2018; Accepted: 12 June 2018; Published: 19 June 2018

Abstract: Together with many other universities worldwide, the University of Göttingen has aimed to unlock the full potential of networked digital scientific communication by strengthening open access as early as the late 1990s. Open science policies at the institutional level consequently followed and have been with us for over a decade. However, for several reasons, their adoption often is still far from complete when it comes to the practices of researchers or research groups. To improve this situation at our university, there is dedicated support at the infrastructural level: the university library collaborates with several campus units in developing and running services, activities and projects in support of open access and open science. This article outlines our main activity areas and aligns them with the overall rationale to reach higher uptake and acceptance of open science practice at the university. The mentioned examples of our activities highlight how we seek to advance open science along the needs and perspectives of diverse audiences and by running it as a multi-stakeholder endeavor. Therefore, our activities involve library colleagues with diverse backgrounds, faculty and early career researchers, research managers, as well as project and infrastructure staff. We conclude with a summary of achievements and challenges to be faced.

Keywords: open science; open access; service portfolio; publishing; repositories; research information

1. Introduction

Together with many other universities worldwide, the University of Göttingen has aimed to unlock the full potential of networked digital scientific communication by strengthening open access as early as the late 1990s. Open science as the paradigm to draw on digital technology for research processes and collaboration and to make these transparent as well as comprehensible, followed these early approaches for open access to research results. Consequently, policies at the institutional level to define and foster open science emerged and have been with us for over a decade now. Experience shows that the transition to open science is a multi-layered process, which builds on communities and communication, services and support, ideas and visions in order to change the conventional research and scholarly communication system.

Bringing open access forward has been defined as one of the strategic goals of Göttingen State and University Library (SUB Göttingen)[1]. When it comes to making open access and open science happen at Göttingen Campus[2], the university library is one of the chief players that provides a wide range of open science services and activities. These include awareness raising and open science training, local services and support for Göttingen's researchers and transforming institutional acquisition budgets from journal subscriptions to open access publishing funds and agreements. All these activities are delivered in a heterogeneous setting: we as a library are responsible for 13 local faculties including a medical school and large Humanities faculty, serve national obligations and offer dedicated infrastructures and support to European digital humanists.

How that plays out in designing aligned services might be highlighted with the following. While a field such as high energy physics has established a rich pre-publication discussion culture taking place on arXiv.org and managed to organize SCOAP3 (Sponsoring Consortium for Open Access Publishing in Particle Physics), a partnership that achieved almost 100% open access for the field's published results, other disciplines are just starting to set up preprint servers (e.g., in biology or chemistry with bioRxiv.org and chemRxiv.org). Even in fields like medicine and health sciences where selection via peer review in journals even decades after arXiv.org seemed to be the only way to publish research results, there are now initiatives to set up a preprint service[3].

Fields like biology or geosciences have developed widely-accepted disciplinary computing sciences, whereas parts of the humanities or social sciences find it hard to even publish in electronic journals, due to fragmentation and economies-of-scale challenges. To meet these disciplinary differences, our library is heavily involved in national and international projects developing infrastructures and services for open access and open science that seek to balance general efforts fit for all disciplines with customization for disciplinary or specific audiences' needs. Our open science activities (which we describe briefly in Table 1) are comprised of electronic publishing and open access, but also reach from research data management, virtual research environments, to digital repository networks, as well as policy making and awareness building.

From a library perspective, the transition to open access both disrupts traditional workflows and broadens the scope of activities. The acquisition aspect—the selection and licensing of resources—increasingly focuses on combining payments for open access publishing such as article processing charges (APCs) with subscriptions and holdings. At the same time, additional support of and services to researchers are needed. In addition, with the shift from print to digital resources, the library as a space is transformed, the latter freeing up space for learning and collaboration. For library employees, these changes can be gradual, but more often, they require further training, and can sometimes lead to restaffing in the long term.

This brings projects into a new perspective. Projects may have been considered merely as add-ons rather than integral entities based on the fact that project staff are often appointed through fixed-term contracts. Due to the ongoing transformation of libraries, projects are increasingly becoming the "new normal" as important agents of change and are used for both stepping up the range and the quality of services. In addition, projects offer an opportunity for experimentation, i.e., to explore, test and evaluate new service areas. Not surprisingly, libraries adopting this approach have the ability to run other change processes as projects, i.e., the line is blurred, and what remains are differences in size and funding streams (board funds from the university's own resources versus third-party funds from external research funding organizations). However, the sustainability of service areas that have

---

[1] Göttingen State and University Library, https://www.sub.uni-goettingen.de/en/about-us/portrait/strategy/.

[2] Göttingen Campus is an alliance between the university and local non-university research institutions, which have come together to promote research, teaching and the training of young researchers; cf. http://www.goettingen-campus.de.

[3] The Yale University Open Data Access (YODA) project, http://yoda.yale.edu/medrxiv. For more information on the debate, see, e.g., [1].

emerged with the activation energy of projects can only be achieved if these are fully integrated into the library's operation and budget planning, ideally right from the start.

In the following, we will outline the application and further development of strategies at Göttingen Campus and highlight a range of activities that are instrumental for the implementation.

Table 1. Overview of mentioned open science projects and initiatives.

Activity/Initiative	Type	Focus	Link
*metrics	Project	Alternative metrics	metrics-project.net
COAR	Association	Repositories	coar-repositories.org
Data Science Summer School	Event	Open data/training	https://tinyurl.com/UGOE-datasummer2018
Deep Green	Project	Open access	deepgreen.kobv.de
DOAJ	Infrastructure	Index for peer-reviewed OA journals	doaj.org
DRIVER	Project	Repositories	driver-repository.eu
European Open Science Cloud (EOSC)	Project	Infrastructure	eoscpilot.eu
FOSTER, FOSTER Plus	Project	Open science training	fosteropenscience.eu
GoeScholar	Infrastructure, service	Repositories	goedoc.uni-goettingen.de
Göttingen eResearch Alliance (eRA)	Service, support	Research data management	eresearch.uni-goettingen.de
Göttingen Research Online (GRO)	Infrastructure, service	Publication data management	gro.uni-goettingen.de
Göttingen University Press	Service, infrastructure	Scholarly publishing	univerlag.uni-goettingen.de
Hacky Hour Göttingen	Community building, event, mailing list	Open science tools	hackyhour.github.io/Goettingen
HIRMEOS	Project	Scholarly publishing	hirmeos.eu
Knowledge Unlatched (Selection Committee 2018)	Initiative	Open access	knowledgeunlatched.org
Open Access 2020	Initiative	Scholarly publishing	oa2020.org
Open Coffee Lectures	Community building, event	Open science	www.sub.uni-goettingen.de/lernen-lehren/kurse-fuehrungen/coffee-lectures/
Open Science Göttingen Meet-up	Community building, event, mailing list	Open science	www.sub.uni-goettingen.de/en/electronic-publishing/open-science/
OpenAIRE	Project, initiative	Infrastructure and network, open science	openaire.eu
Reading Group on Data Science Literature	Community building, event	Training	–
ROpenSci	Initiative	Software tools, community building	ropensci.org
SCOAP3	Initiative	Scholarly publishing, open access	scoap3.org
SUB Göttingen Facebook Page	Community building, outreach	-	facebook.com/SUB.INFO
WG Association of European Research Libraries (LIBER)	Working group (WG)	Research libraries as infrastructure	https://libereurope.eu/strategy/research-infrastructures/committee
WG euroCRIS	Working group	Repositories, current research information systems	www.eurocris.org/community/taskgroups/cris-ir
WG European Commission	Working group	Scholarly publishing	https://preview.tinyurl.com/EC-wg-scholpublishing
WG Knowledge Exchange	Working group	Open access	www.knowledge-exchange.info/projects/project/open-access
WG Research Data Alliance	Working group	Research data management	www.rd-alliance.org/groups/libraries-research-data.html

2. Bridging the Gap between Policy and Practice

Institutional policies on openness, open access, open science or research data endorse and nurture desired practices while leaving room for disciplinary approaches that should be defined at the departmental level. To be effective, such policies need to be reassessed and updated regularly, to ensure their alignment with the principles and practices commonly shared by the wider research community or the legislative framework (e.g., intellectual property rights). Input from researchers is therefore essential for an effective and balanced policy. Yet, it can be difficult for researchers to navigate through these policies and their institutions' supporting services on their own. Librarians provide advice and guidance on open access to university staff, researchers and postgraduate students. In other words, librarians play a key role in the open science movement as they bridge the gap between policy and practice, i.e., act as mediators and enablers through translating open science policies into practice, and vice versa.

Pursuing the goal of making research results of its researchers as widely accessible and usable as possible, the University of Göttingen and the University Medical Center Göttingen (UMG) adopted a joint policy on research data in July 2014 and a revised open access policy in November 2016.[4] The current open access policy recommends authors to retain their rights to ensure unrestricted access to and dissemination of their works; endorses depositing a copy of the manuscript in the institutional repository GoeScholar upon publication and informs researchers about the University's open access options such as the open access publication funds, Göttingen University Press (hybrid publishing model of full open access with print on demand) and further service areas. The 2016 policy builds on the university's initial Open Access Resolution from December 2005 that focused on general benefits of open access, encouraged researchers to engage and promoted free access through self-archiving.

The policy on research data was drafted by several stakeholders in the university (including research support, the legal department and the library). Both the university and the medical center adopted it in July 2014.[5] The policy outlines the responsibilities of data producers and defines available support in the context of research data management. It encourages researchers to ensure unrestricted access to and re-use of research data, in particular of data required to validate results presented in scientific publications. Further, it clearly states that the university supports and advises researchers on data management issues and provides services for data storage and preservation. SUB Göttingen is responsible for the implementation, coordination and continuation of the strategy within the university and connects Göttingen researchers with existing tools and digital information infrastructures.

A common challenge is to effectively communicate institutional policies to the institution's academic community as a whole: these principles should not just look good on paper. Although open access has become a relatively well known concept in many disciplines, uncertainties about common practices and tools still prevail among researchers. The key to successful policy implementation is to send a clear and consistent message across campus engaging all research communities and to equip them with skills needed to turn policies into practice. This can be achieved through several paths, such as the library website, mailing lists, workshops, information and training sessions or informal meet-ups. In addition, to efficiently support researchers, it is essential to create and further develop a network of people across campus that interlinks service and policy areas, covering the library, the research support office and the research integrity office.

---

[4]   University of Göttingen, Official Announcements, No. 65, 6 December 2016, https://www.uni-goettingen.de/de/amtliche-mitteilungen-i-ausgabe-65-06122016/552696.html.

[5]   Research data policy of the University of Göttingen (incl. University Medical Center), http://www.uni-goettingen.de/en/488918.html.

2.1. Raising Awareness and Training for Open Science

Taking open science to the next level first requires researchers' awareness of the importance of openness, followed by skills development such as the adoption of new research practices. The library actively informs about open access services and current open science activities via direct communication with researchers or research support staff, as well as through mailing lists, and organizes events such as roadshows, hands-on workshops or low-threshold events, e.g., our Open Coffee Lectures to reach walk-in audiences. Other events such as summer schools allow in-depth interaction with specific target groups or communities.

A communication and information channel to raise attention for open science and to coordinate efforts was first established in autumn 2016, mainly targeting early career researchers at Göttingen Campus. To date, there are several mailing lists, "Open Science", "Goe Teaching Open Science" and "Hacky Hour Göttingen", collaboratively run by librarians and early career researchers. The "Open Science" mailing list informs subscribers about local and global open science events, such as meet-ups, workshops and webinars. The list also spreads the word about useful tools for research workflows, job postings and recently published reports and research articles. "Goe Teaching Open Science" is used to organize meetings to discuss how open science teaching and training can be better incorporated in research integrity trainings and graduate school level curricula, as well as to collaboratively develop teaching materials for these sessions. Besides mailing lists, SUB Göttingen has been running a Facebook Page[6] since 2011 to inform about open science events hosted at or by the library.

At the European level, the EU-funded project FOSTER Plus[7] engages in open science training of researchers and trainers at the institutional level. It brings together 10 experienced partners across five European countries. In the first project phase from 2014–2016, the project organized over a hundred face-to-face training events across 28 European countries and developed 25 online courses. These activities reached over 6300 participants all over Europe. In addition, the project collected more than 2000 training materials, which were categorized according to an Open Science Taxonomy at the FOSTER portal. The FOSTER portal is an e-learning platform where users can learn about open science or re-use training materials. The current project phase (2017–2019) intensifies and expands these activities. It develops new online courses that go beyond raising awareness and targets disciplinary communities such as the life sciences, the social sciences and the arts and humanities. In some disciplines, open research practices are already the norm, whereas others have just started to explore integrating open science principles into their research routines relatively recently [2]. Therefore, FOSTER provides discipline-specific training and supports knowledge exchange and learning. In addition, the project strengthens the open science training capacity by initiating a trainers' community and also training the trainers. Resources such as the recently released open science training handbook, re-usable training materials and a trainers' directory, where users can find speakers for training events, foster the delivery of training beyond the project. This approach ensures that open science awareness and skills arrive in and grow further at the level of research institutions.

Another initiative that steps up open science knowledge at Göttingen Campus and beyond is the Data Science Summer School[8], a short-term program that welcomes early career researchers from across all disciplines. The course combines theoretical lectures and interactive sessions, giving students the opportunity to directly apply their newly-acquired skills and knowledge through collaborative hands-on training. Participants learn about data management, sharing and processing, as well as different data science methods.

---

[6] SUB Göttingen on Facebook, https://www.facebook.com/SUB.INFO.
[7] Fostering the practical implementation of open science in Horizon 2020 and beyond, https://www.fosteropenscience.eu.
[8] Data Science Summer School, http://www.uni-goettingen.de/de/data+science/575381.html.

2.2. Building Open Science Communities

Elements of the open science agenda are becoming increasingly familiar to early career researchers [3]. However, at the moment, there are only a few opportunities to learn about and to discuss open science topics, such as available options to actively practice open science. The key to improving the current situation is to build up a local open science community and offer an environment where scholars from all career stages and other open science enthusiasts with different backgrounds can come together to meet like-minded people, exchange ideas and experiences and drive open science at and beyond Göttingen Campus.

The Open Science Göttingen Meet-Up launched in autumn 2016 and since then has brought together researchers, librarians and other individuals interested in open science about every three months. Usually, participants agree before each meeting on topics and agenda, whereas library staff members act as facilitators and less as agenda setters. Previous meet-ups included topics such as incentives for practicing open science, raising awareness, open data, researcher profiles and impact metrics. One example is worth mentioning as participants had expressed their interest in sketching and graphic recording to visualize research processes or results. In summer 2017, we organized the visit of Patrick Hochstenbach, digital architect at Gent University Library and artist[9], a colleague we have been working with in the context of digital repositories. He guided participants through an intense and highly instructive workshop that equipped everyone with valuable information, as well as new practical skills on how to conceptualize sketching and create visual graphics, which we applied to express a topic of open science.

Closely related to the meet-ups as a format to engage communities is our Hacky Hour Göttingen[10], initiated by a doctoral student together with librarians, a monthly open meeting that focuses on computational tools and code. In an informal setting, 10–20 participants offer each other support in computational problems and present their approaches, such as how to write a thesis with R Markdown, a basic introduction to MathJax, Jupyter notebooks and an introduction to repositories. No prior knowledge is needed, and everyone, regardless of their career stage, status, experience or background, is welcome to participate, test tools or methods and engage in the discussion. All meet-ups and Hacky Hours are documented through notes on Etherpad, a web-based collaborative real-time text editor, and everyone is invited to join Hacky Hour's Gitter chat (instant messenger) and our mailing list where ideas and questions can be posted before and after the meet-ups. Thereby, Hacky Hour maintains an open communication channel in between meet-ups and is deliberately designed as low threshold, meaning that walk-ins and new members can join the community at any time.

3. Publishing Services and Research Support at Göttingen Campus

To bring open science to full acceptance, publishing options for research results need to be part of the picture, and open access currently seems to be the best fit for a changing research paradigm. Thus, our library strongly supports the goal of maximizing open access to publications and related research outputs, both through its publishing services, run on behalf of the university, as well as being active in the transformation of the scholarly communication system and its political, legal and organizational framework. To meet the latter, several library staff members are active in lobbying or working groups for open science, scholarly communication and open access publishing.

At the service level, user needs determine which and how publishing services are designed and run. Our publishing services take into account that publishing draws on four core functions, namely registration, certification, dissemination and archiving. Certification for example requires that publishing infrastructures meet the expectations of target groups when it comes to citability, review processes or quality control.

---

[9]   https://github.com/phochste.
[10] Hacky Hour Göttingen, https://hackyhour.github.io/Goettingen.

An illustrative example for this approach is the adapted collection policy of GoeScholar, the institutional repository for the University of Göttingen. The initial collection policy covered parallel versions of already published work only, with a strong preference for peer-reviewed articles. The idea was to show Göttingen authors that they would self-archive among peers, meaning that all publications on GoeScholar were of similar origin. Over the years, it became evident that authors wanting to self-archive do not make that decision based on the functionalities of the chosen platform, but rather on whether the platform reaches their intended audiences. Author uploads remained at a very low level, and the steady growth of content on GoeScholar was a result of the repository team's effort. At the same time, research groups kept on requesting an open access platform for primary publication of more informal publication types in a formal (citable) way in open access, such as working papers or report series. The policy therefore opened for primary publications, and the GoeScholar team supports researchers with consulting on publishing concepts, editorial processes such as style sheets or quality control, licensing and persistent identifiers (e.g. DOIs).

Researchers from book-oriented disciplines continue to publish mainly in scientific presses. However, the commercial publishing system continues to fall short in offering affordable open access options for books. As monograph publishing mostly takes place in small to medium-sized publishing houses heavily relying on print sales (including most of the Anglo-American university presses), these presses tend to be highly selective when taking up titles into their publishing program, resulting in scarce publishing options, especially for niche topics, early career authors or those willing to publish open access. Therefore, the university library runs Göttingen University Press (GUP) to offer reliable and affordable publishing options for Göttingen authors. Its open access-focused mission and how it collaborates with a group of other German-language university presses have been thoroughly described by Bargheer and Pabst [4]. GUP books are published in a hybrid model of small print runs combined with an open access version on the press' DSpace-based repository, open for metadata harvesting via OAI-PMH and all equipped with a DOI. Just like most of the newer library-led university presses, it operates with lean workflows: authors submit manuscripts based on templates provided by the press, and digital versions continue to be published as PDF files. Sophisticated XML-based workflows certainly produce digital objects with higher open science and reuse potential. However, as they place additional workload on authors and editors and require activation energy, as well as permanent support from technical staff, they continue to be out of scope for the majority of smaller presses, such as ours. However, some recently-founded presses have benefited from the German Research Foundation (DFG) funding programs, which enabled them to enhance their production processes and to develop alternative business models for monograph publishing (e.g., Heidelberg University Press[11]).

Although open access books have gained momentum at the institutional level over the last few years, they continue to play a more minor role than their social and scientific potential would suggest. Overall, this reflects the fact that open access in book-oriented disciplines, such as the humanities, continues to grow at a slower rate than for example in the natural sciences. This results from a lower standardization level of book publishing and a lack of economies-of-scale ([2,4–6]) in comparison to journal articles, but also with existing reputation-building processes in the mentioned disciplines that would require new reading and validating habits (e.g., accepting digital publications in tenure and promotion).

3.1. Enhancing Institutional Publishing and Integration of Monographs in Open Science Infrastructures

Monographs continue to be important means of communication in the humanities and social sciences; more than papers and other shorter publication formats, they enable scholars to deal with differentiated and complex questions exhaustively. They can open up new research perspectives, i.e., they can be ascribed greater innovative power than articles.

---

[11]   Heidelberg University Press, http://heiup.uni-heidelberg.de/?lang=en.

> Monographs provoke debate, shift paradigms, and provide a focal point for research. It is not surprising [...] that the authors of monographs feel a personal connection with the form and content of the works they publish, nor that monographs play a vital role in the careers of many scholars as key markers of esteem and quality (Crossick, G. [7]).

In addition, since the publication of monographs requires expertise acquired over a long period of time, they help to define scientific profiles and thus gain decisive importance for academic careers. Even if not in the same way in all countries, monographic publications are the condition for acquiring academic qualifications, in Germany, e.g., a PhD or habilitation. The importance of scientific monographs for the Humanities and Social Sciences (HSS) has become increasingly significant with the possibility to publish in open access, as open access enhances the visibility and dissemination of research results [8]. The publication of scholarly monographs in open access has great advantages for scientists as authors and as readers: It increases the visibility of their publications, ensures a wider dissemination of research results in international and interdisciplinary contexts, enables added value such as comprehensive indexing and also allows the innovative features (e.g., annotations or cross-linking) while drawing on the conventional format of the book. However, adopting open access publishing models for scholarly monographs is still slower than for scholarly essays [9,10]. As [11] have shown, scientific journals and articles travel through the digital transformation much more smoothly than books, as they have to overcome fewer technical and conceptual barriers, be it in terms of reading habits, reputation gain or storage concepts. In particular, prestige and reputation play a decisive role, especially if a discipline depends on a narrow circle of traditional high-quality publishers.

In recent years, several infrastructures and services have been developed in order to facilitate the integration of monographs into the open access realm. Nevertheless, the landscape of scholarly publishing is still highly fragmented, with different national, linguistic and subject-specific aspects. While in the Science, Technology and Medical disciplines (STM), the publishing system is strongly concentrated around the top five commercial publishers (Elsevier, Sage Publications, Springer Nature, Taylor & Francis, Wiley-Blackwell) [12], as is shown by their share of papers published by discipline, the situation of the HSS is characterized by the fact that, in addition to the large publishing houses, there are numerous smaller university presses and growing online platforms that bring together several publishers from different national, linguistic and scientific communities. Although a single and unified publishing system, which would cover the whole variety of publication situations and opportunities in Europe, might seem purely utopian or not worthwhile to some people, it cannot be denied that the current uncoordinated situation is a major obstacle hindering the integration of HSS into open science structures.

In order to address the above-mentioned situation, the European network OPERAS [12] initiated the project HIRMEOS (High Integration of Research Monographs in the European Open Science infrastructure, hirmeos.eu), a 30-month EU project funded under the Horizon 2020 program bringing together nine partners from six different countries and five digital publishing platforms: EKT Open Book Press (Greece), Göttingen University Press (Germany), Open Access Publishing in European Networks (OAPEN) (Netherlands), OpenEdition Books (France) and Ubiquity Press (U.K.). The project enables peer reviewed open access books from publishing platforms based on different architectures and software to become an integral part of the open science system by adopting common standards and shared functionalities on these platforms. Participating platforms will for example use the same metadata—authors' ID, documents' ID, Directory of Open Access Books (DOAB) peer-review types, Creative Commons Licenses, usage metrics based on joint standards, citations/reviews, social media impact—and implement a set of common services as a result of the project. This approach allows a natural growth of a horizontally-integrated publication 'ecosystem' able to take up new partners and

---

12   Open access in the European research area through scholarly communication, operas.hypotheses.org/.

platforms. The described process is supported with thorough implementation guidelines for each of the functionalities.

More specifically, the participating platforms will be enriched with tools that enable the identification of the monographs, user authentication and interoperability (via DOI, ORCID, FundRef). Other tools will enable entity extraction (INRIA (N)ERD) and annotation of monographs (Hypothes.is), as well as the collection of usage and alternative metrics data. HIRMEOS will also enhance the technical capabilities of the Directory of Open Access Books (DOAB), the most important indexing service for open access monographs, to provide automated information for inclusion and develop a structured certification system, which will make it possible to document the peer review of each monograph published on the digital platforms involved in the project.

The library contributes to several work packages and leads the work on community outreach and exploitation of project results. In particular, Göttingen is responsible for developing HIRMEOS's communication strategy, strengthening the project's international network and coordinating the assessment of the implemented tools and services. This assessment is particularly important because the increasing digitalization of research and learning is sometimes perceived as a challenge for our attention and ability to reflect (cf. [13–15]). The integrated publication system that HIRMEOS is targeting should primarily support scientific work by simplifying and accelerating basic research activities—the so-called scholarly primitives of writing, finding, commenting, referencing, evaluating, illustrating, presenting [16]—as well as elementary activities in the digital domain: searching in browsers, connecting digital texts, collecting data, scanning and creating digital texts. In order to implement services and tools for digital monographs that are geared at concrete needs and the practices of scientists and students, SUB Göttingen works to get assessments of the different interest groups on the services provided by organizing workshops and webinars with different stakeholders, as well as meetings with the editorial board of the Göttingen University Press.

3.2. From Repositories to Global Open Science Infrastructures

For about two decades now, institutional repositories have provided basic hosting infrastructure for institutional research outputs of all types. Several institutions have broadened the initial scope and created repository systems that allow distinction of parallel peer-reviewed publications and primary publications such as theses, reports or working papers and, more recently, hosting of research data and code. With the rise of integrated Current Research Information Systems (CRIS) in Northern European and increasingly Western European countries, repositories evolved from stand-alone data silos into vertically- or horizontally-integrated systems serving institutional needs, on the one hand, and researchers' needs such as publishing, discoverability and dissemination, on the other. SUB Göttingen currently runs institutional repositories along with several disciplinary repositories for the geosciences, digital humanities and for Anglo-American history and culture that reflect the historically grown research profile of the university.

In addition, SUB Göttingen works closely with the university's research department, the university's department of Strategic Development and Controlling and the Göttingen eResearch Alliance (eRA, see also Section 3.3) in building up Göttingen Research Online (GRO) as a portal for publication and research data. GRO seeks to highlight topics that Göttingen's researchers work on, where they publish and with whom they collaborate. The library's main task in GRO is the innovative publication data management system focusing on researchers' needs to curate and publish individual or group publication lists while complying with the university's institutional reporting and analytical requirements. Further integration of institutional repositories is projected for 2018 to provide full text search and access along with metadata management in one system. GRO will be integrated into the existing university's research information system FactScience to enable publication data reuse for further reporting and management purposes (e.g., performance-based resource allocation).

European open science infrastructures combine institutional and disciplinary distributed infrastructures and create overlay services that enable access to and reuse of European-funded research outputs. Starting with the basic interoperability of repository infrastructures as created by the DRIVER projects (funded by the European Commission in the Sixth and Seventh Framework funding programs) [17], the OpenAIRE project and other initiatives have created additional functionalities, which allow for navigation along a graph of entities based on publications, research data and other research outputs, as well as research institutions and projects. In January 2018, the fourth project phase of OpenAIRE, OpenAIRE-Advance, started. The project aims to sustain the current successful infrastructure, comprised of a human network and robust technical services. OpenAIRE-Advance works towards making open science the default in Europe, reshaping the scholarly communication system towards greater openness and transparency and serving as a trusted pillar of the European Open Science Cloud (EOSC).[13] In its new phase, OpenAIRE works along the following lines (cf. Ibid.):

- Consolidate and optimize services to meet end user needs and create the European Open Science Observatory seamlessly connecting all research artifacts.
- Empower the pan-European Open Science Helpdesk network to increase its national presence and develop capacities to become a pivotal part of open science in national settings.
- Strengthen research community uptake of open science through working with three national research infrastructure nodes (ELIXIR-GR, EPOS-IT, DARIAH-DE)[14] and building bridges to key communities via an open science-as-a-service approach.
- Promote emerging changes in the scientific communication landscape and support the development of the next generation repositories with new functionalities and new technologies.
- Build a global open science network and align policies, practices and services for a truly global and interoperable scholarly commons.
- Outreach beyond researchers to lay the foundations for citizen scientists to leverage the benefits of open science and to bring OpenAIRE closer to industry through an Open Innovation program.
- Collaborate with EOSC-hub[15] towards a concrete implementation of EOSC, creating a joined-up, interoperable set of services to serve the needs of tomorrow's researcher in the context of EOSC.

Besides promoting open science at the local, national and European level, SUB Göttingen is also committed to supporting and further developing international recommendations on information infrastructures in order to align its own developments with global trends. To pursue this goal, SUB is actively involved in several national and international open science organizations and working groups (e.g., expert groups coordinated by the Association of European Research Libraries (LIBER), euroCRIS, the European Commission, Knowledge Exchange, the Research Data Alliance (RDA)).[16]

COAR, the Confederation of Open Access Repositories, is the forum of the international community for repository infrastructure, with the library being one of the founding organizations and host for the legal organization based in Göttingen. In its capacity as an international consortium and forum, COAR brings together repository partners and regional networks of repositories from around the world, including Europe, Latin America and its regional network of LA Referencia, China, Japan, Africa, Australia, Canada and the U.S. Starting with the technical interoperability of repositories [18], COAR's activities aim at the alignment of open access policies, practices, technologies

---

[13] OpenAIRE, Empowering Open Science: Kick Off of the OpenAIRE-Advance H2020 project, press release, 12 January 2018, https://www.openaire.eu/empowering-open-science-kick-off-of-the-openaire-advance-h2020-project.

[14] ELIXIR Greece, a distributed infrastructure for life-science information, https://www.elixir-europe.org/about-us/who-we-are/nodes/greece; EPOS, European Research Infrastructure on Solid Earth, https://www.epos-ip.org; DARIAH-DE, Digital Research Infrastructure for the Arts and Humanities,https://de.dariah.eu/en_US.

[15] EOSC-hub, Services for the European Open Science Cloud, www.eosc-hub.eu/.

[16] LIBER Steering Committee for Research Infrastructures, http://libereurope.eu/strategy/research-infrastructures/committee; euroCRIS CRIS-IR Task Group, https://www.eurocris.org/community/taskgroups/cris-ir; Horizon 2020 Expert Group on the Future of Scholarly Publishing and Scholarly Communication, http://ec.europa.eu/transparency/regexpert/index.cfm?do=groupDetail.groupDetail&groupID=3463; Knowledge Exchange Open Access Expert Group, http://www.knowledge-exchange.info/projects/project/open-access; RDA Libraries for Research Data Interest Group, https://www.rd-alliance.org/groups/libraries-research-data.html.

and services to avoid regional silos and to build a truly global and interoperable scholarly commons. Furthermore, COAR works on recommendations for repositories of the next generation. A recent report outlines 11 new behaviors, as well as the technologies, standards and protocols that will facilitate the development of new services on top of the global network of digital repositories, including social networking, peer review, notifications and usage assessment [19].

3.3. Research Support

Digitally-enhanced research creates new opportunities and challenges for researchers. New tools and platforms are constantly emerging that enable the collection and processing of diverse kinds of research data and other information. One core challenge is to manage and store valuable research data, in such a way that this serves both on-going research and future (re)use, including sharing with the wider research community and other interested parties. At the institutional level, this involves developing guidelines, supporting these with functional information infrastructures and equipping researchers with the skills they need to succeed in today's data-rich and data-driven environment.

To step up support for researchers at Göttingen Campus, SUB Göttingen and the computing and IT competence center GWDG have founded the Göttingen eResearch Alliance (eRA). The multidisciplinary eRA team assists researchers in e-research and data management questions throughout the whole research life cycle, offering support, consultation and training. The eRA is an integral part in the proposal submission process and, in close cooperation with the research office, provides valuable support for applicants to ensure high quality, good practices and alignment with the university's data management policy [20]. Through this process, communication between researchers and eRA is established early on, which is then maintained throughout the course of the research project. During the research phase, the eRA team offers subject-specific and individually-tailored practical workshops and training sessions on research data management. It further supports researchers in successfully implementing research data management and applying digital research methods, such as visualization. Once the project is completed, the eRA team provides researchers with information and support on persistent identifiers, publication of research papers and data and long-term archiving.

4. Analyzing Scholarly Communication

Over the last decade, the digital transformation has led to vast changes in how research is conducted and how research findings are communicated and built upon. In the context of scholarly communication and the ongoing transition to open access, research funders and institutions need to closely monitor the uptake of open access, in all its variations, and not least in terms of costs.

In Germany, the German Research Foundation (DFG) has strongly influenced how universities keep track of articles published in fully-open access journals. Through its "Open Access Publishing" program, which started in 2011, the DFG has supported more than 50 universities including the University of Göttingen to establish support structures for covering open access publication fees. These funds are often managed by the university's library. One funding requirement is the annual reporting of open access publications by researchers affiliated with the university. To comply with this requirement, SUB Göttingen uses various bibliographic data sources, such as the internal research information system maintained by the central research management units to obtain publications to which University of Göttingen researchers have contributed, and the Directory of Open Access Journals (DOAJ) to determine whether the articles were published in quality-assured fully-open access journals.

To date, SUB Göttingen manages one of the largest publication funds for open access publication fees among German universities in terms of the total number of financially supported articles reported to the Open APC initiative[17], an open data effort for sharing information about institutional spending on open access publication fees. Figure 1 shows the annual expenditure of SUB Göttingen

---

[17] https://github.com/OpenAPC/openapc-de.

on publication fees from 2012–2016 aggregated by publisher. While funding for open access articles increased over the period, a slight drop in 2016 can be observed because of less publications in fully-open access journals published by Springer Nature. Our future work will, therefore, focus more on analyzing the overall publication output from researchers affiliated with the University of Göttingen in order to better understand these yearly differences.

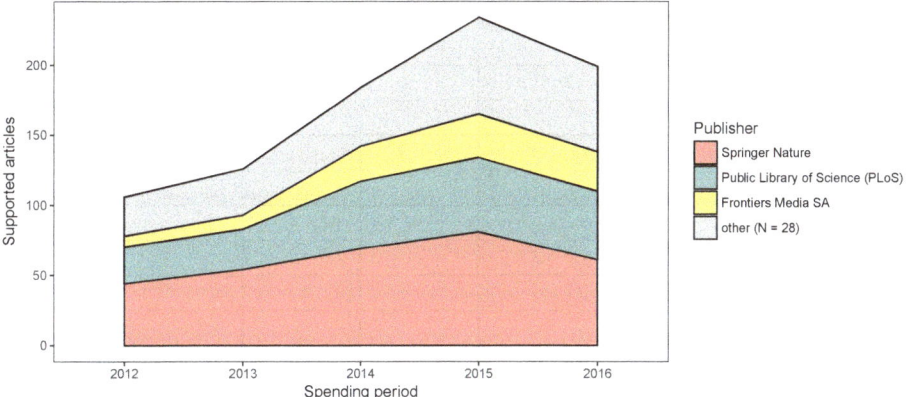

Figure 1. Articles (co-)funded by SUB Göttingen's Open Access Fund. Data source: https://github. com/openapc/openapc-de.

Our results reflect general spending patterns in Germany [21]. Contrary to findings from the U.K. or Austria, where publishing in hybrid open access journals is financially supported, as well, traditional publishing houses typically do not account for the largest share of institutional support. Rather, open access publishers such PLoS and Frontiers SA rank at the top; however, over a quarter of the expenditures was spent on Springer Nature publications, the former BioMed Central journal portfolio. In comparison, Jubb reports that more than half the expenditures on article processing charges spent by a sample of 10 U.K. universities in 2016 went to the three major publishing groups, Elsevier, Springer Nature and Wiley [22].

While reporting workflows for articles published in fully-open access journals are well-established, monitoring of hybrid open access journals remains challenging due to the lack of standardized indexing practices for hybrid open access articles in bibliographic databases [23]. In particular, in the case of hybrid open access, not all publishers share sufficient metadata to enable the identification of open access articles published in subscription-based journals, including licensing information. Moreover, self-archived copies provided by repositories are also difficult to find due to the distributed nature of repositories and the varying degrees of compliance with best-practices for tagging open access full-texts. Methods for monitoring open access to books or conference proceedings are even less established in bibliographic databases [24].

Key to improving insight into the state of open access is both comprehensive and standardized data sources and openly available tools to make the analysis and results transparent and reproducible for others. Promoting this, SUB Göttingen makes its code and, if possible, data sources openly available and actively engages in open science working groups. For instance, code libraries, which facilitate access to Europe PubMed Central [25] and Unpaywall Data [24], a DOI linking service for open access full-texts, have been developed at the SUB and were contributed to the rOpenSci initiative through its on-boarding mechanism, an open peer review process [26]. These software clients enable automated access to data sources that are instrumental for analyzing the uptake of open access, as well as for obtaining full-texts for text-mining purposes. Other examples include an easy-to-use dashboard that presents the current state of hybrid open access publishing based on openly accessible metadata and open source software [27]. Self-organized training sessions, including a Reading Group on Data Science Literature together with other members of the Göttingen Campus complement these activities. All these activities aim at open and re-usable tools for discovering and analyzing scholarly publications, which, in turn, reduces dependences on toll-access data sources and analytical tools.

5. Transforming Acquisition Budgets from Subscriptions to Financing Open Access

One of the main strategies of SUB Göttingen to advance open science is to continuously increase open access to scientific information.[18] This involves the development and negotiation of licensing models that include open access components and the transformation of acquisition budgets by financing open access articles.

A core instrument to increase awareness and uptake of open access publishing among authors is the university's open access publication fund (cf. Section 4). While the DFG has contributed to the fund since 2012, SUB Göttingen has started to gradually move these expenses into its acquisition budget; a process that is foreseen to be finalized by 2020. Since the overall open access expenses have increased over the last five years, this is only possible through a gradual cancellation of subscriptions and the transformation of these means to open access. This process involves close alignment with faculty representatives, in particular with faculties that make use of the OA publication funds. It must however be noted that the overall direct spending on open access publication fees is still rather small, at a level of about 4.3% of the total acquisition budget in 2016 (cf. Figure 1 and SUB statistics).[19]

Additionally, researchers are expected to cover publication charges through project funding. Since some results are published only after a research project is completed, some funders offer additional post-grant funding, for example, the post-grant Open Access Pilot[20] in the European Commission's Seventh Research Framework Programme, which ended in February 2018, and the German Ministry of Education and Research's (BMBF) Open Access fund.[21]

However, the transformation of institutional acquisition budgets is mainly driven by national and international projects and initiatives. Over the last few years, transition efforts have gained momentum, but also faced several challenges. Across Europe, there are similarities, but also differences with respect to the policies and strategies in this context. A few countries strongly promote a gold open access (U.K., The Netherlands), while the rest of the EU countries support a green or combined approach [28].

In order to establish new business models and transition contracts with publishers, research and service institutions need to negotiate with publishers and convince faculties. These new transition contracts, which combine access to journal content with funding to publish in open access, inherit the risk of less flexibility and are hard to finance. The budget management within the libraries has to be adjusted, and even the role of the library might change from deciding what to buy to choosing what to publish in open access.

The German DEAL project[22] aims to conclude nationwide licensing agreements with major academic publishers. An open access component is included in these negotiations. The initiative was commissioned by the Alliance of Science Organisations in Germany, represented by the German Rectors' Conference, the HRK. Despite the effort on both sides, negotiations with Elsevier have not yet resulted in any agreement as of May 2018. Consequently, the University of Göttingen and several other institutions (overall about 200) have canceled their subscriptions for 2017 and 2018. This has taken significant pressure off tight library acquisition budgets. Currently, most universities continue to have access to formerly-subscribed Elsevier journals as the publisher seeks to show their will to cooperate. However, in case Elsevier does cut off access, those institutions in Germany that were not

---

[18] Strategy SUB Göttingen 2018–2021, https://www.sub.uni-goettingen.de/en/about-us/portrait/strategy.
[19] Library statistics 2016, https://www.sub.uni-goettingen.de/en/about-us/portrait/statistics.
[20] FP7 post-grant Open Access Pilot, https://www.openaire.eu/postgrantoapilot.
[21] Bekanntmachung des BMBF, https://www.bmbf.de/foerderungen/bekanntmachung-1404.html.
[22] DEAL project, https://www.projekt-deal.de/about-deal/.

able to cancel subscriptions in the current period will continue to offer inter-library loans. This ensures access to Elsevier's papers for the time being [29] along with researcher's informal ways of getting access to material they want to read.

Agreements with Springer-Nature and Wiley are expected in 2018. If these negotiations succeed, a substantial part of acquisition budgets and scientific outputs will be transformed to open access within the time-frame of the agreements.

Open Access 2020[23], initiated by the Max Planck Digital Library, aims to replace subscription-based business models with economically sustainable and transparent open access publishing models. The national implications of Open Access 2020 are the focus of the National Open Access Contact Point (OA2020-DE)[24], which aims to enable a large-scale open access transformation of scientific journals by 2020. It is commissioned and sponsored by the Alliance of Science Organisations in Germany and collaborates closely with key stakeholders in scholarly publishing, i.e., universities, research institutions, funders, libraries and publishers, to improve the current subscription system. New open access business models are to be developed on the basis of an in-depth analysis of publications and their costs. SUB Göttingen is part of the planning and steering committee of the project.

The Deep Green project[25] focuses on so-called "alliance licenses" containing an open access clause that enables authors from authorized institutions to deposit articles that were published in such licensed journals in an open access repository of their choice with no or only a short embargo period. These licenses are negotiated on a national level and are co-funded by the DFG. SUB Göttingen supports this project in its role as one of the negotiators for alliance licenses [30,31].

Thanks to the international SCOAP3 initiative, 90% of High Energy Physics (HEP) papers are going to be published as open access articles in 2018.[26] SCOAP3 operates on an international level, while each country arranges participation in the partnership by selecting one or more national organizations as so-called representatives. The representatives then arrange the representation in SCOAP3 with all national institutions. Negotiations between the SCOAP3 consortium and scientific publishers like IOP Publishing, Springer, Elsevier, Oxford University Press and Hindawi have achieved the transformation of almost all HEP scientific journals to open access journals. If a journal covers more than one topic, only the HEP section was transformed. All publishing costs are now financed through a centrally-managed fund, such that authors do not need to worry about the financial aspect of publishing. Libraries contribute to SCOAP3 by redirecting the funds that were previously used for subscription fees of HEP literature. Today, these financial contributions correspond to the scientific output of each institution. While the costs for the University of Göttingen remained almost constant after the transition, institutions with very high scientific output face increasing financial contributions. Due to the negotiations, the average cost per open access article in SCOAP3 journals will remain at 1000 Euros maximum for the period of 2017–2019.

As a major publisher for Chemistry, the Royal Society of Chemistry (RSC) now offers an institutional licensing model called "Read and Publish". Having signed such an institutional agreement, SUB Göttingen automatically covers APCs for gold open access publications of affiliated authors in one of the RSC's hybrid journals. This licensing model serves as a pilot for new business processes for the implementation of efficient workflows for handling of these new contracts. According to the ESAC initiative[27], this includes proper author and article identification using ORCID and DOIs, funding acknowledgments and streamlining invoice and reporting processes [32].

---

[23] Open Access 2020, https://oa2020.org/.

[24] The National Open Access Contact Point (OA2020-DE), http://oa2020-de.org/en/pages/about.

[25] Deep Green project, https://deepgreen.kobv.de/de/deepgreen.

[26] SCOAP3, American Physical Society (APS) to join SCOAP3 from 2018, press release, 27 April 2017, https://scoap3.org/aps_joins_scoap3.

[27] Efficiency and Standards for Article Charges (ESAC), http://esac-initiative.org.

While many of these efforts focus on providing open access to STM journal articles, SUB Göttingen also supports the production and funding of open access books. Knowledge Unlatched[28] aims at converting books and journals of renowned publishers, supported by libraries like SUB Göttingen. Librarians from SUB Göttingen accepted the invitation to join the 2018 selection committee and have have helped to choose ebooks together with colleagues around the world.

Last, but not least, the transformation to open access also depends on the authors' personal choices for publication. As it can be difficult for them to evaluate if a journal offers quality services at a reasonable price, SUB Göttingen also supports enabling services such as the Directory of Open Access Journals, which curates a list of open access journals that meet a defined set of quality standards.

6. Research and Experiments as Facilitators of Open Science

Citations (how many and by whom) as the traditional "currency" of the scientific marketplace can be complemented by other measures assessing impact and quality: peer-review, usage statistics and alternative metrics. Together with citation counts, they reflect different angles of impact of scientific outputs [33] as shown in Figure 2.

Figure 2. Four ways to measure impact.

While citation metrics have been around for several decades and are well described, widely known and used (although sometimes without considering their limitations), alternative metrics are comparatively new and still evolving rather dynamically, adding a huge number of several fast changing types of data to the research field. Yet, indicators based on interactions on social media platforms have some very attractive advantages:

- Speed: Online interactions tend to happen very fast so that indicators can be made available immediately after publication of any scientific result and its mention on a social media platform. However, the creation of such metrics requires that platforms offer an API to access and track these interactions and to map publications via unique identifiers.
- Transparency: On social media platforms used for professional purposes, it is common to act under named accounts, i.e., individuals and their activities can be identified and recognized by their peers (versus general purpose platforms that allow, for instance, anonymous comments). Consequently, this results in a transparent picture of interactions. This is also a major argument in favor of alternative metrics. Typical forms of gaming (i.e., manipulation of metrics to an individual's advantage, massively using other people to view, download or like ones' posts) can be detected more easily by software algorithms than the still common practices of citation cartels [34].
- Societal impact: In contrast to citation counts, alternative metrics have the potential to not only reflect impact within the academic community, but also within the general public. This may

---

[28] Knowledge Unlatched, http://www.knowledgeunlatched.org.

arguably be more or less important for some research fields, but in some, cases it would be desirable to determine where scientific findings have an impact or even improve conditions of life.

These advantages and challenges related to citation-based indicators (see also [35]) are core motivations for further investigating alternative metrics such as metrics resulting from interactions on social media platforms. The library leads the *metrics project[29], which is funded by the DFG. The project's main aim is to gain deeper understanding of less developed metrics such as alternative and more specifically social media metrics.

Together with three German partners, the project analyzes data derived from social media platforms to determine if they can be employed in the creation of useful indicators reflecting interactions with scientific outputs. Reliability, accessibility, transparency and repeatability of platforms, as well as metrics aggregators are assessed in a technical work package. Origin, disciplinary differences and perceptions by researchers of scientific communities (social sciences in general and economics more specifically) are analyzed through surveys, interviews and lab experiments. Yet, a broader range of stakeholders is invited to take part in the discussion in community workshops. The first results revealed a greater variety of platforms than anticipated, which were used by researchers in their professional lives and not limited to services targeting researchers: YouTube and LinkedIn were among the top 10 services. This broadens the potential, but also the complexity of any potential metric. Creators of interactions on these platforms exhibit different patterns (e.g., age and career level), which should be taken into account as discussed by [36]. Further research will reveal if and how scientists understand and use social media metrics, how they interpret different levels of aggregation and visualizations of metrics and how reliable different sources of alternative metrics are in practice. The project's findings will benefit a broad range of stakeholders: *metrics users (e.g., researchers, research funders), information services and libraries, but also *metrics providers, with the aim to enable informed use of these metrics and to widen our understanding of the limitations and variation in interpretation.

7. Conclusions

Much has happened since the open access movement's early days at the beginning of the millennium, when the binary model of the green or golden route for open access was promoted to revolutionize scientific communication. Free access to published results continues to play a major part, despite the fact that, for instance, rising APC prices in commercial open access journals reveal new fields of conflict. Enabled by digital technology, research data can be treated as research results in their own right, which has resulted in a need to carefully design management and infrastructure for storing and disseminating them, while at the same time calling for policies or legislation to balance diverging interests. Digital technologies in the research process allow us to conduct research on previously unattainable levels of collaboration and interaction, transparency and comprehensibility, while tenure and promotion procedures only slowly recognize these practices as relevant.

We tried to show that these profound changes on all levels of the scientific communication system do not only affect scientists or publishers, but also result in organizational changes at an infrastructure organization such as our library. In the last five years, it has led to a significant shift in competencies and skills of newly hired or existing staff, requiring them to become research partners who happen to be embedded in the library. In this article, we highlighted how we participate and contribute to various aspects of science and research, on the practical level, with training or in policy making to influence the general setting of science. Our efforts happen against the backdrop that we act on behalf of a highly diverse research campus with disciplines requiring their own research processes and publication cultures. These differences need to be taken into account, given our role to provide our different audiences with content, infrastructure and support throughout the entire lifecycle of research, regardless of the additional effort on staff to align our offers with disciplinary needs. Our efforts will

---

[29] MEasuring The Reliability and perceptions of Indicators for interactions with sCientific productS, http://metrics-project.net.

not lead to more uptake of open science and open access practices if our audiences find themselves outside the scope of our consideration.

Besides our library efforts, further uptake of open science requires a gradual but profound shift of mindsets and social practice, and we anticipate this shift to continue for many more years or decades until it becomes mainstream. Our participation in the described projects leads to quantitative and qualitative growth of activities and staff, but is often based on third-party funding that we have to win in competitive settings. The activation energy from such third-party funds helps us enormously to set up services, but does not solve the challenge to run and extend them in a sustainable fashion and reliably accompany the lengthy shift of mindsets and paradigms. When we started our electronic publishing services around 2003, it was mainly on project money and prototyping services and exploration of whether there would be enough demand to transform them into permanent offers. While this is an understandable management decision, it poses the challenge that, on the one hand, preliminary services create as much or even more effort than routine services and, on the other hand, that services with transformative potential such as open science need time to gain recognition and acceptance.

Libraries are considered to be long-standing partners that are here to stay, and only against this backdrop are we able to reach out to scientists and act as a reliable partner in these newer fields that to many of them seem fast-changing and not yet established. We consider the following activity as our most promising and important. That is, building an open science network together with early career researchers through our Göttingen Open Science meet-ups has been an inspiring experience and has helped to step up knowledge and resulted in new types of collaboration. Making our colleagues from the more traditional parts of a research library aware that supporting open science is not the folly of the few, but the necessary progress we all have to make, has its difficulties. We believe that offering training on open science in-house and at library conferences is a way of sharing our experiences with our direct library colleagues and communities that helps them to come along on the way (plus learn new and exciting things). To end on a positive note, we have taken a broad and inclusive perspective to foster engagement in bringing forward open access and open science at the University of Göttingen. It is therefore the goal for the next few years to further strengthen the local implementation through local, national and international activities, to ensure a smooth shift of core library service areas and to foster and support good open science practices at Göttingen Campus. We are convinced that research libraries like ours are well-fitted hubs for open science activities, able to bridge status groups or disciplinary boundaries and unlock the full social potential of open science.

Author Contributions: All authors contributed to the writing of the paper. B.S. managed the author collective, coordinated the writing and edited the first version of the paper. A.B. organized editing of the revised version and made us all comply with the reviewers' requests.

Acknowledgments: The following projects are related to this work: the EU-funded projects FOSTER Plus, 741839; HIRMEOS, 731102; OpenAIRE2020, 643410; and the German Research Foundation-funded *metrics project. We thank our international and local colleagues in libraries and research for ideas and inspiration, Daniel Bangert for the final language check and last, but not least, our reviewers for their valuable input to improve the article.

Conflicts of Interest: The authors declare no conflict of interest. The founding sponsors had no role in the design of the study; in the collection, analyses or interpretation of data; in the writing of the manuscript; nor in the decision to publish the results.

References

1.	Maslove, D.M. Medical Preprints—A Debate Worth Having. *JAMA* **2018** *319*, 443–444. [CrossRef] [PubMed]
2.	Eve, M.P. *Open Access and the Humanities: Contexts, Controversies and the Future*; Cambridge University Press: Cambridge, UK, 2014. [CrossRef]

3. O'Carroll, C.; Kamerlin, C.L.; Brennan, N.; Hyllseth, B.; Kohl, U.; O'Neill, G.; Van Den Berg, R. (Eds.) *Providing Researchers with the Skills and Competencies They Need to Practise Open Science: Report of the Working Group on Education and Skills under Open Science*; Publications Office of the European Union: Luxembourg, 2017. Available online: https://ec.europa.eu/research/openscience/pdf/os_skills_wgreport.pdf (accessed on 17 June 2018).

4. Bargheer, M.; Pabst, J. Being small is not a fault: Making sense of the newer generation of German-language university presses. *Learn. Publ.* **2016**, *29*, 335–341. [CrossRef]

5. Jubb, M. Academic Books and Their Futures: A Report to the AHRC and the British Library. Available online: https://academicbookfuture.files.wordpress.com/2017/06/academic-books-and-their-futures_jubb1.pdf (accessed on 17 June 2018).

6. Sinclair, M., McCleery, A.; Graham, M.C. Review of Publishing: A Review of Scottish Publishing in the 21st Century—Summary Report. Scottish Arts Council, 2004. Available online: http://www.scottisharts.org.uk/resources/publications/research/pdf/RES3%20Review%20of%20Publishing.pdf (accessed on 17 June 2018).

7. Crossick, G. Monographs and Open Access. A Report to HEFCE, HEFCE, 2015. Available online: http://www.hefce.ac.uk/pubs/rereports/year/2015/monographs/ (accessed on 17 June 2018).

8. Ferwerda, E.; Pinter, F.; Stern, N. A landscape Study on Open Access and Monographs: Policies, Funding and Publishing in Eight European Countries. June 2017. Available online: https://doi.org/10.5281/zenodo.815932 (accessed on 17 June 2018).

9. Eve, M.P. Open Access publishing and scholarly communications in non-scientific disciplines *Online Inf. Rev.* **2015**, *39*, 717–732. [CrossRef]

10. Eve, M.P. Open Access Publishing Models and How OA Can Work in the Humanities. *Bull. Am. Soc. Inf. Sci. Technol.* **2017** *43*, 16–20. [CrossRef]

11. Bargheer, M.; Dogan, Z.M.; Horstmann, W.; Mertens, M.; Rapp, A. Unlocking the digital potential of scholarly monographs in 21st century research. *Liber Q.* **2017**, *27*, 194–211. [CrossRef]

12. Larivière, V.; Haustein, S.; Mongeon, P. The Oligopoly of Academic Publishers in the Digital Era. *PLoS ONE* **2015**, *10*, e0127502. [CrossRef] [PubMed]

13. Baron, N. *Words Onscreen: The Fate of Reading in a Digital World*; Oxford University Press: Oxford, UK, 2015.

14. Carr, N. Is Google Making Us Stupid? The Atlantic, July/August 2008. Available online: https://www.theatlantic.com/magazine/archive/2008/07/is-google-making-us-stupid/306868/ (accessed on 17 June 2018).

15. Pirola, S. *The Academic Book of the Future and Its Readers*; UCL Press: London, UK, 2017. [CrossRef]

16. Unsworth, J. Scholarly Primitives: What Methods Do Humanities Researchers Have in Common, and How Might Our Tools Reflect This? In Proceedings of the Symposium on Humanities Computing: Formal Methods, Experimental Practice, King's College, London, UK, 13 May 2000. Available online: http://www.people.virginia.edu/~jmu2m/Kings.5-00/primitives.html (accessed on 17 June 2018).

17. Van der Graaf, M. *The European Repository Landscape 2008. Inventory of Digital Repositories for Research Output in the EU*; Amsterdam University Press: Amsterdam, The Netherlands, 2009. Available online: https://arno.uva.nl/cgi/arno/show.cgi?fid=150724 (accessed on 17 June 2018).

18. Confederation of Open Access Respositories (COAR). COAR Roadmap: Future Directions for Repository Interoperability. Working Group 2: Repository Interoperability. February 2015. Available online: https://www.coar-repositories.org/files/Roadmap_final_formatted_20150203.pdf (accessed on 17 June 2018).

19. COAR. Next Generation Repositories. Behaviours and Technical Recommendations of the COAR Next Generation Repositories Working Group. 28 November 2017. Available online: https://www.coar-repositories.org/files/NGR-Final-Formatted-Report-cc.pdf (accessed on 17 June 2018).

20. Schmidt, B.; Dierkes, J. New alliances for research and teaching support: Establishing the Göttingen eResearch Alliance. *Program Electron. Libr. Inf. Syst.* **2015** *49*, 461–474. [CrossRef]

21. Jahn, N.; Tullney, M. A study of institutional spending on open access publication fees in Germany. *PeerJ* **2016**, *4*, e2323. [CrossRef] [PubMed]

22. Jubb, M. Monitoring the Transition to Open Access: December 2017. Report Commissioned by Universities UK. Available online: http://www.universitiesuk.ac.uk/policy-and-analysis/reports/Pages/monitoring-transition-open-access-2017.aspx (accessed on 17 June 2018).

23. Björk, B.-C. Growth of hybrid open access, 2009–2016. *PeerJ* **2017**, *5*, e3878. [CrossRef] [PubMed]

24. Piwowar, H.; Priem, J.; Larivière, V.; Alperin, J.P.; Matthias, L.; Norlander, B.; Haustein, S. The state of OA: A large-scale analysis of the prevalence and impact of Open Access articles. *PeerJ* **2018**, *6*, e4375. [CrossRef] [PubMed]

25. Levchenko, M.; Gou, Y.; Graef, F.; Hamelers, A.; Huang, Z.; Ide-Smith, M.; Iyer, A.; Kilian, O.; McEntyre, J. Europe PMC in 2017. *Nucleic Acid. Res.* **2017**, *46*, D1254–D1260. [CrossRef] [PubMed]

26. Ram, K., Ross, N.; Chamberlain, S. A model for peer review and onboarding research software. In *CEUR Workshop Proceedings. 1686 Proceedings of the Fourth Workshop on Sustainable Software for Science: Practice and Experiences (WSSSPE4), Manchester, UK, 12–14 September 2016*; Allen, G., Carver, J., Choi, S.-C.T., Crick, T., Crusoe, M.R., Gesing, S., Haines, R., Heroux, M., Hwang, L.J., Katz, D.S., et al., Eds.; CEUR Workshop Proceedings: Aachen, Germany, 2016. Available online http://ceur-ws.org/Vol-1686/WSSSPE4_paper_13.pdf (accessed on 17 June 2018).

27. Jahn, N. About the Hybrid OA Dashboard. 2018. Version of 11 June 2018. Available online: https://subugoe.github.io/hybrid_oa_dashboard/about.html (accessed on 17 June 2018).

28. Kita, J.-C.; Duchange, N.; Ponsati, A. Open Access Publishing Policies in Science Europe Member Organisations: Key Results from Science Europe and Global Research, Science Europe, Report D/2016/13.324/8, October 2016. Available online: http://www.scienceeurope.org/wp-content/uploads/2016/10/SE_OpenAccess_SurveyReport.pdf (accessed on 17 June 2018).

29. Matthews, D. German Universities Plan for Life without Elsevier. Times Higher Education (THE). 2017. Availabe online: https://www.timeshighereducation.com/news/german-universities-plan-life-without-elsevier (accessed on 17 June 2018).

30. Hillenkötter, K. Die Open-Access-Komponente in den DFG-Geförderten Allianz-Lizenzen. *Bibl. Forsch. Prax.* **2012**, *36*, 300–304. [CrossRef]

31. Schmidt, B.; Shearer, K. Licensing Revisited: Open Access Clauses in Practice. *Liber Q.* **2012**, *22*, 176–189. [CrossRef]

32. Geschuhn, K.; Stone, G. It's the workflows, stupid! What is required to make "offsetting" work for the open access transition. *Insights* **2017**, *30*, 103–114. [CrossRef]

33. Priem, J.; Taraborelli, D.; Groth, P.; Neylon C. Altmetrics: A Manifesto. 26 October 2010. Available online: http://altmetrics.org/manifesto (accessed on 17 June 2018).

34. Franck G. Scientific communication—A vanity fair? *Science* **1999**, *286*, 53–55. [CrossRef]

35. Wilsdon, J.; Allen, L.; Belfiore, E.; Campbell, P.; Curry, S.; Hill, S.; Jones, R.; Kain, R.; Kerridge, S.; Thelwall, M.; et al. *The Metric Tide: Report of the Independent Review of the Role of Metrics in Research Assessment and Management*; HEFCE: Stoke Gifford, UK, 2015. [CrossRef]

36. Lemke, S.; Mehrazar, M.; Peters, I.; Mazarakis, A. Evaluating Altmetrics Acts Through Their Creators—How to Advance? In Proceedings of the Workshop Altmetrics 17 at the 4th Altmetrics Conference (4:AM), Toronto, ON, Canada, 26–29 September 2017. Available online: http://altmetrics.org/altmetrics17 (accessed on 17 June 2018).

Article

Data-Driven Transition: Joint Reporting of Subscription Expenditure and Publication Costs

Irene Barbers [1,*,†] , **Nadja Kalinna** [1,2,†] **and Bernhard Mittermaier** [1,†]

1   Forschungszentrum Jülich, Central Library, D-52425 Jülich, Germany; n.kalinna@fz-juelich.de (N.K.);
    b.mittermaier@fz-juelich.de (B.M.)
2   RWTH Aachen, University Library, D-52062 Aachen, Germany
*   Correspondence: i.barbers@fz-juelich.de
†   These authors contributed equally to this work.

Received: 14 February 2018; Accepted: 12 April 2018; Published: 23 April 2018

Abstract: The transition process from the subscription model to the open access model in the world of scholarly publishing brings a variety of challenges to libraries. Within this evolving landscape, the present article takes a focus on budget control for both subscription and publication expenditure with the opportunity to enable the shift from one to the other. To reach informed decisions with a solid base of data to be used in negotiations with publishers, the diverse already-existing systems for managing publications costs and for managing journal subscriptions have to be adapted to allow comprehensive reporting on publication expenditure and subscription expenditure. In the case presented here, two separate systems are described and the establishment of joint reporting covering both these systems is introduced. Some of the results of joint reporting are presented as an example of how such a comprehensive monitoring can support management decisions and negotiations. On a larger scale, the establishment of the National Open Access Monitor in Germany is introduced, bringing together a diverse range of data from several already-existing systems, including, among others, holdings information, usage data, and data on publication fees. This system will enable libraries to access all relevant data with a single user interface.

Keywords: open access; APC; workflow; journal subscription; offsetting; publication fee; monitoring; transition

1. Introduction

The open access publishing model is an inherent part of scientific publishing today, and needless to say it affects the long-term tasks of academic libraries in procuring scholarly content. This content is no longer solely available through the traditional model of journal subscriptions, but increasingly in the form of accessible online content that is free of charge. This relatively new area of responsibility that falls upon libraries includes supporting affiliated scientists with the publishing process, as well as offering workflows and infrastructure such as institutional repositories or publication funds to handle article processing charge (APC)-financed open access publications. Many libraries manage publication funds to cover these costs and therefore have to report on this expenditure. Although this role has been established recently with the growing acceptance of and demand for open access publishing, there are still challenges associated with the large-scale transition to open access. One of these challenges is the reconciliation of parallel expenditure for subscription fees for closed access content and the rising costs for publishing in open access journals, which at some point in the future could make subscription costs obsolete. Libraries should record data for both types of expenditure and they need to implement joint reporting to manage the shift from subscription budget to publication budget calculations. Section 2 will illustrate why it is important to develop workflows to collect data on publication charges and how libraries should be involved in this process. Section 3 then presents a method to create a joint reporting of subscription costs and publication costs through adapting two separate systems to enable combined queries. Section 4 then shows examples for results and discusses the use of joint reporting. Further to this, in Section 5 we provide an outlook on the National Open Access Monitor, a reporting system in Germany at the national level.

2. Workflows for Collecting and Using Data on Publication Charges

In this section, the relatively new roles of libraries regarding open access publishing will be presented. One of them is a comprehensive service in the field of scientific publishing, which comprises the development of workflows for collecting and using data on publication charges. The collection and usage of data on publication charges aim to address the need for reliable expenditure data, not only when it comes to budget plans and negotiations with publishers for new agreements like "read and publish" contracts (combining subscription with open access publishing) for the individual research institution, but also for national agreement negotiations and overviews of the costs of scientific publishing. As open access publishing increasingly becomes a requirement, in particular for the APC-funded business model, the question arises as to who is responsible for managing the growing number of publication fee payment processes. Originally, these fees were charged to the publication's authors and were known as "author fees". However, there is a high level of administrative effort involved and authors realized that when they processed the APC payment themselves, it often took them more than one hour. This was revealed in a survey for a Knowledge Exchange report in 2017, in which authors said that "streamlined administrative procedures" would be of great help, and they would make expenditure become more transparent [1] (p. 14). Another UK study about the total costs of open access inferred that the management of gold open access could take two hours per article [2] (p. 2 and p. 17). A number of libraries therefore started to process these payments as a service provided in the field of scientific publishing. However, the question regarding who is currently responsible for the management of publication fees is not easy to answer, since it is handled in various ways—even within one country with different scientific institutions. A study by Solomon and Björk to estimate per-article expenditure for the publications of research-intensive universities in the USA and Canada indicates that there was no reliable data on publication fees collected in the USA and Canada (publication data collected between 2009 and 2013), since they used data from the APC payment repositories of four European institutions [3] (p. 5). In the UK, Wellcome Trust and Research Councils UK (RCUK) cover the majority of APCs for publications that contain publicly-funded research results. Pinfield et al. (2015) examined the payment responsibilities of 23 universities in the UK and stated that the APCs of these institution were mostly financed by the two aforementioned organizations [4] (pp. 1757–1758). In addition, Pinfield/Finch (2014) reported that the institutions' libraries often manage these payments centrally (ibid., p. 1752). In German universities and non-university research institutions it is more common practice for affiliated libraries assist their publishing scientists, particularly when they choose open access journals [5] (p. 87). The German Research Foundation (DFG) has, similarly to the Wellcome Trust or RCUK, established the program for research infrastructure known as "Scientific Library Services and Information Systems (LIS)", which comprises DFG funding for open access. German universities can apply for these funds, which "are intended as start-up funding to set up an open access publication fund [...]" [6] (p. 3). It is mostly the university libraries that are responsible for managing these open access funds, for example the Leibniz Universität Hannover (TIB) [7].

However, thinking of ways to finance through external funding options, some argue that libraries cannot simply be declared as the responsible institutions that centrally take care of publication charge payments. There are organizational issues due to structural conditions such as the two-tier library system in Germany. In such cases, the separation of a library system into a central library and several independent institute libraries affects the assignment of university-wide tasks of the university library. Nevertheless, the central management of payment by the libraries is highly desirable. Libraries have supplied scientific literature from closed access publishers for many years. The nature of this library service is currently changing, however, with at least one-third of scholarly journal literature being freely available due to open access publishing [1] (p. 14). Giving the responsibility of managing publication payments to libraries is a good idea, since, as mentioned before, they have been negotiating subscription contracts with publishers for years. This is a great advantage when it comes to the reconciliation of parallel expenditure for subscription fees because they have the financial data available. Furthermore, they often report on the publications output (bibliography) of their research institutions, meaning they are already involved in the field of scientific publishing. Non-university research institutes often run their own publication funds and have therefore implemented open access policies to communicate the support and services they offer in terms of open access publishing and strategies for approaching the transition. We, the Central Library of Forschungszentrum Jülich, are a non-university research library with over 200 publications per year for which invoices are processed, amounting to roughly 400,000 EUR in APCs, hybrid publication charges, and associated costs (see Section 3). According to our Open Access Strategy, "the Central Library has the task of supporting the transition from subscription journals to open access and to control expenditures for subscription journals in such a manner that sufficient funds are available for gold open access publication fees (article processing charges, APCs)" [8]. This claim is compliant with the OA2020 initiative's mission statement, that in order to be successful in the transition process it is necessary to "establish transparency with regard to costs and potential savings" [9]. Therefore, collected data can be used to prepare for negotiations with publishers when it comes to discussing offsetting publication costs against subscription costs or of flipping journals from the hybrid model to the full open access model. To summarize, it should not fall to the authors to contend with APC management. The libraries have experience managing subscription agreements and budget plans, and also often take care of external funding budgets (DFG, RCUK, etc.) and bibliographies. The library should therefore be responsible for processing all publication fee invoices, including page or colour charges, and invoices for article processing charges (APCs) for publishing in full or hybrid open access journals. If this is not implemented, there will be little opportunity to monitor the overall costs of subscription and publishing [10] (p. 325). However, there is a need for optimization articulated even in cases where libraries such as the German Max Planck Digital Library are in charge of payment management. Responsible staff at the Max Planck Digital library for example remarked that in contrast to the proven structures in managing journal subscriptions "the management of publication costs is still largely based on manual processes" [5] (p. 87). They also mentioned the great need for standardization in this area, as articulated by the British Research Information Network (RIN) (ibid.). The RIN did not publish any new findings in this regard on its website in the meantime [11]. Despite that, the MDPL described that the expenses for licenses, subscriptions and publication fees should be brought together to be able to evaluate publishers' offers, but they do not explain how they are achieving that reconciliation of parallel expenditure [5] (p. 88). In accordance with these statements, Vierkant et al. outlined that it is currently hardly possible to automate the APC workflows [12] (p. 164). This means that publication fee management must be performed manually, which in turn implies that the library must cooperate closely with the authors. If an author is planning a submission, he/she should inform the library in good time. When the library or the research institution as a whole has distributed an open access strategy/policy in which funds and prepayment methods are also communicated, authors tend to get in contact with the library on time for payment reasons. This enables the library to check the corresponding author's affiliation, the business model offered by the journal, and the total applicable publication fees. The library also clarifies if there is a cooperation contract with the publisher[1]. These conditions affect the fund from which the publication can be paid for and the payment process itself, as these agreements often imply other payment methods, such as payment from a prepayment account to reduce single invoices

---

[1] For example the publishing agreement between Frontiers and the Helmholtz Association.

and a reduction in publication fees by receiving discounts granted in such cooperation agreements. This emphasizes the complexity of the APC market, which must be considered when establishing workflows and systems to collect and use publication fee data [3] (p. 7). The MDPL also brings up this subject by commenting upon the hurdle of intensive dialogue with each individual publisher/provider which must take place, as the administrative process varies from provider to provider [5] (p. 88). Therefore librarians must be familiar with the changing market of scientific publishing and ways of distributing published research results. Keller described the growing need for competences in this field with the term "publishing literacy", which comprises "the in-depth understanding of new (digital) possibilities of scholarly communication and the skills of the individual researcher to select the best format to present, publish and disseminate his results and ideas" [13] (p. 158). The author describes this skill as an important aspect of information literacy and as a "key focus of the work of academic librarians" in supporting the author adequately (ibid.). This task includes checking for green open access options offered by publishers and implementing the procedures that automatically make the permitted manuscript version available in the library's repository after the applicable embargo period has elapsed. However, the above-mentioned good practice requirements give rise to the question as to whether there is a suitable place and a proven workflow for storing and reporting on data on publication fees in academic libraries. Vierkant et al. note that there is no established approach so far [12] (p. 158). The majority of universities and research libraries run online repositories with metadata on the institution's publications. However, these repositories do not provide a means of managing invoicing data by default. Nevertheless, some academic libraries, such as the University of Regensburg, have started to implement APC management within their repositories [14]. In order to create a fast and practical way of handling publication fees, we initially set up a database using the software MS Access. We called this the Publication charge-Reprint-Colour Charge-Cover (PROCC) database. The following data is entered into this database for each publication that incurs charges:

- Title
- Source (name of journal or e-book)
- DOI
- Publisher
- Corresponding author
- Institute
- Status of payment, cost type (e.g., permission, APC, colour charges), price, invoice, and date processed
- Special contract (prepayment account, offsetting)

The PROCC database comprises a simple, user-friendly interface where the data can be easily inputted. Data storage and maintenance is server-sided (see Section 3). The database can be easily queried to determine the total expenditure, for example, per publisher, per year, or per cost type. However, running a repository for all publications by our institution implies that we have to maintain two separate databases, which in turn means that there are data overlaps because metadata such as title, author, and journal is recorded both in the repository and in the PROCC database. In other words, the database containing publication costs exists separately from the repository's record of the publication. They are only connected by the ID number of the related record, which has to be entered manually. As Wagner pointed out, the publishing process should be changed to avoid multiple records of the same items of data [15] (p. 43). Such time-consuming workflows should be optimized by using established systems. A clear disadvantage of our separate database is the manual data input, which leads to duplication (title, author, source, institute, etc.) which is moreover non-transparent because the expenditure is not accessible by the scientific institutes. For these reasons, a decision has been made to shut down the PROCC database. Comparable to the plans of the University of Regensburg and in cooperation with Deutsches Elektronensynchrotron (Hamburg/Zeuthen) (abbreviated as DESY), we have expanded our shared repository infrastructure [16] to include the functionality of recording publication fees. In this context, an Extensible Markup Language (XML)-based format including cost information in the Open Archives Initiative—Protocol for Metadata

Harvesting (OAI-PMH) interface has been developed in order to be harvested by the University Library of Bielefeld, which releases datasets for the Open APC Initiative [17]. At the moment, we still store the data on fees in both databases (the PROCC database and the APC management tool in the repository) and we will continue to do so until we have a solution for connecting the repository with the electronic resource management system (ERMS). Until then, we can exploit the advantages of the SQL-based PROCC database, which enables joint reporting with the expenses for subscription costs as it shares the same SQL server as the ERMS.

3. Electronic Resource Management System and Publications Database—Joint Reporting System

During our search for methods of gathering data for joint reporting, we found that such methods are mostly depicted in a general way, for example "gathering data from volunteer libraries" to calculate the "total cost of ownership", as described by the authors of [4] or [18]. However, where and how institutions collect or even combine both kinds of data at a local level has not been reported. This lack of information shows the need to share examples of methods, which is what we are currently attempting to achieve.

Our requirements for the joint reporting system include the immediate availability of data with subsequent daily updates. The use of our established two local systems has proven to be an obvious and practical approach. Data on subscription journals and on publication fees are updated in both systems in an ongoing daily workflow and can be used for real-time reporting. Additional advantages can be seen in the use of skills developed for the established workflows, the continuation of the established workflows themselves, and the avoidance of duplicate data storage.

Having described the process and workflows for recording data on publication expenditure in the previous section, the following section will provide details on how subscription costs are captured with the help of an electronic resource management system (ERMS) and how automated joint reporting of expenditure for subscriptions and publications has been established. An ERMS is defined by Verminsky and Blanchat as: "an internal system or software program to assist in the maintenance of licensed electronic resources, such as databases, ebooks, and ejournals. An ERMS may include a means to track license agreements including license and copyright terms, renewals, access management, and collection development" [19] (p. 235). ERMSs are in most cases not part of library management systems [20], but stand alone, which makes the integration of electronic resource management into a library's workflows challenging. In addition, ERMSs do not provide the technical or organizational framework to handle a publication fee workflow.

Our institution operates its own ERMS [21] which is built as an SQL Server database. Development started in 2007 [22], shortly after the library switched its subscription model from print to e-only wherever possible. The ERMS provides information about journal metadata and access information, imported from the "Elektronische Zeitschriftenbibliothek" ("Electronic Journals Library"), hosted by the University Library of Regensburg [23]. Certain licensing information such as subscription costs, cost codes, and licensing codes are not managed in the EZB database, but are stored and managed inside the local ERMS. COUNTER usage reports [24] are collected on a regular basis from publishers' platforms or their usage report providers, and uploaded into the ERMS. Licensing information and usage data are then used to provide reporting in several views, tailored to the needs of collection development. These views present reports detailing subscription costs, usage data, and cost per download analysis for each publisher as well as at the individual journal title level. This includes in-depth analysis of package subscriptions, time-lines, and usage data broken down by year of publication as well as usage reports for open access publishers and open access journals.

One step towards the goal of supporting the shift away from subscription budgets to open access publication budgets is to monitor both budgets closely in order to be able to track developments. We therefore implemented several reports into our ERMS monitoring web interface, showing the number of publications by journal and the publication costs at the journal level and publisher level. The only source for these reports is the PROCC database, as described in the previous section. To go one step further in bringing both sides together, SQL statements across the two databases provide reports which unite subscription costs, downloads, cost per download, and publication costs per journal into one single view. Both databases run on the same SQL Server and reports are displayed within one single web interface built with SQL Server Reporting Services. The main obstacle when creating joint reports is that the ERMS presents subscription information at a different level than the PROCC database, which presents information on publications. On the one side, we have information about licensing at the journal level, package level, or publisher level, whereas on the other side, data on publication expenditure is presented at the article level. To align these different levels, publication costs must be aggregated first at the journal level. This is achieved by initially creating a view of publication costs at the journal level which is then used to serve as a source for the combined query to join subscription data and publication data. Additionally, a common identifier for journal titles is necessary in both databases, and as the identifier of the EZB, termed EZB-ID, is already in use in the ERMS, the same identifier was added to the journal table in the PROCC database. Another possible identifier would be the identifier used in the "Zeitschriftendatenbank – ZDB" [25]. The use of ISSN has been proven unsuitable as there are too many inconsistencies in this identifier. Aggregating reports at the publisher level is an additional challenge. As there exist no authorized forms for publishers in the commonly used knowledge bases, publisher names used in ERMS are often different to publisher names used in the PROCC database. Again, we regularly find different levels of aggregation and allocation of journals. In the past, we used to allocate journals to hosts rather than publishers in the ERMS, as usage reports come from the hosts. Publishers and hosts often differ. Highwire [26] is a good example. It is an organization that serves as a host for multiple publishers and societies. All journals hosted by Highwire used to be joined under the same label in ERMS in the past. However, joint reporting with publication expenditure means that this allocation of journals no longer meets the purpose of reporting. To match publishers in both ERMS and PROCC databases, several adjustments had to be made in both databases. As a first step, the bigger hosts in ERMS, where several publishers and societies had been summarized together, have been split up so that those publishers are now represented individually. The second step was to insert the data on ERMS publishers into the PROCC database publishers table to match the publisher names and thus to be able to join the respective publishers tables in SQL statements for the creation of reports.

As we are building on established structures of the ERMS that were originally designed for the sole purpose of usage reporting, some other adjustments were necessary. In the past, reporting was only performed for those journals where usage data was provided and where subscription costs had been incurred. The philosophy had always been that the usage data of journals with no subscription costs was not of central interest, as there was no cost per download as such to calculate. This also meant that initially whenever a journal had no usage reported and/or no subscription expenditure recorded, it did not show up at all, even if publication charges had been incurred. In other words, if a certain journal was not already captured by ERMS, it would not show up in the joint reporting interface, even if publication fees had been allocated to it in the PROCC database. One measure in opening up ERMS structures has therefore been to input open access journals from well-known publishers manually on a regular basis in ERMS. This can be done by exporting so-called "green" journals from a chosen set of publishers from our knowledge base, the EZB. Another idea would be to harvest selected data from the Directory of Open Access Journals (DOAJ) [27]. However, an automated harvesting process for relevant open access journals is still desirable.

4. Results and Further Use of Joint Reporting

One of the major benefits of joint reporting is that the complete range of a given publisher's portfolio, be it of subscription journals, hybrid, or open access journals, can be viewed and analysed in a single report with all the relevant data aggregated. The joint view thus provides us with new key figures like total expenditure per journal and total expenditure per publisher. Factoring publication fees into the calculation broadens the scope and brings a fresh perspective to the traditional method of collection development through cost-per-download analysis. Additionally, the automated joint reporting serves as the basis for further analysis and visualization of the institutional expenditure on subscriptions and publications as a whole and with a focus on the most important publishers. The visualization is presented as the Open Access Barometer [28] on the institution's website and constitutes an example of the visibility and further use of the data. The purpose of presenting the information on the website is to advocate open access within our institution and to demonstrate the library's efforts towards supporting our institution's open access goals through the considered collection development. The total expenditure, number of the institution's own publications, cost per publication, and distribution of expense types are documented for the 12 most important publishing houses (according to expenses and number of publications). Comments on the cost structure and the transition status of the individual publishers are additionally exclusively available on the intranet. Figure 1 shows the shares in the total number of publications of the most important publishing houses (according to expenses and number of publications) where journal articles with a corresponding author from our own institution were published in 2017, and shows the shares of total expenditure for those same 12 publishers. "Total expenditure" adds the sum of subscription fees and publication fees paid to the publishers in 2017.

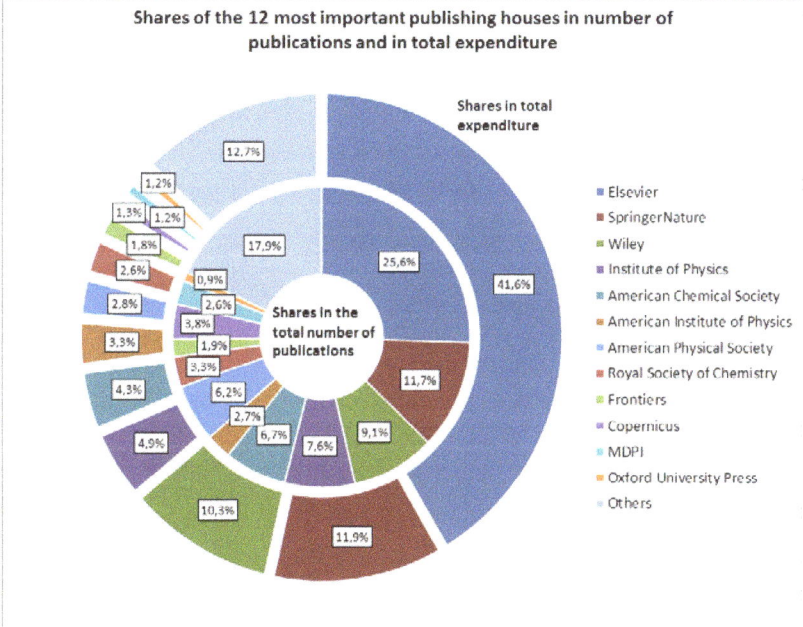

Figure 1. Shares in the total number of publications and in total expenditure in 2017. Source: Forschungszentrum Jülich.

The three biggest publishers with the highest shares in the number of publications (Figure 1) together account for access to 62.3% of all subscribed journals and for 70% of subscription expenditure Table 1. The table shows the shares of subscribed journals compared to the shares of expenditure for the nine subscription publishers from our previous sample.

Table 1. Shares of the number of subscribed journals and of subscription expenditure.

Publisher	Share of the Number of Subscribed Journals	Share of Subscription Expenditure
Elsevier	51.5%	50.3%
- Elsevier Subscribed Journals	2.4%	39.7%
- Elsevier Freedom Collection	49.1%	10.6%
Springer Nature	9.0%	9.1%
- Springer Subscribed Journals	0.8%	3.7%
- Springer Cross Access	5.8%	0.4%
- Nature Subscribed Journals	0.4 %	4.3%
- Nature Complete	1.9%	0.7%
Wiley	1.8%	10.6%
Institute of Physics	1.8%	4.7%
American Chemical Society	1.4%	5.2%
American Institute of Physics	0.4%	3.2%
American Physical Society	0.3%	2.6%
Royal Society of Chemistry	1.0%	2.7%
Oxford University Press	3.6%	1.0%
Others	29.5%	10.7%
Total for all publishers	100%	100%

Figure 2 presents the proportion of the types of cost for each publisher. The chart shows that hybrid publication charges and associated costs are more significant than gold open access expenditure for the traditional subscription publishers. The exception here is SpringerNature, which has a large proportion of APC expenditure due to a high number of publications in both Nature Communications and Scientific Reports.

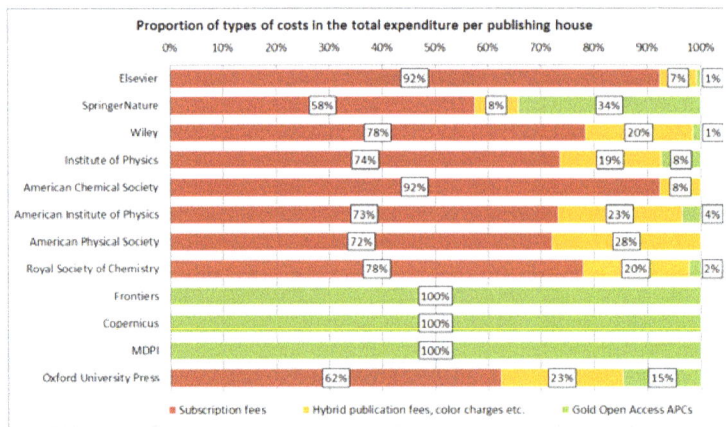

Figure 2. Proportion of types of costs in 2017. Source: Forschungszentrum Jülich.

For almost all the publishers, we can see that their average hybrid publication charges are higher than their average gold open access APC Table 2. This corresponds with the findings of a Universities UK report [29] that shows the difference in APC price bands for full open access journals and hybrid journals.

Table 2. Average publication expenditure by type of cost.

Publisher	Average APC in EUR	Average Hybrid Publication Charge in EUR	Average Color Charge in EUR	Average Cover Charge in EUR	Average Page Charge in EUR
Elsevier	1017	2092	1049		925
Springer Nature	1840	2634	1763		
Wiley	1017	2416	1198	1242	1924
Institute of Physics	1346	1901	1565		405
American Chemical Society		1127			
American Institute of Physics	2042	1950			473
American Physical Society		1269	1643		
Royal Society of Chemistry	516	1659		1117	
Frontiers	1650				
Copernicus	1447				
MDPI	1049				
Oxford University Press	2130	2450	1050		900
Others	1209	1052	1113		1252

The figures shown in Tables 2 and 3 are based on the publication fees that were processed by our library in 2017. It is worth noting that the number of instances for APCs and other charges (Table 3) does not correspond to the number of journal articles with corresponding authors from our institution used for Figure 1. This is partly due to the corresponding author articles being published in subscription journals, where no publication fees are incurred. Furthermore, publication fees can be paid for by institutions other than our own and some authors do not use the library's publication workflow services. It should also be noted that fees can vary for a single publisher depending on the journal selected for publication.

Table 3. Total instances and total sum of publication fees.

	APCs	Hybrid Publication Charges	Color Charges	Cover Charges	Page Charges
Total instances	138	69	33	6	28
Total sum of fees	209,064 EUR	117,166 EUR	39,038 EUR	7076 EUR	33,397 EUR
Total average publication fee	1510 EUR	1698 EUR	1183 EUR	1179 EUR	1193 EUR

What use can we make of these findings? The joint reporting enables control over expenditure in a manner that places us in a position to make fully informed decisions on collection development in the light of the transition process. Download metrics and the calculation of cost per download are still of significance for the detailed collection development of subscription journals, since these metrics are informative for cancellation and/or renewal decisions at the single-journal or package levels. However, data on the types of cost, shares of subscription expenditure, and publishing fee rates help to create an overall picture, which together with the key figure of "total expenditure per publisher" will indicate where attention should be focused in terms of negotiation strategy. Over the course of the next few years, we will be able to create views on the development of expenditure and keep track on shifts in proportion to demonstrate the progress of transition and collected data can be used to prepare for negotiations with publishers.

5. The Broader Perspective: A National Open Access Monitor for Germany

The system described in the previous sections can be adopted by any academic library. In addition to some programming skills, it is necessary to

- maintain an ERMS with an appropriate interface
- download COUNTER statistics of subscribed journals and store them in a database
- maintain the bibliography of the institution with authority data for journals and publishers
- record the open access and non-open access publications fees paid by the institution, again using authority data for journals and publishers

However, in most cases not all requirements are met, which means that the number of libraries utilizing such a system is quite limited. Furthermore, it would be rather uneconomical if all libraries were to develop and implement such systems independently. This was one of the reasons behind establishing the National Open Access Monitor in Germany. It originated within the framework of the OA2020 movement, where the German Alliance of Research Organisations [29] established a National Contact Point [30] in 2017. One of the tasks of this National Contact Point is to establish a data monitor [31]. This data monitor, which is still under construction, received a powerful boost by a grant from the Federal Ministry of Education and Research (BMBF). The BMBF had established a National Open Access Strategy for Germany in autumn 2016, which included the idea of the National Open Access Monitor. In a subsequent call, the Central Library of Forschungszentrum Jülich was the successful applicant for this task; the project started in January 2018. According to the National Open Access Strategy [32], the Open Access Monitor should *"track the quantitative status of Open Access in Germany in a reliable manner. (...) If institutions are able to quantify the share of Open Access in their publications, they will also be able to identify areas that are weaker in Open Access and foster Open Access in a more targeted manner. It is also planned that monitoring will show what sources and amounts of funds are used for obtaining scientific information and for financing publications (both for Open Access and the subscription-based model). In this way, the changeover to Open Access can be structured in a tailored manner."* This means that the Open Access Monitor has a broad focus—not only open access, but also subscription, and not only a from national perspective but also with the local view of single institutions. Academic publishing is currently a mixed economy, consisting both of the open access model and the subscription model, and it will remain so in the foreseeable future. Therefore, data from both models has to be gathered. Some of the data is available only at the local level and therefore must be collected there. This data includes expenditure (both for APCs and subscriptions), journal holdings, and usage data. Some of the data are already available in databases and therefore does need not to be collected at the local level. This includes publication and citation data. The National Open Access Monitor does not intend to collect the data directly from the participating institutions nor to build a new system comprising all necessary functions to do so. In contrast, for reasons of economy and acceptance in the community, the Monitor will rely on systems which already exist or which are currently being developed (Table 4).

Table 4. Sources for the National Open Access Monitor.

System	Data	Operator
Global Open Knowledgebase (GOKb) [33]	Authority records for journals and publishers	Staatsbibliothek zu Berlin and VZG
Virtual International Authority File (VIAF) [34]	Authority records for institutions	OCLC
LAS:eR [35]	Licenses and license fees	hbz, VZG, University Libraries of Frankfurt and Freiburg
National Statistics Server [36]	COUNTER statistics	University Libraries of Frankfurt and Freiburg
KB-database [37]	Publications and citations	Kompetenzzentrum Bibliometrie
BASE [38]	Publications	University Library Bielefeld
OpenCitations [39]	Citations	David Shotton and Silvio Peroni
Open APC	Publication fees	UB Bielefeld

License information will come from LAS:eR, a system currently being developed within the framework of a DFG project. It is intended to be a free and open ERMS, avoiding the many problems associated with commercial systems on the market. Today, the extent to which libraries will use this system is unclear. However, we are optimistic that there will be reasonable uptake: it is intended to establish a private Lots Of Copies Keep Stuff Safe (LOCKKS) network at a national level [40], where the licensing rights of the respective members will be maintained in LAS:eR. Usage information will be incorporated as COUNTER statistics. An easy option is participation in the National Statistics Server, where institutions can maintain their usage statistics; on their side, only the Standardized Usage Statistics Harvesting Initiative (SUSHI) [41] credentials have to be provided. Institutions that do not use this fee-based service could provide their COUNTER statistics directly. For publication and citation data, a number of sources[2] are used because no single source fits all purposes: BASE contains publications from all journals, but not from all institutions (and from some institutions not covering the complete bibliography), because institutions have to participate actively. The Web of Science [42] comprises both publication and citation information, but not for all journals. No interaction on behalf of the institutions is necessary, so the coverage for the indexed journals is very good. The Web of Science will be accessed via the bibliometric database of Kompetenzzentrum Bibliometrie, where the affiliations of German institutions have already been normalized and cleaned. The idea is to calculate ratios between the number of publications in the Web of Science and the number of publications in BASE at the level of publishers for a number of institutions with an excellent coverage in BASE. These ratios can then be used to extrapolate for other institutions. OpenCitations is freely accessible and contains citation data from most publishers. As of January 2018, notable exceptions are Elsevier and the American Chemical Society. Publication fees can be taken from Open APC. Here, an increase in participation of institutions and a broader coverage of types of publication fees is desirable. All systems

---

[2]   Additionally, the use of Crossref metadata is considered.

share a common feature in that they do not contain data at a 100% level; in some cases, the figure is much lower. Therefore, it will be an important goal of the project to identify and develop means of increasing the participation of institutions in collecting data and delivering it to the respective systems. A key problem is authority control: some systems do not have validated authority records[3]; while others implement authority control but utilize their own, proprietary scheme[4]. To map data from different sources, it is therefore necessary to validate different proprietary schemes against a master file of authority records. For institutions, we use the Virtual International Authority File (VIAF), and for journals and publishers the Global Open Knowledgebase (GOKb). GOKb will be a machine-readable excerpt of the "Zeitschriftendatenbank—ZDB", the worlds' largest database for serials. GOKb already exists, but will undergo a fundamental update in the near future. The National Open Access Monitor will amalgamate this data in a PostgreSQL 10 database. It will come with a user interface that allows access to the data. A dedicated rights management for the regulation of access to the database in various usage scenarios will be implemented:

- Institutions will have access to their own data from a single user interface, in most cases for the first time.
- Negotiators for transformation agreements will have all relevant data concerning a specific publisher at hand.
- On behalf of the BMBF, the status and progress of open access can be monitored on a national scale by Forschungszentrum Jülich or other parties.
- Scientists can use the data for research on the publishing system.

6. Conclusions and Outlook

Open access has brought a change in the roles and systems of academic libraries. A dedicated open access strategy is desired, funds have to be established and maintained, and a central payment process managed by the library is desirable. This will allow publication cost data to be collected and stored in an appropriate system, which should be connected to the institutions' bibliography/repository and augmented with subscription expenditure information. If a library currently has only a bibliography or a repository in place, it is worth considering expanding their system's capacity to cover publication fees instead of creating a new system in parallel. This system, of course, still has to be connected to an ERMS. The collection of this data is not an end to itself. The information helps the library in its reporting duties and in dealing with questions of budget allocation. It enables librarians to engage in negotiations with publishers about offsetting publication costs against subscription costs or flipping journals from the hybrid model to the full open access model. Since we suggest that offsetting should only be seen as an intermediate step within the transition process [43], the importance of detailed expenditure control cannot be stressed enough. Negotiations can only be pursued on the basis of solid data. Offsetting agreements must have valid data on a larger scale at hand, potentially at a national level. Without such data, endeavours such as the DEAL negotiations [44] cannot be pursued. At a minimum, the current expenditure levels and the publication numbers must be at hand. To this end, anticipatory aggregation at the national level is convenient and economical. Furthermore, this approach reduces the burden on individual institutions to maintain such a system on their own. To some extent, however, the collection of data will still reside with each institution.

Important conclusions we can draw from our experiences:

- It is important to use normalized data/authority files. Otherwise, reporting at any intermediate level (e.g., the publisher's level) involves tedious manual work. Without controlled data, ease of reporting is only feasible at a small-scale level (e.g., single articles) or at the top level.

---

[3] Example: Names of journals and publishers in BASE.
[4] Example: Names of journals and publishers in Web of Science.

- It makes sense to use one single system that incorporates both (open access) publication information and subscription information.
- At a national level, data should be available in stock and not collected on demand. The latter involves multiple requests for the delivery of data, sometimes on short notice, and therefore rather poor compliance and a higher workload for the local libraries.

Author Contributions: Irene Barbers is responsible for Sections 3 and 4; Nadja Kalinna is responsible for Sections 1 and 2; Bernhard Mittermaier is responsible for Sections 5 and 6.

Conflicts of Interest: The authors declare no conflict of interest.

Abbreviations

The following abbreviations are used in this manuscript:

APC	Article Processing charges
ERMS	Electronic Resource Management System
OAI-PMH	Open Archives Initiative—Protocol for Metadata Harvesting
PROCC database	Publication charge-Reprint-Colour Charge-Cover database
SUSHI	Standardized Usage Statistics Harvesting Initiative
XML	Extensible Markup Language
LOCKKS	Lots Of Copies Keep Stuff Safe

References

1. Knowledge Exchange: Paying for Open Access. The Author's Perspective 2017. Available online: http://doi.org/10.5281/zenodo.438037 (accessed on 17 April 2018).
2. Research Consulting UK: Counting the Costs of Open Access. The estimated Cost to UK Research Organisations of Achieving Compliance with Open Access Mandates in 2013/14, 2014. Available online: http://www.researchconsulting.co.uk/wp-content/uploads/2014/11/Research-Consulting-Counting-the-Costs-of-OA-Final.pdf (accessed on 17 April 2018).
3. Solomon, D.; Björk, B.-C. Article processing charges for open access publication—The situation for research intensive universities in the USA and Canada. *PeerJ* **2016**, *4*, e2264.
4. Pinfield, S. The "Total Cost of Publication" in a Hybrid Open-Access Environment: Institutional Approaches to Funding Journal Article-Processing Charges in Combination With Subscriptions. *J. Assoc. Inf. Sci. Technol.* **2016**, *67*, 1757–1766.
5. Sikora, A.; Geschuhn, K. Management of article processing charges—Challenges for libraries. *Insights* **2015**, *28*, 87–92.
6. Deutsche Forschungsgemeinschaft. Guidelines Open Access Publishing. DFG form 12.20—02/17. Available online: http://www.dfg.de/formulare/12_20/12_20_en.pdf (accessed on 13 February 2018).
7. Leibniz Information Center for Science and Technology University Library: Leibniz Universität Hannover's Open Access Publishing Fund. Available online: https://www.tib.eu/en/publishing-archiving/open-access/financing-open-access/publishing-fund-leibniz-universitaet/ (accessed on 13 February 2018).
8. Forschungszentrum Jülich. Open Access Strategy of Forschungszentrum Jülich. Available online: http://www.fz-juelich.de/zb/EN/Expertise/open_access/oa_strategy_fzj/oa_strategy_node.html (accessed on 21 April 2018).
9. OA2020, Mission Statement. Available online: https://oa2020.org/mission/ (accessed on 9 January 2018).
10. Frick, C. Empfehlungen für Workflows zur Übernahme von Publikationsgebühren. In *Praxishandbuch Open Access*; Söllner, K., Mittermaier, B., Eds.; De Gruyter Saur: Berlin, Germany; Boston MA, USA, 2017; pp. 323–330, ISBN 978-3-11-049406-8. Available online: https://www.degruyter.com/downloadpdf/books/9783110494068/9783110494068-037/9783110494068-037.pdf (accessed on 30 January 2018).
11. The Association of Commonwealth Universities. Research Information Network: APC Payments. Available online: https://www.acu.ac.uk/research-information-network/apc-payments (accessed on 30 January 2018).

12. Vierkant, P.; Siegert, O.; Deinzer, G.; Gebert, A.; Herbstritt, M.; Pampel, H.; Tobias, R.; Wagner, A. Workflows zur Bereitstellung von Zeitschriftenartikeln auf Open-Access-Repositorien—Herausforderungen und Lösungsansätze. *Das Offene Bibliotheksjournal* **2017**, *4*, 151–169.

13. Keller, A. Publikationskompetenz als neues Aufgabengebiet für Bibliotheken: Eine australische Fallstudie. *Bibliothek Forschung Praxis* **2015**, *39*, 158.

14. Deinzer, G. Managing APCs with institutional repository software (EPrints). In Proceedings of the 11th International Conference on Open Repositories, Trinity College, Dublin, Ireland, 13–16 June 2016. Available online: https://epub.uni-regensburg.de/35536/ (accessed on 30 January 2018).

15. Wagner, A. Publizieren ist Nicht Genug. In *Der Schritt Zurück als Schritt Nach Vorn—Macht der Siegeszug des Open Access Bibliotheken Arbeitslos? In Proceedings of the 7. Konferenz der Zentralbibliothek Forschungszentrum Jülich WissKom 2016, Jülich, Germany, 14–16 June 2016*; Mittermaier, B., Ed.; Forschungszentrum Jülich GmbH Zentralbibliothek, Verlag: Jülich, Germany, 2016; pp. 23-45, ISBN 978-3-95806-146-0.

16. JOIN[2]—Just anOther INvenio INstance. Available online: https://join2-wiki.gsi.de/cgi-bin/view (accessed on 16 January 2018).

17. INTACT Open APC. Available online: https://www.intact-project.org/openapc/ (accessed on 20 December 2017).

18. Shamash, K. Article Processing Charges (APCs) and Subscriptions: Monitoring Open Access Costs 2016. Available online: https://www.jisc.ac.uk/reports/apcs-and-subscriptions (accessed on 18 March 2018).

19. Verminsky, K.A.; Blanchat, A. *Fundamentals of Electronic Resources Management*; Facet Publishing: London, UK, 2017; ISBN 9781783302307.

20. Kowalak, M.; Sabisch, A. Electronic Resource Management. In *Neue Formen der Erwerbung*; Göttker, S., Wein, F., Eds.; De-Gruyter Saur: Berlin, Germany, 2013, p. 150, ISBN 9783110255508.

21. Heinen, I. Das Jülicher Electronic Resource Management System. *B.I.T. Online* **2011**, *14*, 41–43.

22. Aumeier, F.; Heinen, I. Inhouse-Lösung für das Jülicher Electronic Resource Management-System. *Bibliotheksdienst* **2007**, *41*, 322–330.

23. Elektronische Zeitschriftenbibliothek. Available online: https://ezb.uni-regensburg.de/ (accessed on 9 January 2018).

24. COUNTER. Available online: https://www.projectcounter.org/ (accessed on 30 January 2018).

25. Zeitschriftendatenbank. Available online: http://zdb-katalog.de/index.xhtml (accessed on 9 January 2018).

26. Highwire. Available online: https://www.highwirepress.com/ (accessed on 9 January 2018).

27. Directory of Open Access Journals. Available online: https://doaj.org/https://doaj.org/ (accessed on 9 January 2018).

28. Forschungszentrum Jülich, Zentralbibliothek, Open-Access-Barometer. Available online: http://www.fz-juelich.de/zb/EN/Expertise/open_access/oa_barometer/oa_barometer_node.html (accessed on 9 January 2018).

29. Fraunhofer Gesellschaft. Allianz der Wissenschaftsorganisationen. Available online: https://www.fraunhofer.de/de/ueber-fraunhofer/wissenschaftspolitik/StellungnahmenAllianzderWissenschaftsorganisationen.html (accessed on 30 Janualy 2018).

30. OA 2020 DE. Nationaler Open Access Kontaktpunkt. Über. Available online: http://www.oa2020-de.org (accessed on 30 January 2018).

31. Mittermaier, B. Datenarbeit und "Nationaler Kontaktpunkt Open Access"—Ein Interview mit Dr. Bernhard Mittermaier. *ABI Technik* **2017**, *37*, 293–296.

32. German Federal Ministry of Education and Research (BMBF). Open Access in Germany. The Strategy of the German Federal Ministry of Education and Research. Available online: https://www.bildung-forschung.digital/files/170419_Open_Access_english.pdf (accessed on 11 February 2018).

33. GOKB—Global Open Knowledge Base. Available online: http://gokb.org (accessed on 30 January 2018).

34. VIAF—Virtual International Authority File. Available online: https://viaf.org/ (accessed on 30 January 2018).

35. Hochschulbibliothekszentrum des Landes Nordrhein-Westfalen (hbz). Projekte: LAS:eR. Available online: https://www.hbz-nrw.de/projekte/LASeR (accessed on 30 January 2018).

36. Nationaler Statistikserver. Available online: https://statistik.hebis.de/stats/site/login (accessed on 30 January 2018).

37. Kompetenzzentrum Bibliometrie. Dateninfrastruktur. Available online: http://www.forschungsinfo.de/Bibliometrie/index.php?id=infrastruktur (accessed on 30 January 2018).

38. Universitätsbibliothek Bielefeld. BASE Bielefeld Academic Search Engine. Available online: https://www.base-search.net/ (accessed on 30 January 2018).

39. Open Citations. Available online: http://opencitations.net/ (accessed on 30 January 2018).

40. FIZ Karlsruhe. Nationales Hosting Elektronischer Ressourcen (NatHosting). Available online: https://www.nathosting.de/download/attachments/2490483/NatHosting_Projektbericht_mit_Anlagen.pdf?version=1&modificationDate=1476708609000&api=v2 (accessed on 5 January 2018).
41. NISO. Standardized Usage Statistics Harvesting Initiative (SUSHI) Protocol (ANSI/NISO Z39.93-2014). Available online: http://www.niso.org/standards-committees/sushi (accessed on 5 February 2018).
42. Clarivate Analytics. Available online: https://clarivate.com/products/web-of-science (accessed on 30 January 2018).
43. Geschuhn, K.; Stone, G. It's the workflows, stupid. What is required to make, 'offsetting' work for the open access transition. *Insights* **2017**, *3*, 103–114.
44. Mittermaier, B. From the DEAL eEngine Room—An Interview with Bernhard Mittermaier 2017. Available online: http://libreas.eu/ausgabe32/mittermaier_en/ (accessed on 30 January 2018).

Case Report

Getting Scientists Ready for Open Access: The Approaches of Forschungszentrum Jülich

Thomas Arndt †[iD] and Claudia Frick *,†[iD]

Central Library, Forschungszentrum Jülich GmbH, 52428 Jülich, Germany; t.arndt@fz-juelich.de
* Correspondence: c.frick@fz-juelich.de; Tel.: +49-2461-61-6206
† These authors contributed equally to this work.

Received: 16 February 2018; Accepted: 23 May 2018; Published: 25 May 2018

Abstract: Many scientific institutions are faced with the question of how they should inform their scientists and scientific coordinators about the option of publishing open access. This task is one that libraries have taken upon themselves: libraries are familiar with the market participants and have years of experience in teaching information and publication literacy. This case report looks at two approaches taken by the Central Library of Forschungszentrum Jülich in 2017. It highlights the motivation, strategy, resources and implementation, as well as the first evaluation of both approaches. The first approach was a redesign of the training courses offered by the Central Library with a focus on the target groups and new contents. The second approach was implemented as part of International Open Access Week and involved offering an information event tailored to each scientific institute. The event was customized to meet the needs of the target group defined by each institute, the institute itself, and was organized individually. As a result of these efforts, the open access rate increased over the last few months and at 48% open access in 2017, Forschungszentrum Jülich is well on its way to achieving the open access goals set by the Helmholtz Association.

Keywords: open access; information services; training; publishing literacy; marketing

---

1. Introduction

Open access represents the transition from the classic model of a paying readership to free knowledge for all. On the one hand, scientific libraries are actively driving this change; on the other hand, they are subject to it themselves, have to react to the changed requirements and must adapt themselves and their structures. No individual department in the Central Library of Forschungszentrum Jülich is responsible for open access. Instead, the topic is relevant in each of its areas, including information services and marketing. Accordingly, open access as a cross-cutting issue is part of the library's training program, as well as its marketing activities.

Forschungszentrum Jülich, as a member of the Helmholtz Association, encourages its researchers to publish their scientific findings open access. In 2016, the Helmholtz Association adopted an open access policy, which defines 100% open access as a goal for all peer-reviewed publications starting from publication year 2023, which has to be reported at the beginning of 2025 [1]. Forschungszentrum Jülich also has its own publication guideline, which encourages scientists to publish green open access by depositing the post-prints of their peer-reviewed journal articles in the institutional repository.[1] To support green open access, the Central Library of Forschungszentrum Jülich implemented an institutional repository back in 2006. In 2012, it then combined this institutional repository with its former publications database in the form of the JuSER publications portal [4]. In addition to

---

[1] The definitions of green and gold open access used in this case report follow, e.g., [2,3].

the publication guideline, ForschungsztentrumJülich implemented a very clear and detailed open access strategy in 2015 [5]. It explicitly encourages the publication of the scientific findings of Forschungszentrum Jülich in gold open access journals. To support gold open access, the Central Library began paying publication charges in 2013, and in 2016, it established a publications fund for article processing charges [6], which explicitly excluded the payment of hybrid open access fees to prevent double dipping [7]. The publications fund has been very well accepted, and its expenditure increased by 40% from 2016 to 2017 [8].

Although the term open access is widespread among librarians and stakeholders of the open access movement, many scientists are not familiar with the implications, the potential or the impact of open access. To change this, information on open access has been gradually integrated into the library's information services and its training program over the last few years. In addition, the Central Library holds dedicated events like International Open Access Week [9]. Nevertheless, scientists have only gradually become aware of open access, and the number of open access publications has increased slowly. In 2017, the Central Library attempted to close this information gap anew since increasing awareness of open access is a struggle and the information must be communicated repeatedly and prepared and presented in new creative ways [10]. Therefore, the training program was extended and revised (see Section 2), and as part of International Open Access Week, individual events were offered for each of the 70 research institutes at Forschungszentrum Jülich. These events focused on the specific needs and workflows of scientists in each institute, and the series of events was called "Open Access Week on Tour" (see Section 3).

2. Training Program

Forschungszentrum Jülich offers its employees a broad internal training program, which is revised annually and published at the beginning of each year. The Central Library participates in this program, offering training courses in information literacy and publishing literacy [11] in response to the changing role of the library [12–14]. The spectrum of training courses for 2017 in the fields of publishing literacy and open access was expanded and redesigned.[2] The strategic objectives behind this project on new open access training courses were to close existing knowledge gaps, to reduce individual and thus time-consuming consultations and to raise the awareness among scientists of open access and scientific publishing. Based on the description of the initial situation and a stakeholder analysis, the following sections will highlight the gaps and problems in the 2016 training program, present the detailed project goals for 2017 and describe the concrete solution and training courses offered.

2.1. Initial Situation

The training courses offered by the Central Library of Forschungszentrum Jülich in 2016 comprised a total of 26 training courses. Sixteen of these training courses can be assigned to the field of information literacy and seven to the field of publishing literacy. The three remaining training courses do not fall under these categories and included, among other things, a workshop for administrative staff working in institute libraries.

Two of the seven courses in the field of publishing literacy dealt with bibliometric aspects, two with literature management programs and three with the writing and publishing of scientific papers. Two of the latter three training courses took three hours each and only marginally touched upon the subject of open access. The remaining training course was one hour long, focused exclusively on open access and the related services offered by the Central Library and was called "Open Access". One of the issues of the 2016 training program regarding open access was the focus on that single training course. This approach failed to recognize that many scientists are not aware of what open access is, how it

---

2   The redesign of the 2017 training program was part of a project within the framework of the study program Library and Information Science at the Cologne University of Applied Sciences. The project report was published open access [15].

affects them and why they should deal with it. In brief, there was a lack of scientific context. A separate training course entitled "Open Access" is therefore unattractive for scientists and does not explain the benefits for them because it is not related to the research circle [16]. Furthermore, this course failed to address administrative staff or scientific coordinators in the research institutes. They also have to deal with open access and often have practical questions, but are deterred by too much theory. Additionally, with only a single training course per year, new developments and questions that arise repeatedly during the consultation process cannot be promptly incorporated into the annual training course and must instead be answered anew on an individual basis. This is very time-consuming.

The individual author consultations have already led to a continuous enhancement of the information presented on the intranet of Forschungszentrum Jülich in the past, e.g., new FAQs or a detailed description of the difference between green and gold open access. Instead of only using this up-to-date link between questions of authors and information services of the Central Library on the intranet, this project aims to incorporate this information quickly and directly into the training courses throughout the year.

The strategic goals of revising the training program were to expand the range of training courses in the field of open access in order to close the existing gaps, to reduce the individual support effort, to link the term open access to the research cycle and to impart the most important competences in the field of scientific publishing to the scientists of Forschungszentrum Jülich. The objectives were to develop training ideas and content and to ensure that the course instructors were the librarians directly involved in scientific publishing. The project on new open access training courses did not include a special evaluation of the training courses since standard evaluations of courses that are part of the official training program are performed by the Human Resources Development Department of Forschungszentrum Jülich.

2.2. Stakeholder Analysis

A stakeholder analysis for the project was prepared according to Alama and Gühl ([17], pp. 58–60). Stakeholders are divided into five categories: political environment, work environment, professional environment, organizational environment and projects in the environment. The result is shown in Figure 1. This stakeholder analysis, carried out in preparation of the project, played a key role in identifying the target groups of the new training courses and the actors within the library. It also provided important starting points for marketing, such as addressing the Executive Board[3] and pointed out relevant incentives for the course participants, such as the guidelines of the research funders and the Helmholtz Association with which they have to comply.

The primary stakeholder in the political environment of the project is the library management. It is in turn influenced by the Board of Directors of Forschungszentrum Jülich. Forschungszentrum Jülich itself is a member of the Helmholtz Association. Since the Helmholtz Association is financed by public funds, the public can also be regarded as a stakeholder in the last instance. Other political stakeholders are research funders like the European Commission since their guidelines must also be taken into account for funded projects.

The political environment hosts the driving stakeholders for this project. As previously stated in Section 1, the Helmholtz Association adopted an open access policy with the goal of 100% open access in 2023 [1], and Forschungszentrum Jülich also has its own publication guideline, which encourages scientists to publish green open access by depositing the post-prints of their peer-reviewed journal articles in the JuSER publications portal. Many research funders have additional guidelines containing open access components, for example Horizon 2020 [18], BMBF [19] and Deutsche Forschungsgemeinschaft [20]. Due to these political considerations, the topic of open access

---

[3]   The Executive Board consists of the Board of Directors of Forschungszentrum Jülich and the managing directors of the research institutes.

is becoming increasingly important and is a central component of publishing literacy for scientists and scientific coordinators.

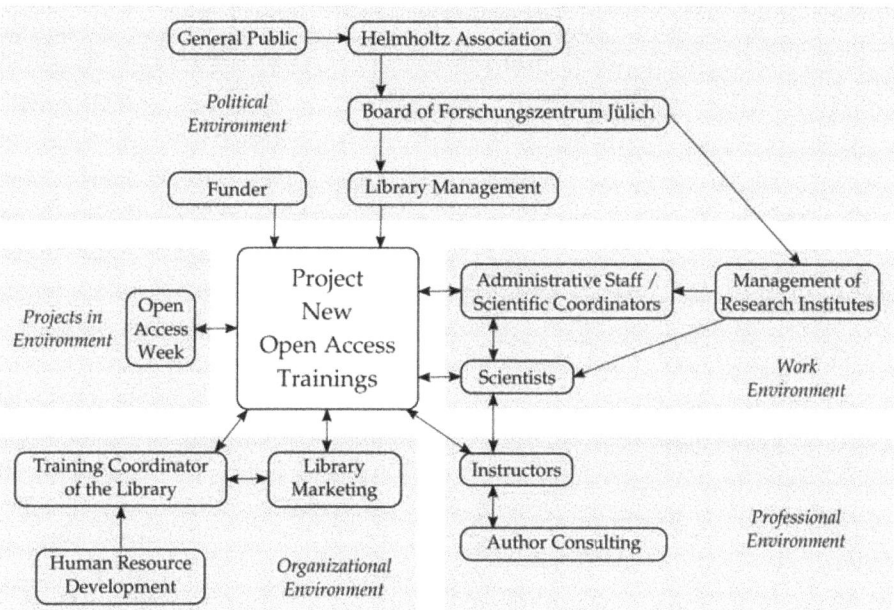

Figure 1. The stakeholder analysis of the project, which divides the stakeholders into five areas: political environment, work environment, professional environment, organizational environment and projects in the environment. The importance of stakeholders is reflected by their proximity to the project in the center.

The work environment contains the two stakeholders who are the target groups of the new training courses: the administrative staff, including scientific coordinators, and the scientists. They are located in the research institutes and are the most important stakeholders [21]. The management of the research institutes is comprised therefore of second-instance stakeholders in the work environment, who are themselves influenced by the political environment.

In the professional environment, the instructors of the training courses act as stakeholders. They are either part of the individual author consultation in the scientific publishing team or are strongly related to this team. As stated in Section 1, open access is a cross-cutting issue in the library. Therefore, the organizational environment includes the stakeholders involved in the creation and marketing of the training program within the library. This implies lively and early communication between all participants from the different teams of the library. This is achieved through joint preliminary meetings and continuous consultations. The results are always documented and, if necessary, distributed to all stakeholders within the library by e-mail. In addition to the training coordinator at the Central Library and library marketing, the professional environment also includes the Human Resources Development Department of Forschungszentrum Jülich, responsible for preparing the internal training program and the evaluation of the training courses included in the official training program.

Another project situated in the environment interacted strongly with the project on new open access training courses: International Open Access Week at Forschungszentrum Jülich, organized by the Central Library. This project will be presented in Section 3.

2.3. New Training Courses

Based on the previously-identified gaps and issues regarding publishing literacy and open access and on the questions that arise daily during individual author consultations (see Section 2.1), the scientific publishing team developed three new training courses for 2017 in cooperation with the training coordinator at the Central Library. These new courses focus strongly on the target groups of administrative staff and scientists. In principle, the training courses should be generally understandable and comprehensible to both target groups. The aim was to link the topic of open access to everyday administrative and academic life, as suggested by Schmitz [16]. As in previous years, all of the courses were publicized in the printed training program, on the intranet sites of the Central Library and the Human Resources Development Department and via a mailing list in the Human Resources training newsletter. In the following section, each training course and the related additional marketing activities are presented separately.

2.3.1. Training Course "Publication Fees"

The "Publication Fees" training course was prepared and conducted by the staff member who was also responsible for processing publication fees in the Central Library. The aim of this course was to explain the most important terms within the context of publication fees and to provide information and skills in dealing with different types of publication fees, the selection of journals and the specific publishing formalities at Forschungszentrum Jülich. The number of participants was limited to 12, and the course was planned to last 45 min. The course was designed mainly for administrative staff dealing with publication fees and was therefore conducted in German. It was held twice on two different dates.

The additional marketing activities prior to the first run consisted of an e-mail sent to the staff working in the institute libraries about two weeks before the event. The e-mail invitation targeted these employees and simultaneously asked them to forward the training invitation to potential, interested parties at the respective institute. As a result, both runs of the training course were fully booked.

The training content addressed questions that were frequently asked in individual consultations and was partially based on past training courses. After a general introduction to the topic of open access and an introduction to the different routes, the most important publication guidelines were briefly outlined in order to clarify the importance of the topic. The aim was to turn the participants into multipliers to communicate the topic of open access and its relevance to their research institutes. The main part of the training course then dealt with publication fees and how they are handled at Forschungszentrum Jülich [6].

The first run of the training course took longer than the scheduled 45 min as many questions arose, including general questions about open access, giving rise to a need for discussion. Presentation slides and contact details were sent to the participants as a follow-up. Furthermore, feedback from the participants, which was given in the feedback form of the Human Resources Development Department, presented in person or sent by e-mail, was incorporated into the second run.[4] The suggestion that an English-language version should be offered was passed on to the project team planning International Open Access Week at Forschungszentrum Jülich, as described in Section 3.

---

[4]   The first run received a total grade of 1.61 from the participants, twelve of whom completed the feedback form of the Human Resources Development Department of Forschungszentrum Jülich, with a better grade of 1.42 for the content of the training course. The second run received a total grade of 1.54 from the participants, four of whom completed the feedback form, again with a better grade of 1.06 for the content of the training course. The grading translates to 1 for very good, 2 for good, 3 for satisfactory, 4 for adequate and 5 for poor.

2.3.2. Training Course "Publications and Research Funders"

The training course "Publications and Research Funders" was prepared and conducted by the librarian who was involved in the revision of the publication guideline of Forschungszentrum Jülich in 2017. The aim of the training course was to explain the most important publication guidelines to the participants and to provide them with information and skills on the various aspects, in particular the open access components. The number of participants was limited to 12, and the training course was planned to last one hour. The major target groups of the course were scientific coordinators and senior scientists dealing with third-party funding. The training course was held in German.

The response to the initially performed marketing activities related to this training course was not as successful as expected. Although information on the training course had been sent to the administrative staff of the institute libraries, not even a single enrollment had been received one week before the course. To remedy this, individual scientists in the research institutes and well-known scientific coordinators were contacted in person. In addition, the participants of the first run of the "Publication Fees" training course were contacted. As a result, two-thirds of the places were booked for the training course.

The content and structure of the training course explicitly included the creation of a common basis for all attendees [22]. All technical terms related to open access were explained in a clear and concise manner, as suggested by Dawson [10]. Starting with a formal introduction to the topic of publication guidelines, the most important guidelines for the scientists of Forschungszentrum Jülich were outlined and presented briefly. The common feature of the presented guidelines was identified as open access, which was then addressed in the subsequent part of the course. After a general introduction to open access, the most important terms in the publication process were introduced, and the open access specifications of the most relevant publication guidelines, for example, of Horizon 2020 [18], BMBF [19] and Deutsche Forschungsgemeinschaft [20], were described in detail. The aim was to work in a solution-oriented manner and to explain to the participants what they can and must do in order to comply with these guidelines. Finally, the most important services of the Central Library were presented in a compact format, and contact details were provided. A detailed reference list and useful links completed the slides.[5]

The training course was designed openly and included time for questions and a discussion that also touched upon topics not directly related to the presented publication guidelines. Overall, this created a very communicative and pleasant atmosphere. After the training course, the participants were sent the slides and contact details by e-mail. The slides were also published open access [22]. Feedback was very positive, and a suggestion was made to make the training course mandatory for all scientists dealing with third-party funding.[6]

2.3.3. Training Course "How to Publish"

The aim of the training course "How to Publish" was to explain the entire publishing process of journal articles to new scientists and to provide information and expertise on the various steps involved, particularly in regard to open access. The training course was prepared and conducted by a librarian with experience in publishing scientific papers. A senior scientist of Forschungszentrum Jülich was asked to act as an additional instructor. The senior scientist gave real life examples and shared personal experiences with the participants. The number of participants was limited to 12,

---

[5] Quote from the feedback form: "For a one hour tutorial the material was just right, with plenty of references if needed for more detail."

[6] Quote from the feedback form: "This course should be *mandatory* for anyone involved with an EU project, whether as coordinator or WP leader. The instructor, Dr. Claudia Frick, really knows her material and can convey exactly what is needed to bring the dissemination side of project management up to DFG/HGF or EU standards." The training course received a total grade of 1.15 from the participants, seven of whom completed the feedback form.

and the training course was planned to last two hours. Since the major target group of this training course was scientists, the training course was conducted in English.

This training course was advertised during the introduction to the Central Library for new employees. Several scientists registered directly for the course, and it was fully booked within a short time. Despite this, only one-third of the registered participants showed up. Presumably, the time frame between registration and the training course was too long, and a reminder may have increased the number of the participants. Accordingly, the instructors will send training course reminders in advance of each training course via e-mail starting in 2018.

The content of the training course addressed new scientists who have no or only minor experience in scientific publishing. After some basic information about the research cycle and the different publication types, the training course focused on academic papers including a short excursion to open and closed access journals. The main part of the training course covered the workflow of publishing a peer-reviewed journal article. The workflow was shown step by step, enriched with background information, and was visualized using an example journal article published by the instructor. All steps of the workflow were outlined, including reviewer comments. The subsequent part focused on what happens after an article has been published and introduced open access as a natural part of the workflow. The training course closed with a summary of all services offered by the Central Library for all stages of the publication workflow.

The training course benefited from the cooperation with the senior scientist who presented major insights far beyond the experience of the instructor. The training course was designed openly and included time for questions and discussions. The atmosphere was very communicative.[7] Presentation slides and contact details were sent to the participants as a follow-up. The slides were also published open access [2]. The participants circulated the information within their research institutes, which led to the course being repeated as a personal consultation in 2017 with a smaller group of participants and without the senior scientist.

In 2018, this training course is again part of the training program, and the senior scientist has also agreed to act as an additional instructor. The content will be updated to include some issues suggested by the participants on the feedback form, e.g., information about authorship and scientific conduct. Additionally, an e-mail reminder will be sent in advance of the training course.

3. Open Access Week

As part of International Open Access Week from 2011 to 2016, the Central Library ran the webinar "Science is open – an introduction to open access", which was offered by the Helmholtz Open Access Project Coordination Office. The first aim was to provide basic information on open access and to raise awareness of open access. The second aim was to stimulate contact between different stakeholders. The webinar was run at the Central Library and targeted PhD students. Following the webinar, Central Library experts answered questions on open access, the JuSER publications portal and other services offered by the Central Library. There were always less than 10 participants in the webinar (see Section 4).

Combined with the "Open Access" training course addressing scientists (see Section 2.1), this webinar addressing PhD students during International Open Access Week was insufficient to achieve the goals set by the driving political stakeholders (see Section 2.2). Therefore, library marketing initiated additional events as part of Open Access Week 2016. Two days of the Open Access Week were dedicated to short English-language events about open access and the services offered by the Central Library. During the remaining three days, invited publishers who cooperate with the Central Library ran webinars outlining their approaches to open access and their services for authors

---

[7] The training course received a total grade of 1.34 from the participants, three of whom completed the feedback form, with the best grade for the didactic method.

affiliated with Forschungszentrum Jülich. All of these webinars and events took place in the Central Library. Unfortunately, there were very few participants. The Central Library experts noticed a lack of understanding of the distinction between gold open access and green open access and of the impact of these differences. Additionally, the relevance and usability of the JuSER publications portal was questioned by the participants.

Overall, this project in 2016 was deemed successful in increasing awareness of the term open access at Forschungszentrum Jülich. All employees were informed about the event in leaflets, posters, e-mails, intranet articles or newsletter articles. However, the project proved unsuccessful in informing many scientists of what open access is, how it affects them and why they should deal with it. Following the evaluation of Open Access Week 2016, the Central Library decided on a different approach for 2017: to provide separate events in German and English, to focus on the services offered by the Central Library and particularly to actively increase the level of participation. The approach combined local events in the Central Library, webinars and events at the research institutes. The latter was called "Open Access Week on Tour".

3.1. Training Courses and Events Join Forces

Following the experiences in 2016, it was decided to focus only on one specific topic from the area of open access during the events of Open Access Week 2017. In order to meet the request for bilingualism and comply with user suggestions (see Section 2.3.1), the event "Publication Fees–Covering Costs for Scientific Publications" was offered in English. In addition to the usual presentation mode as a face-to-face training course in the rooms of the Central Library, the course was also offered as a webinar.

During International Open Access Week, another event explaining the basics of open access was advertised in English as a Q&A session in the Central Library and offered in German as an introductory webinar. The basis was provided by the experiences of the instructors who created the introduction to the Central Library for new employees and attended previous webinars offered by the Helmholtz Open Access Project Coordination Office.

In the run-up to Open Access Week 2017, marketing activities for open access were intensified. Employees of Forschungszentrum Jülich were informed about topics relevant to open access by means of internal news items. These topics were:

- JuSER as an OpenAIRE-compliant repository
- Combating the fear of predatory journals
- Increasing the range and reputation of the Journalof large-scale research facilities [23]
- Termination of agreements with Elsevier by Helmholtz centers [24]

Flyers and posters were created and distributed for Open Access Week 2017. On the Monday of International Open Access Week, Central Library employees manned an information stand in the staff canteen of Forschungszentrum Jülich. Under the heading of "Open Access and further developments in scientific publishing", information about open access was actively provided, discussions with scientists took place and the Open Access Week events and the new "Open Access Week on Tour" series of events were promoted. This series was designed for Open Access Week 2017 with the main aim of disseminating detailed information on open access to scientists by offering individual sessions at each research institute of Forschungszentrum Jülich.

3.2. Top-Down Marketing

The Central Library defined an additional communication strategy for open access. The intention of this strategy was not to only address the scientists directly, but to also target management at the research institutes of Forschungszentrum Jülich identified as the main influencers in the stakeholder analysis (see Section 2.2). This approach was supported by Prof. Wolfgang Marquardt, Chairman of the Board of Directors. In 2015, he had set the objective that: "Our share of open access publications should consistently be 10% above the global average." [25] With the support of the Board of Directors in accordance with the Open Access Policy of the Helmholtz Association [1], three communication measures were defined and implemented.

- Corporate Communications featured an article in the in-house magazine "intern" of Forschungszentrum Jülich [26] and issued an additional press release.
- The official bodies of Forschungszentrum Jülich were used to circulate information, for example the open access rate was placed on the July agenda of the Jour Fixe of the Executive Board in 2017.[8] Furthermore, the "Open Access Week on Tour" was mentioned at the Executive Seminar of Forschungszentrum Jülich.
- Referring to the gap between ambition and reality, an internal memo was sent from the management of the Central Library to the heads of all 70 research institutes of Forschungszentrum Jülich offering an event of "Open Access Week on Tour" at their institutes. It was signed by the open access representative of Forschungszentrum Jülich and delivered one day after the aforementioned Jour Fixe.

As part of this communication strategy, the "Open Access Week on Tour" series of events was planned to take place at some of the respective research institutes presented by instructors of the Central Library and the library management. The institutes determined the location of the event, the organizational framework and the language and co-determined the content, target group, group size and scope of the event. The target groups ranged from the management of the research institute to doctoral seminars and plenary meetings.

The marketing approach of open access described above enabled many institutes to be reached. The institutes at Forschungszentrum Jülich are largely independent. They often decide for themselves whether and to what extent they implement the suggestions of the Executive Board. In order to pursue the open access objective, they themselves can pass on information internally, ideally involve the Central Library or do nothing at present. From the point of view of the Central Library, five events would have been a success. Up to the end of April 2018, information events had been held at seventeen of the 70 research institutes. Three institutes were visited before International Open Access Week 2017; fourteen appointments were arranged subsequently, also for 2018; and nine additional institutes expressed interest. A total of 215 employees attended the events. The directors of the institutes were welcomed at almost all events. Additional events of the "Open Access Week on Tour" have been scheduled for 2018. A closer look at the institutes that already hosted an event or expressed their interest did not reveal any pattern or trend regarding the disciplines or the open access rates prior to the event, which confirms the cross-disciplinary success of the broad marketing approach.

3.3. Presented Content at "Open Access Week on Tour"

The information presented at the research institutes during the events of "Open Access Week on Tour" was customized to meet the needs and wishes of each research institute in accordance with Dawson [10]. Each presentation was composed of three main modules as shown in Table 1. The slides of the event at Peter Grünberg Institut: Functional Nanostructures at Surfaces (PGI-3) were published open access as examples [27]. The modularized presentation included consistent parts such as general information and the services offered by the Central Library related to open access. The submodule relating to motivation for the "Open Access Week on Tour" included a slide that was then customized for each institute. It showed the current open access rate of Forschungszentrum Jülich (see Section 4 for detailed information) and compared it to the rate of the research institute.

---

8   This Jour Fixe is a long-term scheduled, monthly working meeting of the Executive Board.

Table 1. The modularized structure of the content presented at the events in the research institutes, including the submodules and details of whether they were consistent or had to be customized for each research institute before the event.

Module	Submodule	Feature
general information	definition of open access	consistent
	motivation	customized
	routes to open access	consistent
	publication guidelines	consistent
	impact of open access	consistent
courses of action	information about the journals in which the scientists of the research institute published	customized
services offered by the Central Library	author's advice	consistent
	handling of publication fees and publications fund	consistent
	JuSERpublications portal	consistent

In addition, the slides dealing with the potential courses of action were customized based on those journals in which the research institute published in recent years. With the help of these customized slides, the training course identified and addressed the specific needs of each research institute, as suggested by Tappenbeck [28]. The published journal articles were extracted from the JuSER publications portal, and each journal was categorized as closed or gold open access. These data were additionally enriched with the self-archiving policies of all closed access journals. Figure 2 shows an example list of the journals in which a given research institute of Forschungszentrum Jülich published in recent years. One-third of the journals shown in the example are gold open access journals, whereas two-thirds are closed access journals. Only half of these closed access journals have an embargo period compliant with the maximum embargo period of six months accepted by Horizon 2020.

Knowing the number of published articles per journal, in addition to the information given in Figure 2, enables the research institute to calculate the maximum open access rate it could achieve without changing its publication behavior simply by using gold and green open access options. This in turn allows the institute to develop its own open access strategy based on real numbers and publication information. Since the impact factor of a journal is important for several research institutes and scientists [21], it was added to the journal list. It was used to highlight the actual influence of open access on citations, the increasing number of open access journals with an impact factor and a detailed explanation of how the impact factor is calculated.

The presentation closed with the benefits of green open access in the institutional JuSER publications portal, such as automatic harvesting by the repository of the European Commission [29] and indexing in BASE (Bielefeld Academic Search Engine) [30] and Unpaywall [31]. Finally, personal contact details on information concerning the different services and of the instructor were given.

A discussion followed the presentation about the different routes to open access, the different players involved and possible courses of action. Scientists themselves can decide to publish gold or green open access. Scientists who are also editors of journals can support the transition of scholarly journals to gold open access [32]. The Central Library promotes the transition to open access. It has established the publications fund for gold open access and offers an institutional repository where scientists simply have to upload their post-prints, and the library then checks the self-archiving policies of the journals for green open access. In addition, the Central Library is involved in negotiations with major academic publishers as part of the DEAL project aiming to achieve nationwide licensing agreements that will lead to automatic open access for all journal articles published by German scientists [33]. This currently concerns all journals highlighted in red in Figure 2 since all of them are

Elsevier journals, but it also addresses the journals published by Springer and Wiley. After the events, the slides were sent to the research institute staff by e-mail.

Title	Publisher	Journal Type	Embargo	Manuscript Type
Atmospheric chemistry and physics	Copernicus / EGU	Open Access		
Atmospheric measurement techniques	Copernicus	Open Access		
Journal of geophysical research / Atmospheres	Wiley / AGU	Closed Access	6	Publisher's Version
Bulletin of the American Meteorological Society	AMS	Closed Access	6	Publisher's Version
Geophysical research letters	Wiley / AGU	Closed Access	6	Publisher's Version
Earth's future	Wiley / AGU	Open Access		
Journal of the atmospheric sciences	AMS	Closed Access	6	Publisher's Version
Geoscientific model development	Copernicus	Open Access		
Annales geophysicae	Copernicus	Open Access		
International journal of modern physics / B	World Scientific Publishing	Closed Access	12	Post-Print
Reviews of geophysics	Wiley / AGU	Closed Access	6	Publisher's Version
Advances in meteorology	Hindawi	Open Access		
International journal of coal geology	Elsevier	Closed Access	24	Post-Print
Journal of climate	AMS	Closed Access	6	Publisher's Version
Atmospheric research	Elsevier	Closed Access	24	Post-Print
Atmospheric environment	Elsevier	Closed Access	24	Post-Print
Faraday discussions	RSC	Closed Access	12	Post-Print
Tellus / B	Wiley	Open Access		
Analytical and bioanalytical chemistry	Springer	Closed Access	12	Post-Print
Chemical geology / Isotope geoscience section	Elsevier	Closed Access	24	Post-Print
PLoS one	PLoS	Open Access		
Journal of the American Society for Mass Spectrometry	Springer	Closed Access	12	Post-Print
Journal of geophysical research / Space physics	Wiley / AGU	Closed Access	6	Publisher's Version
Journal of quantitative spectroscopy & radiative transfer	Elsevier	Closed Access	24	Post-Print
Journal of applied meteorology and climatology	AMS	Closed Access	6	Publisher's Version
Journal of paleolimnology	Springer	Closed Access	12	Post-Print
Review of scientific instruments	AIP Publishing	Closed Access	0	Post-Print
Annals of geophysics	INGV	Open Access		
Atmosphere	MDPI	Open Access		

Figure 2. This figure shows an example list of the journals in which a research institute of Forschungszentrum Jülich published in recent years. This list is enriched with information on the journal type and whether green open access is possible in the case of closed access journals. The embargo period is given in months from the date of publication in the journal for the related manuscript type. Closed access journals that meet the embargo period accepted by Horizon 2020 are highlighted in green, and those that also meet the embargo period accepted by the Helmholtz Association are highlighted in yellow. Closed access journals whose embargo period is not accepted by any of the above mentioned institutions are highlighted in red. The presented embargo periods were collected in April 2018.

4. Results and Lessons Learned

The new training courses in 2017 concerning open access attempted to address the needs and wishes of scientists and administrative staff. Feedback was very positive. During the training sessions, lively discussions took place, both between the instructor and the participants and among the participants themselves. Open access was recognized and accepted as a relevant topic within the daily lives of scientists. Based on the experiences with the training program in 2017, the same training courses will also be offered in 2018. In addition, a stand-alone training course entitled "Open Access" will be relaunched, since the topic is now well known throughout Forschungszentrum Jülich.

Feedback on the "Open Access Week on Tour" series of events was used by the Central Library to improve the presentation and adapt it to the expectations of the participants. This includes, for example, highlighting keywords on the slides and a visualization of the course of action. The comprehensive range of information on open access on the intranet of Forschungszentrum Jülich was expanded in response to the questions and suggestions of participants. For example, a link list for services with short descriptions of the services was created under the heading "Open Access Tools – Useful Websites". The existing FAQs for the JuSER publications portal were revised and extended, for example to include an entry on "How should projects (funding, collaboration) and (doctoral) programs be entered?"

Direct feedback from the scientists revealed their major concerns: the potential lower reputation of open access publications, which was mostly linked to the impact factor of the journals instead of real citations of individual articles, the lack of importance of open access in the evaluation process of science output and some legal issues regarding self-archiving of their published articles. The presentation and the ensuing discussion addressed these issues very well, and the attendees realized that they can easily increase their open access rate with the support of the Central Library. They also realized how their work and the research community in general benefits from such efforts.

Figure 3 shows the success of the approaches and efforts of the Central Library in preparing scientists for open access. Until 2016, open access was only touched upon in a few training courses. These courses were attended by a lower number of participants than the 2017 training courses with a focus on open access. Looking at the results of the evaluation of the information events, the same pattern is clear: the number of participants in the "Open Access Week on Tour" series of events in 2017 exceeded the number for individual events of the previous years.

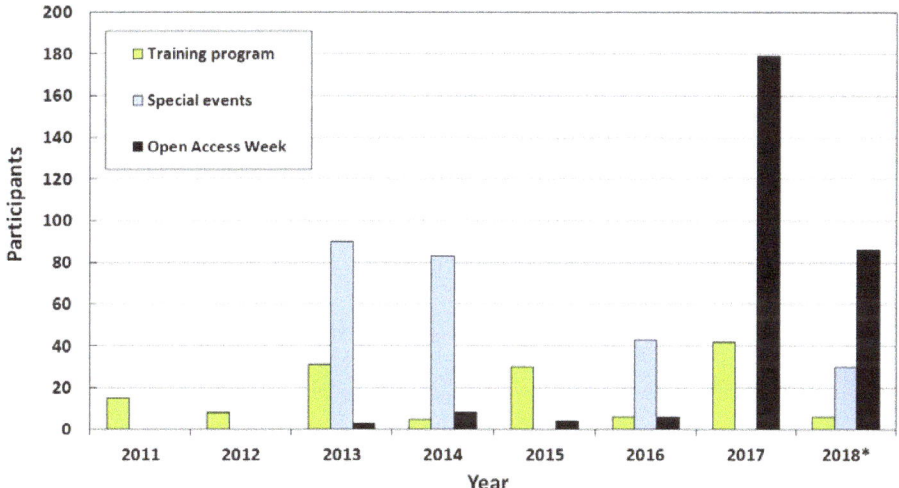

Figure 3. Number of participants in open-access-relevant training courses (green), events (blue) and International Open Access Week (black). In 2017, 42 scientists took part in open access training courses. In 2013, 31 scientists took part in open-access-related training courses. In 2013, 90 attended an event on copyright issues, in 2014, 83 a publishing house presentation on successful publishing, and in 2016, 42 an information event on research data management, all of which mentioned open access. In 2017, 179 scientists took part in the events organized as part of Open Access Week (black), and in 2018, 85 scientists have participated so far. Numbers for 2018* only from January to April.

The Central Library can now draw on its own experience for future goals and projects. The following points emerged as most important:

- A combination of several approaches is necessary to raise awareness of open access and to change the behavior of scientists regarding scientific publishing.
- A stakeholder analysis helps to identify the target groups of potential training courses and reveal their motivational factors for marketing.
- The specific marketing for events and the dissemination of general information should take place on several levels and be aimed at both stakeholders and target groups several times and in several ways.
- The implementation of training courses in the library and on site in the institutes must be flexible in terms of time and content.

- Standard content for training courses and presentations, such as basic information, concepts and course materials, should be enriched with customized data and tailored to address the level, background and discipline of the participants.
- The change in established communication channels will be noticed and, in addition to achieving the project goals, result in an increase in the reputation of the library as an innovation driver.

Overall, the approaches of the Central Library and its initiatives supporting scientists were appreciated, and feedback from both scientists and management on the new training courses and Open Access Week events was very positive. This feedback was reflected in an increase in the open access rate (see Figure 4). The open access rate for the publication year 2017 increased from 39% in July 2017 to 48% in April 2018. In addition, many authors also supplied open access versions of their publications from previous years.

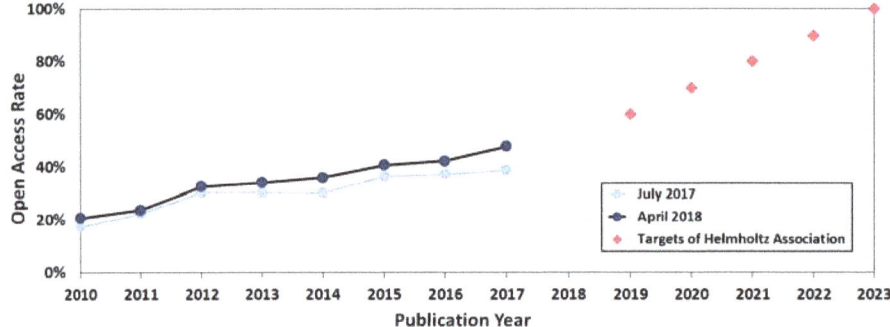

Figure 4. The open access rate of Forschungszentrum Jülich before the Open Access Week on Tour (July 2017, light blue) and in April 2018 (dark blue). The targets set by the Helmholtz Association are highlighted in red.

The open access rate was placed again on the April agenda of the Jour Fixe of the Executive Board of Forschungszentrum Jülich in 2018. The Central Library reported on the content of the events, the institutes visited and the improved open access rate. Due to the objectives of the Helmholtz Association and the support of Jülich's Board, the Central Library will continue to visit institutes and include the "Open Access Week on Tour" concept in its regular training program in 2019. With this outcome and the ongoing effort of all stakeholders, hopes are high that the targets set by the Helmholtz Association will be attained.

Conflicts of Interest: The authors declare no conflicts of interest.

References

1. Open Access Policy of the Helmholtz Association, 2016. Available online: http://os.helmholtz.de/open-sci ence-in-der-helmholtz-gemeinschaft/open-access-richtlinien/open-access-richtlinie-der-helmholtz-geme inschaft-2016/open-access-policy-of-the-helmholtz-association-2016/ (accessed on 24 May 2018).
2. Frick, C. *How to Publish—From Finished Manuscript to Publication in a Scientific Journal*; Slides, Training Course; Forschungszentrum Jülich Gmbh: Jülich, Germany, 2017. Available online: http://hdl.handle.net/2128/15 670 (accessed on 24 May 2018).
3. Piwowar, H.; Priem, J.; Larivière, V.; Alperin, J.P.; Matthias, L.; Norlander, B.; Farley, A.; West, J.; Haustein, S. The state of OA: A large-scale analysis of the prevalence and impact of Open Access articles. *PeerJ* **2018**, *6*, e4375. [CrossRef] [PubMed]
4. JuSER: Jülicher Shared Electronic Resources. Available online: https://juser.fz-juelich.de/ (accessed on 24 May 2018).

5. Open Access Strategy of Forschungszentrum Jülich. Resolution of the Board of Directors of 24 November 2015. Available online: https://www.fz-juelich.de/zb/oa_strategie_en (accessed on 24 May 2018).

6. Publication Fund/Publication Charges at Forschungszentrum Jülich. Available online: https://www.fz-juelich.de/zb/publication_funds (accessed on 24 May 2018).

7. Mittermaier, B. Double Dipping in Hybrid Open Access—Chimera or Reality? 2015. Available online: http://hdl.handle.net/2128/8611 (accessed on 24 May 2018).

8. Expenditures of Forschungszentrum Jülich on Article Processing Charges Published as Part of the Open-APC Data Set. Available online: https://treemaps.intact-project.org/apcdata/fzj-fb/#publisher/is_hybrid=FALSE (accessed on 24 May 2018).

9. International Open Access Week. Available online: http://openaccessweek.org/ (accessed on 24 May 2018).

10. Dawson, D. Effective Practices and Strategies for Open Access Outreach: A Qualitative Study. *J. Libr. Sch. Commun.* **2018**, *6*, eP2216. [CrossRef]

11. Shapiro, J.J.; Hughes, S.K. Information Literacy as a Liberal Art? *Educ. Rev.* **1996**, *31*, 31–35.

12. Keller, A. Publikationskompetenz als neues Aufgabengebiet für Bibliotheken: eine australische Fallstudie. *Bibl. Forsch. Prax.* **2015**, *39*, 158–162. [CrossRef]

13. Meyer-Doerpinghaus, U.; Tappenbeck, I. Informationskompetenz neu erfinden: Praxis, Perspektiven, Potenziale. *o-bib* **2015**, *2*, 182–191. [CrossRef]

14. Horstmann, W.; Jahn, N.; Schmidt, B. Der Wandel der Informationspraxis in Forschung und Bibliothek. *Z. Bibl. Bibliogr.* **2015**, *62*, 73–79. [CrossRef]

15. Frick, C. *Publikationskompetenz und Open Access im Schulungsprogramm des Forschungszentrums Jülich*; Report; Cologne University of Applied Sciences: Cologne, Germany, 2017. Available online: http://hdl.handle.net/2128/15668 (accessed on 24 May 2018).

16. Schmitz, S. Open-Access-Beratung in der Bibliothek: Wie berate ich meine Zielgruppe? Fortbildungsworkshop auf der Jahrestagung der Arbeitsgemeinschaft für Medizinisches Bibliothekswesen (AGMB) in Basel (07.–09.09.2015). *GMS Med. Bibl. Inf.* **2015**, *15*, Doc26. [CrossRef]

17. Alam, D.; Gühl, U. *Projektmanagement für die Praxis. Ein Leitfaden und Werkzeugkasten für Erfolgreiche Projekte*; Springer: Berlin/Heidelberg, Germany, 2016.

18. Guidelines to the Rules on Open Access to Scientific Publications and Open Access to Research Data in Horizon 2020, Version 3.2. 21 March 2017. Available online: http://ec.europa.eu/research/participants/data/ref/h2020/grants_manual/hi/oa_pilot/h2020-hi-oa-pilot-guide_en.pdf (accessed on 24 May 2018).

19. Open Access in Germany: The Strategy of the German Federal Ministry of Education and Research. September 2016. Available online: https://www.bildung-forschung.digital/files/170419_Open_Access_english.pdf (accessed on 24 May 2018).

20. Guidelines for the Use of Funds: International Research Grants with Guidelines for Final Reports. Available online: http://www.dfg.de/formulare/2_012e/2_012e.pdf (accessed on 24 May 2018).

21. Depping, R. Publikationsservices im Dienstleistungsportfolio von Hochschulbibliotheken. Eine (Neu-)Verortung in der wissenschaftlichen Publikationskette. *o-bib* **2014**, *1*, 71–91. [CrossRef]

22. Frick, C. *Publikationen und Drittmittel—Welche Richtlinien Müssen bei Geförderten Projekten Beachtet Werden?* Slides, Training course; Forschungszentrum Jülich Gmbh: Jülich, Germany, 2017. Available online: http://hdl.handle.net/2128/15669 (accessed on 24 May 2018).

23. Journal of Large-Scale Research Facilities (JLSRF). Available online: https://jlsrf.org/ (accessed on 24 May 2018).

24. Helmholtz Centers Terminate Agreements with Elsevier. Press Release of Helmholtz Association from 25 August 2017. Available online: https://www.helmholtz.de/en/current_topics/press_releases/article/artikeldetail/helmholtz_centers_terminate_agreements_with_elsevier/ (accessed on 24 May 2018).

25. Van Ackeren, J. Open Access: Reading Free of Charge. *INTERN* **2016**, *1*, 21.

26. Van Ackeren, J. Open Access: What's Jülich's Stance? *INTERN* **2017**, *3*, 10–11.

27. Frick, C. *Open Access Week on Tour—Peter Grünberg Institut, Functional Nanostructures at Surfaces (PGI-3)*; Slides. Presentation; Forschungszentrum Jülich Gmbh: Jülich, Germany, 2018. Available online: http://hdl.handle.net/2128/18283 (accessed on 24 May 2018).

28. Tappenbeck, I. Das Konzept der Informationskompetenz in der Bibliotheks- und Informationswissenschaft: Herausforderungen und Perspektiven. In *Handbuch Informationskompetenz*; Sühl-Strohmenger, W., Ed.; De Gruyter: Berlin, Germany, 2012; pp. 156–166. [CrossRef]

29. OpenAIRE. Available online: https://www.openaire.eu/ (accessed on 24 May 2018).
30. BASE: Bielefeld Academic Search Egine. Available online: https://www.base-search.net/ (accessed on 24 May 2018).
31. Unpaywall. Available online: http://unpaywall.org/ (accessed on 24 May 2018).
32. Solomon, D.J.; Laakso, M.; Björk, B.-C.; Suber, P. (Eds.) Converting Scholarly Journals to Open Access: A Review of Approaches and Experiences. Copyright, Fair Use, Scholarly Communication, etc. 2016. Available online: http://digitalcommons.unl.edu/scholcom/27 (accessed on 24 May 2018).
33. Project DEAL. Available online: https://www.projekt-deal.de/ (accessed on 24 May 2018).

Article

Converting the Literature of a Scientific Field to Open Access through Global Collaboration: The Experience of SCOAP3 in Particle Physics

Alexander Kohls * and Salvatore Mele

CERN, CH-1211 Geneva 23, Switzerland; salvatore.mele@cern.ch
* Correspondence: alexander.kohls@cern.ch

Received: 23 February 2018 ; Accepted: 3 April 2018; Published: 9 April 2018

Abstract: Gigantic particle accelerators, incredibly complex detectors, an antimatter factory and the discovery of the Higgs boson—this is part of what makes CERN famous. Only a few know that CERN also hosts the world largest Open Access initiative: SCOAP3. The Sponsoring Consortium for Open Access Publishing in Particle Physics started operation in 2014 and has since supported the publication of 20,000 Open Access articles in the field of particle physics, at no direct cost, nor burden, for individual authors worldwide. SCOAP3 is made possible by a 3000-institute strong partnership, where libraries re-direct funds previously used for subscriptions to 'flip' articles to 'Gold Open Access'. With its recent expansion, the initiative now covers about 90% of the journal literature of the field. This article describes the economic principles of SCOAP3, the collaborative approach of the partnership, and finally summarizes financial results after four years of successful operation.

Keywords: CERN; journal flipping; gold open access; particle physics; SCOAP3

---

1. Collaboration in Particle Physics (and Its Scholarly Communication)

Particle physics (also called High Energy Physics—HEP) is the paradigm of international scientific cooperation. After World War II many research centres around the world started building increasingly powerful accelerators. Between 1951 and 1954, twelve European countries founded CERN [1], the European Organization for Nuclear Research, with the objective to "*increase international scientific collaboration*" and to rebuild their cooperation in the spirit of 'science for peace'. Many decades, successful accelerators, and a couple of Nobel prizes later, CERN now counts 22 Member States [2]. These jointly finance and govern the Organization for the benefit of their scientific community and particle physicists worldwide. Indeed, the CERN scientific program is open to all countries, and over 13,000 researchers from more than 70 nations use the CERN infrastructure by participating in numerous different experiments [3]. The CERN LHC program has come to epitomize big science: a particle accelerator of 27 km circumference, protons accelerated to almost the speed of light, beams colliding billions of times per second at the core of four large experimental apparatuses, hundreds of petabyte of data recorded, and collaborations of several thousands scientist analysing them. CERN's mission of providing infrastructure for large scale collaborations is one of the pillars of the SCOAP3 Open Access initiative.

Another pillar is the peculiar scholarly communication practice of the field. Particle physics grew fast between the late 1940s and through the 1970s. Experimental physicists gathered at dozens of laboratories around the world, theoretical physicists at hundreds of universities. Accelerators' energy was increased fast, entire zoos of new particles where theorized and discovered. Exchange of information needed to be quick, at a time where the fastest way to communicate was airmail. Traditional scholarly communication practices (i.e., writing an article and waiting for it to appear in print on the shelves of academic libraries a couple of years later) was simply not an option to support the scientific vigour of the time. In order to accelerate the distribution of the latest experimental results or new theories, it became common practice instead to mail 'preprints' of scientific papers to the key research centres and physics departments active in the field, at the same time of submission to scholarly journals [4].

With the emergence of e-mail servers in the late 1980s, this system was ready for disruption, both to provide a level playing field (only the most renewed sites would receive all preprints, sent by other researchers hopeful for attention—and mailing lists to which preprints were sent by important institutions would be occasionally pruned to save postage and print, leaving out colleagues at peripheral institutes [5]) and to be able to retrieve on demand interesting preprints, knowing authors and succinct abstracts. Thanks to Paul Ginsparg, then at Los Alamos National Laboratories, arXiv [6] was born in 1991. Following the wider adoption of the idea of the World Wide Web in the HEP community, after its inception at CERN in 1989 [7], arXiv[1] then became the preprint server with the functionalities expected by a 'Green Open Access Repository' [8] of today. Its universal adoption quickly meant that almost the entirety of the literature then appearing in peer-reviewed journals in the field would appear on the arXiv [9]. After a quarter century, about 60% of all articles ever written in particle physics have appeared on the arXiv as preprints.

Back to CERN, it is interesting to note that in its original spirit as a locus of open cooperation, the CERN founding Convention [1] includes in the Organization's mission "[...the] *sponsoring of international co-operation in nuclear research, including co-operation outside the Laboratories* [which] *may include in particular* [...] *the dissemination of information*". Moreover, the Convention sets out, that "[...] *the results of its experimental and theoretical work shall be published or otherwise made generally available*".

In summary, (i) CERN's role to provide infrastructure to the particle physics community; (ii) its spirit of fostering international cooperation; (iii) a scholarly communication environment where universal Green Open Access had since long effectively dis-intermediated the role of journals as tools of dissemination, all together created the conditions for the inception of the SCOAP3 Open Access model. It was driven by the vision of leveraging the cooperative models of particle physics, to convert to Open Access its final peer-reviewed literature at no burden for authors.

This article is structured as follows. After this introduction which has laid out the background of scholarly communication and collaborative infrastructure in the field, Section 2 describes the SCOAP3 business mode, Section 3 illustrates the way SCOAP3 divides across countries its costs, Section 4 presents the collaborative structure of the partnership. Finally, Section 5 discusses the SCOAP3 financial results to date, and Section 6 offers some concluding remarks.

2. The SCOAP3 Business Model

The SCOAP3 Business Model was first developed by a dedicated working group[2] and presented in 2007. The original mission remains fully relevant, and is still the daily driving principle of the initiative. SCOAP3 aims to "*provide open and unrestricted access to all HEP research literature in its final, peer-reviewed form*... [and] ...*centralize all OA expenses that will therefore not have to be directly borne by authors and research groups*" [10]. In this context, and in the rest of this article, HEP research literature is defined as original research articles that have been submitted by their authors to arXiv under one of its HEP categories[3] [11].

The legal framework, the financing model, as well as the governance of the initiative follow the well-tested examples of large experimental collaborations at the LHC. Thereby, CERN acts as the 'Host Organisation' of the initiative in the same way that it hosts experiments in accordance with

---

[1] http://arxiv.org.
[2] The working group consisted of 26 members from the physics and library communities and was mandated by leading European HEP funding agencies, HEP laboratories and library consortia to explore the possibility of converting HEP scientific publishing to Open Access [10].
[3] hep-ex, hep-lat, hep-ph, hep-th.

its principles [1]. A multitude of institutions, in this case mainly academic libraries, then use this infrastructure to achieve an overarching objective which only their worldwide collaboration and financial cooperation could make possible. Through the transfer of this knowledge and governance model, academic libraries, and their worldwide community, can be empowered to affect global changes in Open Access.

The key Open Access innovation, and ultimately the success, of SCOAP3 is indeed the continuous and constructive tripartite collaboration of the library community, national funding agencies and commercial and society publishers of high-quality HEP journals. All these participants are part of the SCOAP3 'recirculation of funds' business model, displayed in Figure 1 and described in the following.

(1) CERN, for the benefit of SCOAP3, enters into contracts with publishers of HEP journals (again following the example of experiments hosted at CERN, on whose behalf CERN contracts). Depending on the journal's fraction of HEP content, the contract may cover the entire journal or only the HEP fraction. Publishers are centrally paid for their services by SCOAP3. All HEP articles are immediately published Gold Open Access under a Creative Commons Attribution (CC-BY) licence[4] and authors retain the copyright in their work.

(2) Under the terms of the SCOAP3 contracts, participating publishers reduce subscription fees for all their customers, in a way commensurate with the content becoming Open Access. A reconciliation process took place before launching the operation to determine the exact amounts of reductions under mutually accepted principles. This process can be complex when SCOAP3 journals form part of a large package deal or consortia arrangement, and the successful conclusion creates the financial leverage to support then the operation.

(3) The reduction of subscription fees releases funds in the library system that SCOAP3 partners use to pay their contributions to the initiative. As they redirect funds previously spent to access content that is now Open Access, initial participation in SCOAP3 is often cost-neutral for individual libraries. This is an important change in the role of libraries, and one increasingly gaining attention. Through a synoptic view of subscription investment, and Open Access opportunities, libraries can be instrumental in the process of making published content immediately available Open Access, both from researchers from their institutions and globally.

(4) The publication process for researchers does not change when a journal becomes part of SCOAP3. Authors do not need to pay Open Access fees, nor need to be distracted by any administrative matter. Everything is handled centrally, without any interaction with the authors who, 'magically' comply with even the strictest institutes 'or funders' Open Access mandates[5]. By design, this is a departure, from so called 'author-pays' models where authors, or their institutions directly, cover publication fees. Creating the 'invisible infrastructure' SCOAP3, and in a comparable way, also the emerging national and institutional-wide agreements with selected publishers, aim to realise the largest amount of advantages for authors and readers in parallel. This, in turn, allows a fact-based approach for institutions, and libraries in their new role of managing Open Access therein, to articulate the shifting of publication costs, and process, to a central institutional point rather than the author level.

(5) In some countries, national funding agencies support the initiative with additional financial contributions to SCOAP3 beyond the contributions from academic libraries. This is particularly relevant in countries that are very active in particle physics as discussed in Section 3.

(6) A guiding principles of SCOAP3 is to remove any barriers or burden for authors to achieve Open Access, and give to any reader access to any article in the field. This creates a possible financial shortfall as some institutes in particular countries, or some countries overall, could choose not to participate to the initiative, without any disadvantages for their authors. CERN, as the host organization of SCOAP3, initially covers such shortfalls while the initiative is still

---

[4] https://creativecommons.org/licenses/by/4.0/. This license, and its previous version, are used for all SCOAP3 articles. They allow the widest possible dissemination and reuse of the work.
[5] E.g., the Research Councils UK [12] or the Austrian Science Fund (FWF) [13].

growing. Indeed, from its start in January 2014, more than 1300 new universities from 28 countries as well as 2 intergovernmental organizations joined SCOAP3, consistently reducing this shortfall as the realization of Open Access opportunities matures globally.

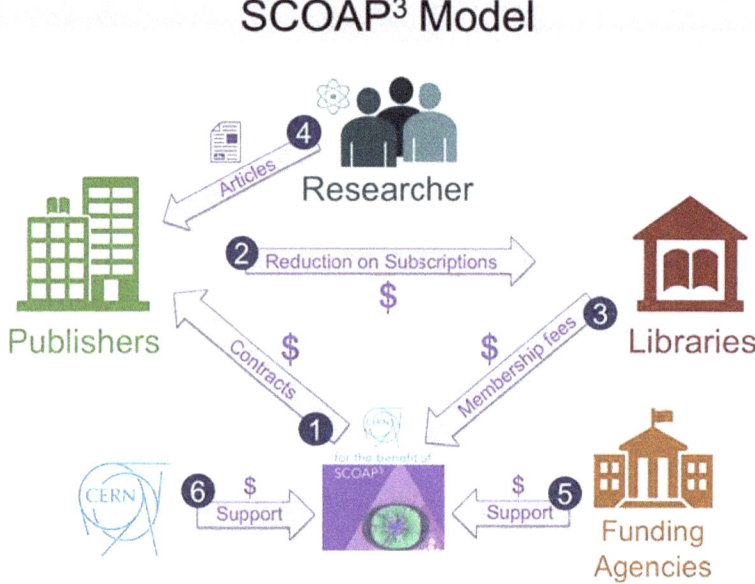

Figure 1. Main stakeholders and financial flows in the SCOAP3 Business Model.

3. The SCOAP3 'Fair Share' Principle

A key factor in the SCOAP3 partnership is a commonly-accepted and unambiguous mechanism to allocate costs across literally thousands of participating libraries. SCOAP3 introduced a 'fair share' principle, based both on the tradition of academic libraries consortia, and inspiration from the budgets of large-scale HEP experiments.

The cost-allocation scenario starts from two observations. The first is that the costs of peer-review are now sustained at the author-side rather than the reader-side, and therefore need to be correlated with the quantity of authorship. The second is that SCOAP3 contracts between CERN and publishers are designed as service contracts, suggesting that costs be allocated in proportion to the usage of such service, which again points to the quantity of authorship.

Both large-scale collaboration, with thousands of authors in about 10% of HEP papers, and wide-spread multi-institute collaboration across countries, make it impractical to allocate costs based, say, on first or corresponding authors.

SCOAP3 adopted such an allocation at country level. Each country would be responsible for a fraction of the total budget in proportion with the number of their 'signatures' in the literature, i.e., individual authors affiliated to institutes in that country. The detailed mechanics of this calculation are described by Krause, Lindqvist, Mele [14], and in particular the way to fairly resolve frequent cases of multiple affiliations.

All SCOAP3 participating countries have agreed that their 'fair share' also includes an additional contribution above the volume of their publication, to fairly give Open Access opportunities to researchers from low- and medium-income countries, whose institutions cannot be reasonably expected to have the means to support the initiative.

While allocating costs of an Open Access initiative based on authorship may seem like an obvious approach, it could lead to financial imbalances in the SCOAP3 vision of converting an entire field to Open Access. Indeed, contributions to SCOAP3 are intended to be financed by redirecting funds previously used to subscribe to SCOAP3 journals. While this model works well at a global scale, there could be differences between the aggregate amount of reductions in subscription fees of all institutions in a country, compared to this country's 'fair-share' contribution.

In particular, countries with a relatively high research intensity in the field, might face a funding gap, as the aggregate reductions in academic libraries' subscriptions are not sufficient to support a comparatively high 'fair share'.

To address the funding gaps in some countries with insufficient redirected library funds, SCOAP3 collaborates with several funding agencies [15]. Most libraries continue to contribute on a cost-neutral basis while a central agency tops up the missing funds. This is particularly attractive for funding bodies with a vision to implement Gold Open Access. The fact that most Gold Open Access costs are already covered by the re-direction of subscriptions, makes the actual costs for agencies relatively low compared to full payment of publication fees, often called Article Processing Charges[6].

At this moment, such arrangements are not present in all countries with a funding gap. In some, academic libraries have made an effort to contribute beyond their aggregate reductions at the service of their research communities. In others, a gap persists and is temporarily filled by CERN.

Finally, as mentioned in Sections 4 and 5 below, some countries are not yet engaging with SCOAP3 and their 'fair share' is currently also met by CERN.

4. The SCOAP3 Collaboration Structure

The SCOAP3 organisation closely mimics that of the large experimental collaborations at CERN. At the time of writing, SCOAP3 consists of more than 3000 libraries from 43 countries [15]. To accommodate widely varying national academic structures, research libraries or funding agencies join the collaboration in several ways. In many countries, one central organisation, most often an existing library consortium, represents all research libraries in the country. In other countries, several established consortia participate in parallel. Funding agencies, orchestrating the SCOAP3 participation, might either participate in their own right as additional partners in that country, or support financially the country's participants. At the moment of writing, beyond nation states, also three intergovernmental organisations with a stake in the field, participate in SCOAP3 with the same rights and obligations as individual countries. The first is CERN as a partner, through its library. The second is the International Atomic Energy Agency, IAEA. The third is the Joint Institute for Nuclear Research, JINR, an organisation similar to CERN, that represents some of its 18 Member States in the initiative. The different participation models are shown in Figure 2.

As for all large multilateral endeavours, good and participative governance is at the core of the SCOAP3 initiative. It is interesting to describe as, to our knowledge, this is the first time a large Open Access initiative has adopted a similar model. All participating countries are represented in the SCOAP3 Governing Council [16] which steers the strategic direction of SCOAP3, establishes the rules of the collaboration, and discusses all key financial aspects (e.g., new contracts with publishers). Every country or intergovernmental organisation is represented at the Governing Council. Following the collaborative spirit SCOAP3 is built on, the partnership aims for unanimity for all decisions.

The Governing Council appoints the members of the SCOAP3 Executive Committee. This board follows the geographical and institutional diversity of the SCOAP3 partnership and is responsible for the operation of the initiative and closely collaborates with the SCOAP3 Operations team at CERN. The Executive Committee receives support from dedicated community working groups. Such working

---

[6] A fee usually charged on a per-article basis by the publisher to make a publication available Open Access. It covers the article production costs as no subscription fees can be generated for the Open Access content [8].

groups are also established by the Governing Council for a specific purpose (e.g., financial audit, repository services, survey of strategic opportunities) [16].

The role of CERN as the host organisation of SCOAP3, comes with some specific responsibilities. CERN provides in-kind resources such as operations personnel, technical and administrative infrastructure, and hosts the regular governance meetings. At the time of writing, the CERN SCOAP3 Operations team employs about 1.5 FTE staff to assure the operation of the initiative. To assure constant alignment of the SCOAP3 vision and CERN's own Open Access approach, CERN is entitled a dedicated representative in the SCOAP3 governing bodies. Beyond CERN's staff investment, some small IT infrastructure and the management of a dozen service contracts, the the administrative overheads of SCOAP3 are comparable to those of any membership organization which is coordinating, and invoicing, about four dozen partners. Indeed, a key part of the SCOAP3 model is the indispensable nation-by-nation role of contacts which organise their domestic community and liaise with the international governance.

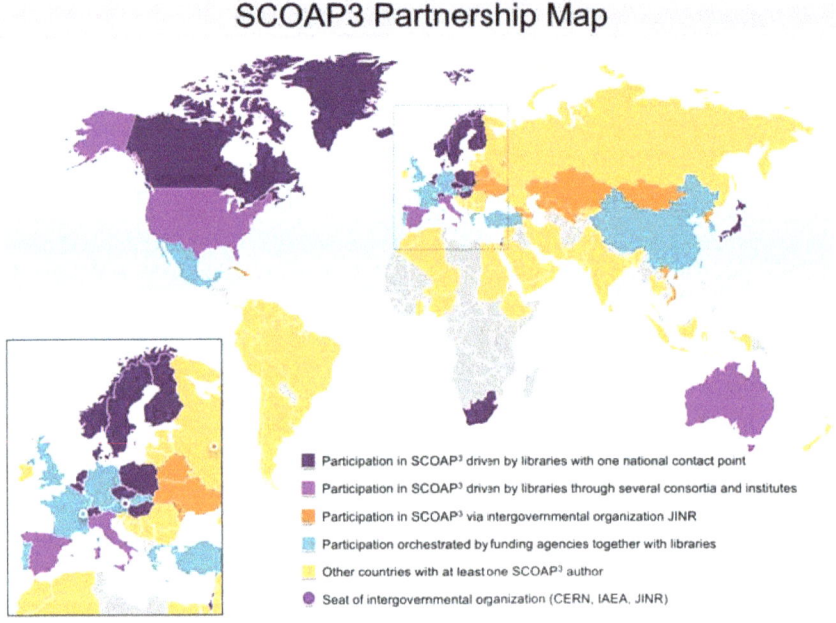

Figure 2. SCOAP3 Partner Countries by type of participation as well as countries with at least one author publishing in SCOAP3 journals (as of February 2018).

5. Financial Results

As a result of a competitive tendering process, CERN, for the benefit of SCOAP3, entered into contracts with 11 commercial and society publishers for its first 3-year cycle (2014–2016) as shown in Table 1. These contracts determine nominal journal-specific Article Processing Charges (APCs). However, the SCOAP3 arrangements have a very important difference with respect to a simple agreement to cover APCs for a set of authors. To ensure contracts fit within the overall partnership's budget, SCOAP3 has introduced a capping mechanism. If the number of published articles in a journal exceeds a certain annual maximum, originally defined as the volume of publications in that journals within some yearly growth, every additional article has then to be made Open Access at no additional cost [17]. As a result, SCOAP3 contracts focus on the notion of a total amount required to convert an entire journal (or the HEP fraction thereof) to Open Access. Between 2014 and 2016, SCOAP3 supported the publication of 13,368 articles [18].

Table 1. List of publishers and journals participating in the first 3-year cycle of SCOAP3 (2014–2016), alongside the nominal charge per article (effective charges differ, and are calculated as described in the text), the fraction of the journal covered by SCOAP3 and the number of articles covered over the first three years of the initiative.

Publisher	Journal	Nominal APCs	HEP Coverage	SCOAP3 Articles 2014–2016
Elsevier	Nuclear Physics B	2000 USD	100%	1008
Elsevier	Physics Letters B	1800 USD	100%	2654
Hindawi Publishing	Advances in High Energy Physics	1000 USD	100%	512
IOP Publishing/Chinese Academy of Sciences	Chinese Physics C	1000 GBP	7%	91
IOP Publishing/German Physical Society	New Journal of Physics	1200 GBP	3%	25
IOP Publishing/SISSA	Journal of Cosmology and Astroparticle Physics	1400 GBP	31%	654
Jagiellonian University	Acta Physica Polonica B	500 EUR	22%	56
Oxford University Press/Japanese Physical Society	Progress of Theoretical and Experimental Physics	1000 GBP	36%	255
Springer/Italian Physical Society	European Physical Journal C	1500 EUR	100%	1830
Springer/SISSA	Journal of High Energy Physics	1200 EUR	100%	6283

Between 2014 and 2016, the SCOAP3 partnership disbursed a total 13.8 million Euros to publishers for making 13,368 articles Open Access. The average investment per article[7] was of 1032 Euros per article over the first three years. This average investment per article for journals in this 'quality' range[8] compares positively to other Open Access initiatives[9].

It is important to note that all running costs of SCOAP3 beyond the payments to publishers are borne by CERN, within its mission of providing infrastructures for the field and its commitment to Open Access. All governance roles are non-remunerated and on a voluntary basis. Therefore, the actual cost for the SCOAP3 partnership itself is limited to the payments to publishers.

More than three-quarters of the 13.8 million Euros of Open Access fees (2014–2016) were financed by the re-direction of funds previously used for subscriptions in participating libraries. Funding agencies in some research-intensive countries contributed a top-up of these funds, if redirected subscription funds from libraries were not sufficient. In aggregate, these two sources represent 92% of the SCOAP3 financing.

---

[7] The notion of investment per article (IPA) might be in this context a more interesting one than an APC for two reasons. The first is that the structure of the SCOAP3 contracts, and their summed investment from the partnership, increasingly diverges from the notion of paying a single fee for a single article in a ('hybrid') journal. The second is that, effectively, access and reuse of the articles will stand indefinitely after this initial public 'investment' in such a common good.

[8] We use this word encompassing both the perception of the HEP community, as well as objective indicators of quality based on citation counts.

[9] Recent studies, analysing actual Open Access fees paid by European institutions, calculated average Article Processing Charges in the range of 1900–2000 Euros [19,20].

The missing 8% can be attributed to a few individual institutions, and a few countries, not yet participating in SCOAP3 but having a significant HEP authorship (as presented in Figure 2). For the initial phases of SCOAP3, CERN is covering this shortfall under the guidance of its own governance.

SCOAP3 extended its operation for a second 3-years cycle, from 2017 through 2019. A total of 8 journals are covered in this period, with article numbers growing to an expected total above 15,000, for a maximum expenditure of 14.7 million Euros. Therefore, the average investment per article is expected to remain stable around 1000 Euros [21].

6. Conclusions and Recent Developments

Thanks to the tripartite involvement of academic libraries, funding agencies and publishers, in a multi-lateral international collaboration hosted at CERN, SCOAP3 has been successful in delivering its objective *"to provide open and unrestricted access to all HEP research literature…"* [10]. In the following, this statement is quantitatively assessed, and compared to recent developments.

The total volume of HEP journal publications can be estimated as follows. All relevant literature in the field is indexed in the InspireHEP database[10]. For the year 2017, InspireHEP lists 7023 HEP articles (following the arXiv-based, author-driven, self-categorization explained in Section 2) [22]. About two dozen journals have a significant amount of HEP articles so defined. A long tail of journals publishes less than 25 HEP articles per year[11]. It is practically impossible to convert such a long tail to Open Access, and we ignore this small fraction of articles. From the remaining 6640 articles, 53% were supported by SCOAP3 during the first year of its second cycle, as detailed in Table 2.

Table 2. 2017 High Energy Physics (HEP) articles by journal group.

Journal Group	2017 HEP Articles	Share
SCOAP3 Journals	3499	53%
APS Journals	2400	36%
Other Journals	741	11%

The largest outstanding amount of article was published in journals by the American Physical Society. In April 2017, CERN and the American Physical Society (APS) announced that from January 2018, APS would participate in SCOAP3 with the HEP content of three journals [23] and therefore increasing the SCOAP3 coverage to 89% of the journal literature in the field.

In summary, the vision of SCOAP3 has been almost entirely realized. In a recent public webinar, the SCOAP3 governance announced that it is investigating which opportunities could exist, to extend its Open Access model to cover some of the remaining 11% of journal publications.

Acknowledgments: The authors wish to thank all members of the SCOAP3 governance, and in particular the current and former members of the SCOAP3 Executive Committee, for their shared vision, intellectual contributions, moral support and financial commitment. SCOAP3 would not be possible without the generous support of many colleagues in various CERN services which contributed expertise and enthusiasm over a decade of preparation and operation of this initiative.

Author Contributions: Both authors worked on this manuscript and carried out the analysis and discussion jointly.

Conflicts of Interest: The authors are members of CERN personnel, and CERN is the Host Organisation of SCOAP3. Both are directly involved in the initiative: A.K. holds the position of SCOAP3 Operations Manager; S.M. led the initiative before the start of operations, and is appointed by CERN to the SCOAP3 governing bodies.

---

[10] https://inspirehep.net.
[11] 383 articles published in 77 journals.

Abbreviations

The following abbreviations are used in this manuscript:

APC	Article Processing Charge
APS	American Physical Society
CC-BY	Creative Commons Attribution License
CERN	European Organization for Nuclear Research
FTE	Full-Time Equivalent
HEP	High-Energy Physics
IAEA	International Atomic Energy Agency
IPA	Investment Per Article
JINR	Joint Institute for Nuclear Research
LHC	Large Hadron Collider
OA	Open Access
SCOAP3	Sponsoring Consortium for Open Access Publishing in Particle Physics

References

1. CERN Convention for the Establishment of a European Organization for Nuclear Research. CERN, 1953. Available online: https://council.web.cern.ch/en/content/convention-establishment-european-organization-nuclear-research (accessed on 20 February 2018).
2. CERN Member States. Available online: http://www.webcitation.org/6xNGDH2oU (accessed on 20 February 2018).
3. CERN Distribution of all CERN Users by Location of Institutes on 5 July 2017. OPEN-PHO-CHART-2017-007. Available online: https://cds.cern.ch/record/2290407 (accessed on 20 February 2018).
4. Heuer, R.-D.; Holtkamp, A.; Mele, S. Innovation in Scholarly Communication: Vision and Projects from High-Energy Physics. *Inf. Serv. Use* **2008**, *28*, 83–96, doi:10.3233/ISU-2008-0570.
5. Goldschmidt-Clermont, L. Communication Patterns in High-Energy Physics. *HEP Libr. Webzine*, 2002, 6. Available online: http://webzine.web.cern.ch/webzine/6/papers/1/index.html (accessed on 21 February 2018).
6. Editorial: Keep Posting. *Nat. Phys.* **2016**, *12*, 719, doi:10.1038/nphys3862. Available online: https://www.nature.com/articles/nphys3862 (accessed on 21 February 2018).
7. Berners-Lee, T.J. Information Management: A Proposal. CERN, 1989. CERN-DD-89-001-OC. Available online: https://cds.cern.ch/record/369245 (accessed on 20 February 2018).
8. Suber, P. What is Open Access. In *Open Access*; MIT Press: Cambridge, MA, USA, 2012; pp. 1–27, ISBN 978-02-6230-252-4.
9. Gentil-Beccot, A.; Mele, S.; Brooks, T.C. Citing and Reading Behaviours in High-Energy Physics. *Scientometrics* **2010**, *84*, 345–355, doi:10.1007/s11192-009-0111-1.
10. Bianco, S.; Ellestad, O.H.; Ferreira, P.; Friend, F.; Gargiulo, P.; Hanania, R.; Henrot-Versille, S.; Holtkamp, A.; Igo-Kemenes, P.; Jarroux-Declais, D.; et al. Towards Open Access Publishing in High Energy Physics: Report of the SCOAP3 Working Party. CERN, 2007. CERN-OPEN-2007-015, ISBN 978-92-9083-292-8. Available online: https://scoap3.org/files/Working_Party_Report.pdf (accessed on 21 February 2018).
11. SCOAP3 Invitation to Tender—Technical Specification. CERN 2012. Available online: https://scoap3.org/files/Technical_Specification.pdf (accessed on 20 February 2018).
12. RCUK Policy on Open Access. Available online: http://www.rcuk.ac.uk/documents/documents/rcukopenaccesspolicy-pdf/ (accessed on 17 January 2018).
13. FWF Open Access Policy. Available online: http://www.webcitation.org/6xNFwtASf (accessed on 20 February 2018).

14. Krause, J.; Lindqvist, C.M.; Mele, S. Quantitative Study of the Geographical Distribution of the Authorship of High-Energy Physics Journals. CERN, 2007. CERN-OPEN-2007-014. Available online: https://cds.cern.ch/record/1033099 (accessed on 20 February 2018).
15. SCOAP3 Participating Countries. Available online: http://www.webcitation.org/6xNFlBz9R (accessed on 20 February 2018).
16. What is SCOAP3: Governance. Available online: http://www.webcitation.org/6xNFpARKE (accessed on 20 February 2018).
17. Romeu, C.; Gentil-Beccot, A.; Kohls, A.; Mansuy, A.; Mele, S.; Vesper, M. The SCOAP3 Initiative and the Open Access Article-Processing-Charge Market: Global Partnership and Competition Improve Value in the Dissemination of Science. CERN, 2016. CERN-OPEN-2014-037, doi:10.2314/CERN/C26P.W9DT. Available online: https://cds.cern.ch/record/1735210/ (accessed on 20 February 2018).
18. SCOAP3 Phase 1 Journals. Available online: http://www.webcitation.org/6xNG2CUt1 (accessed on 20 February 2018).
19. Ahlborn, B.; Ambler, C.; Andrae, M.; Apel, J.; Becker, H.-G.; Bertelmann, R.; Beucke, D.; Blume, P.; Blumtritt, U.; Braun, K.; et al. *Datasets on Fee-Based Open Access Publishing across German Institutions*; Bielefeld University: Bielefeld, Germany, 2018. doi:10.4119/UNIBI/UB.2014.18.
20. Shamash, K. Article Processing Charges (APCs) and Subscriptions—Monitoring Open Access Costs. *JISC*. 2016. Available online: https://www.jisc.ac.uk/sites/default/files/apc-and-subscriptions-report.pdf (accessed on 15 January 2018).
21. SCOAP3 Forum 2017 Presentation. Available online: https://scoap3.org/wp-content/uploads/2017/12/Webinar-Dec-2017.pdf (accessed on 15 January 2018).
22. InspireHEP. Available online: http://inspirehep.net/?ln=en (accessed on 17 January 2018).
23. SCOAP3 News: APS Joins SCOAP3. Available online: http://www.webcitation.org/6xNFQb5iD (accessed on 20 February 2018).

Article

Open Access in Vocational Education and Training Research

Karin Langenkamp , **Bodo Rödel** * , **Kerstin Taufenbach and Meike Weiland**

Federal Institute for Vocational Education and Training (Bundesinstitut für Berufsbildung—BIBB), Robert-Schuman-Platz 3, 53175 Bonn, Germany; langenkamp@bibb.de (K.L.); taufenbach@bibb.de (K.T.); weiland@bibb.de (M.W.)
* Correspondence: roedel@bibb.de; Tel.: +49-228-107-2411

Received: 25 January 2018; Accepted: 2 July 2018; Published: 5 July 2018

Abstract: The article presents a research project at the Federal Institute for Vocational Education and Training in Germany and reflects the perspective of researchers in the field of vocational education and training (VET). It investigates the technical and structural, policy-related, and normative and inherent academic research conditions exerting an influence on the acceptance, dissemination, and use of Open Access (OA). The research project focuses on the German-speaking countries. VET research represents an interlinking of various related academic research areas, rather than comprising a stand-alone discipline. Therefore, the assumption must be that the results of the project will be at least partially transferable to other fields within the social sciences and the humanities and will thus contribute towards findings with regard to OA across the whole of the latter domain. The background to the project is underpinned by science communication and by media theory. The empirical basis of the study has its foundations in a Sequential Mixed Method Design with a qualitative strand, followed by a quantitative strand. The qualitative exploration via focus groups will lead to hypotheses for the online survey. The online survey will be aimed at academic researchers from various disciplines who share common ground in that they address topics that are related to VET research. The realisation of the research project is planned for 2018–2020.

Keywords: Open Access; vocational education and training research; social sciences; humanities; sociology of science

1. A Research Project at the Federal Institute for Vocational Education and Training (BIBB) in Germany

The research project that is presented here refers to the German dual system of vocational education and training (VET), which is characterised by companies and vocational schools acting as learning venues. Research in the field of VET is performed in few specialised extra-university research institutes, as well as at universities. Vocational education and training research is concerned with, among other things, training occupations, the vocational school system, didactics, methodology, career guidance, career orientation, and various target groups, such as company training staff, trainees, examiners, and vocational school teachers. Publishing with Open Access is also becoming increasingly more significant in vocational education and training research.

Since 2010, researchers at BIBB have been conducting extensive work on the subject of Open Access. For this reason, BIBB formally adopted an Open Access Policy in March 2011. In 2014, it also signed up to the "Berlin Declaration on Open Access to Knowledge in the Sciences and Humanities". Then, in 2016, BIBB signed an "Expression of Interest in the Large-scale Implementation of Open Access to Scholarly Journals" in order to support the "Open Access 2020" initiative.

As part of the implementation of its Open Access Policy, by now, all BIBB publications are made directly accessible in accordance with the "gold open access" principle. At the institutional level,

BIBB is thus playing a pioneering role in the field of Open Access in vocational education and training research. The BIBB library supports the overall Open Access strategy by establishing a specialist repository for vocational education and training research. In this context, the question of the conditions of acceptance, dissemination, and use of Open Access in vocational education and training research is of special interest.

2. Open Access as an Area of Debate within Vocational Education and Training Research in Germany

Free access to academic research literature is central to the concept of Open Access. "Free" relates to three aspects in this regard.

1. Access is free of charge. Readers do not normally need to pay for electronic access to academic research literature. No usage or licensing fees are incurred. Because editorial processing, if the necessary production and graphic preparation of the manuscripts in the run-up to publication, is nevertheless necessary and causes costs the process is currently usually financed via so-called Article Processing Charges (APC). This means that the author or institution funds the appearance of the article as an Open Access publication. The financing of OA is a problem area subject to much extensive debate. The expectation is that this aspect will also be of significance to the field of vocational education and training. For this reason, it has been taken into account within the scope of the research project.
2. Licensing is as open as possible. Legal protection of OA publications frequently takes place via a form of licensing, which fosters the dissemination of academic research literature rather than by means of copyright, which at least in Germany is highly author-centric. Creative Commons Licences (CC Licences) are one example of a common licensing model. This aspect is also likely to play a role in German VET research, and will therefore form part of the further course of the research project.
3. Open Access publications should be as easy to find as possible. The aim is that academic research literature should be simple to access and that availability should not be hindered by technical restrictions. For this reason, a standardised and meaningful meta data structure needs to be in place. Repositories or similar instruments are also required in order to provide permanent storage. Access should be unproblematic, e.g., via download therefore suitable file formats need to be used.

In the OA debate, a distinction is drawn between the two publication pathways of "gold open access" and "green open access". Gold open access refers to initial publication of an article in OA journals or in the form of an OA monograph. Works are thus available on the Internet free of charge immediately following publication. Green open access denotes the additional publication in repositories of academic research works, which have already been issued in printed form by a publishing house. This may either take place at the same time as print publication or at a later date following the expiry of an "embargo". Repositories may either be institutional in nature, e.g., belonging to an institute of higher education, or be disciplinary repositories that collect literature from a single area of academic research. Examples of disciplinary repositories that relate to the field of vocational education and training research are SSOAR, PsyDok, EconStor, and peDOCS. The Federal Institute for Vocational Education and Training is currently working to establish an internationally aligned repository for vocational education and training research (VET Repository), and this is scheduled to go live in 2018.

In Germany, various stakeholders at both the policy making and academic research level are undertaking tremendous efforts to drive forward Open Access. Examples of the strides made include the OA Strategy adopted by the Federal Ministry of Education and Research in 2016 "Open Access in Deutschland" [Open Access in Germany] and the "OA 2020—initiative for the large-scale transition to Open Access", as initiated by the Max Planck Digital Library, and to which BIBB has also signed up.

In the field of science, technology and medicine (STM) OA is a well-established publication model and its benefits are widely recognised [1] (p. 29). Based on our experiences, we submit the hypothesis that the humanities and social sciences[1] tend to exhibit a greater degree of reticence. OA endeavours in this area are also an object of criticism in Germany. Within the field of vocational education and training research, the supposition is that scepticism and uncertainty are more prevalent because the status of knowledge regarding the topic of OA is lower. This particularly applies in respect of questions that are relating to quality standards, usual financing models, and licensing. Within the scope of an unpublished feasibility study carried out by BIBB for the establishment of a repository, various interviews were conducted with academic researchers in the field of vocational education and training. These were guided expert interviews on the use of Open Access and repositories for academic publications. The Repository project was also presented at a conference that was hosted by the Vocational Education Division at the German Educational Research Association (DGfE). The attitudes that are expressed in the interviews and the controversial debate that occurred during the presentation suggest that views regarding OA tend to be sceptical [3,4].

Only two investigation results on OA as a publication model in the humanities and social sciences in Germany are currently available:

Ulrich Herb: "Open Science in der Soziologie" *[Open Science in sociology]* [5] and Doris Bambey: "Fachliche Publikationskulturen und Open Access. Fächerübergreifende Entwicklungstendenzen und Spezifika der Erziehungswissenschaft und Bildungsforschung" *[Specialist publication cultures and Open Access. Cross-disciplinary tendencies and specific characteristics of the educational sciences and education research]* [6].

The work that was carried out by Herb [5] focuses on the topic of Open Science and provides an inventory within the discipline of sociology. According to Herb, the term Open Science describes a cultural shift in practice and communication in academic research. Computer-aided work and digital communication are facilitating a more effective and more open exchange of information within the academic research community and are fostering the transfer of results to society. Open Access to academic research publications, research data and research software in a way that is limited by as few financial, technical, and legal barriers as possible is expanding transparency and opportunities for quality assurance of academic research work. Better provision of information is increasing the efficiency of academic research and is enhancing the innovation that takes place on the basis of research findings by making it easier to transfer knowledge to trade and industry and to society [7].

Within this context, Herb views Open Access as one of several sub-sections of Open Science. The author investigates the dissemination of Open Science on the basis of a literature study and presents arguments for and against. He also explores the extent to which the openness of academic research is encouraged and has already been realised. In addition, he uses database analyses to compare the status quo of Open Science in German-language sociology with the area of STM. In his investigation, Herb [5] (p. 417) arrives at the conclusion that in the area of sociology OA does not appear in any way to be a phenomenon that has been disseminated to a below-average extent (. . .). The main focus is on specialist journals; monographs seldom being published in OA form. Herb surmises that this could be connected to the OA publishing houses' lack of reputation [8]. Because sociology is a related academic discipline of vocational education and training research, the supposition is that the reputation of publishers could also play a part in the decision of whether to publish a VET research text via OA or in a closed-access publishing house. It is unclear whether the role of the publishing houses has a similar level of significance to that identified by Herb in the field of sociology. It remains to be seen whether the importance of the reputation of publishing houses will emerge as a possible inherent condition within

---

[1] In accordance with Max Weber, we understand social sciences to include all research disciplines which analyse the phenomena of human co-existence. We generally relate the term humanities, particularly with regard to the clear way in which it is delineated from the sciences, to the tradition of thought which emerged in Germany following the Enlightenment [2].

the academic research system with regard to acceptance of Open Access within the further course of the research project, and particularly in the exploratory phase of data collection.

According to Herb, greater emphasis should also be placed on the broader reach of OA publications. However, he also notes that there is an absence of studies dealing with this thematic area (…) [5] (p. 418). The author also identifies that there is absolutely no tradition of OA in sociology in the field of research data and software. The same applies in respect of "Open Review" or "Open Metrics" procedures. Herb [5] (p. 419) thus arrives at the following overall conclusion with regard to Open Science. The culture of open knowledge is not widespread in sociology. Even in the case of Open Access to journals (…), there is very little evidence of open information within the meaning of Open Definition.[2] Open Access journals in the field of sociology very rarely use licences that meet the requirements of Open Definition.

Bambey [6] presents the current status of OA in the educational sciences and uses a literature analysis to investigate the effect of specialist and socio-cultural constellations on publication behaviour. She also looks at the constellations of publishing houses on the market and at information structure conditions. In addition, Bambey takes an empirical survey as the basis for analysing the user behaviour of readers at the peDOCS Repository, which is a full-text database.

She concludes that, (…) the respective specialist cultural starting points and economic constellations of interests very strongly [determine] how the Open Access paradigm materialises, the impact it achieves and the acceptance it enjoys" [6] (p. i). Therefore, the important conditions from Bambey's point of view are the specialist cultures and the economic interests that are associated with the dissemination of academic research texts. She states that both of these exert an influence on the acceptance and impact or dissemination of OA. She further concludes that status-related differences in publication behaviour are becoming visible. Bambey writes that more than half of the professors surveyed have already published via Open Access (…), whereas this is true to a much lesser extent for the group of young academic researchers [6] (p. 277). The intention is for the research project to draw on these considerations and results with the goal of identifying conditions that favour the acceptance, dissemination, and use of OA. A further objective is to investigate whether the dependency between publication behaviour and status of the person and an influence of specialist cultures from related disciplines can also be found in vocational education and training research.

The "Study of Open Access Publishing" (SOAP) is a further important source that has looked specifically at OA in the humanities and social sciences. This was a project financed by the European Commission. During the period from 2009 to 2011, it studied the attitudes that were adopted towards Open Access by academic researchers all over the world and also examined their experiences of OA publications [10]. The study concluded that respondents were highly supportive of OA, although financing and quality assurance were viewed as major hurdles. Pending more precise analysis of the investigation, one criticism that must be levelled is that respondents were contacted via mailing lists from cooperating OA publishing houses such as BioMed Central or Thomson Reuters, and the supposition must therefore be that they were already familiar with OA. 52 percent of participants stated, for example, that they had already published an OA article.

Against this background, the research project will investigate the issue of which technical and structural, policy-related, and normative conditions (legislation), and which conditions inherent within the field of vocational educational and training research are effective with regard to the acceptance, dissemination, and use of Open Access as a publication model. In doing so, the attitudes, evaluations, and inhibitions of researchers in their role as authors are to be disclosed for this field of academia. The project will also look at the area of conflict between authorship and use of academic research

---

[2]   Herb refers to the definition produced by the Open Knowledge Foundation [9] "Open means anyone can freely access, use, modify, and share for any purpose (subject, at most, to requirements that preserve provenance and openness)". The aim of the research project is to investigate this assessment and to examine which conditions exert an influence on the acceptance and dissemination of OA within the field of vocational education and training research.

publications. Authors are always users of academic research publications, and this means that their interests in these two capacities may diverge.

Because vocational education and training research includes contents from various disciplines [11] (p. 610), [12] (p. 79), and given the fact that these are influenced by a range of academic research approaches and work methods and by different publication traditions and behaviours [13] (p. 658), the supposition must be that the results that emerge from the research project regarding publishers' conduct and attitude towards OA in VET research will be at least partially transferable to other social sciences and humanities.

3. Background to the Research Project with Regard to Media Theory and Research on Science Communication

The research project is based on media theory and research into science communication in order to identify, describe, and reflect developments in the field of Open Access. The aims are to create an understanding of the economic relevance of knowledge and of science, and to present the sequences of science communication and the publication systems that vary according to disciplines. These form the context for the research issue centring on the conditions governing the acceptance, dissemination, and use of Open Access.

The transformation of the work and industrial society into a knowledge society [14] (p. 19), which began in the 1990s, and the consideration of knowledge as a production factor alongside land, capital, and labour have ushered in a new economic era by establishing specific infrastructures for the distribution of knowledge [14] (p. 19). Lyotard [15] (p. 31) emphasises the increase in the significance of knowledge in terms of its value as a commodity. Within this context, the focus is no longer primarily on the utility value of knowledge. The emphasis has now shifted to its exchange or sale value [16] (p. 104). This economisation of knowledge is also not being held up by the science system and by the publication and communication structure that pertains there. Academic publishers are now using the massive price increases that have ensued in the wake of this development to achieve impressive returns on sales in a field, which was once non-commercial [15] (p. 31), [17] (p. 7). Publishing houses are benefiting from one particular aspect of research knowledge in this regard. Research results published in such media usually need to be original. This means that research results may not already have been published either in whole or in part. Publication in relevant academic journals turns research knowledge into a unique commodity, the dissemination of which is then managed by the publishing houses. This circumstance is joined by a further economisation factor in the shape of the constantly growing number of research publications. Taubert/Weingart [18] (p. 23) trace various reasons for this development. One such cause is the increasing quantitative measurement and the evaluation of research outcomes. This is leading to "salami slicing", i.e., the dividing up of research results across several individual publications. Two further phenomena are "cascading peer review", the passing on of rejected manuscripts within a publishing house or between publishers for the purpose of publication in a less prestigious journal, and a growth in the number of publications in so-called "predator journals[3] [18] (p. 23). The authors also state that the possibility of secondary publication is also leading to an increase in the publication volume.

This growth in research publications is both making it harder for researchers to assess the relevance of results as well as hampering the work of academic research libraries. In their capacity as infrastructure institutions of universities and research institutions, the remit of the latter is to facilitate full access to current research results for researchers. For this reason, libraries face the dilemma of not being able to fall back on lower cost research results, and are thus compelled to pay the rising prices of publication media. This further complicated by the fact that most academic research journals (up to

---

[3] The term "predatory journal" was popularised by the American librarian Jeffrey Beall in 2010. It describes journals which
    publish articles in exchange for fees without having a transparent quality assurance procedure in place [19].

50.1% of the high ranking journals in the Web of Science) are in the hands of six major publishing houses. This means that a small number of stakeholders is able to exercise a monopoly. This is a significant economic factor, which, in combination with falling or stagnating library budgets, is leading to the so-called "journal crisis", as this development has also been referred to since the 1990s [18] (p. 12), [20] (p. 11).

Alongside the economisation of knowledge, the opportunities that are brought by digitalisation are also fostering a shift in the formal communication of science, for which Taubert/Weingart [18] (p. 5) deem an examination of the claim to truth of research results by specialist colleagues (peer review) to be essential. The consequence of the so-called revolution in information and communication technologies has been that: The Internet has fundamentally changed the practical and economic realities of distributing scientific knowledge and cultural heritage. For the first time ever, the Internet now offers the chance to constitute a global and interactive representation of human knowledge, including cultural heritage and the guarantee of worldwide access [21] (p. 1). This has brought about a change in mass media communication and in the science communication system [22] (p. 5). The research and publication cycle has become digital. Regardless of publication media, researchers are able to act in an unhindered and free way in publishing their texts via the "green open access road" by using such means as self-archiving in the form of secondary publication on their own websites, on Web 2.0 platforms or in repositories. There are also the opportunities that are afforded by "gold open access", via which an article appears as an initial publication in a freely accessible OA journal or in the form of an OA monograph [17] (p. 10). For the sake of completeness, mention should be made at this point that manufacturing costs for the creation of high-quality products are also incurred in the case of OA publications.

Although the prospects associated with OA for a higher degree of reception of an author's own publications and for better availability of research results are obvious [23] (p. 35), OA tends to be a recognised publication medium in the natural sciences, rather than in the social sciences and humanities, where it has not yet made its mark. In order to answer the question as to why the publication behaviour of researchers in the field of STM is significantly different to those in the humanities and social sciences, it will be helpful to take a look at the necessity for publication in academic research journals. The number of publications in renowned journals that deliver a high impact factor [24] (p. 35) and presence in prestigious places [25] (p. 237) continue to be important for professorial appointments, recruitment procedures, and the granting of tenure. Researchers still need to build up a reputation and stabilise their record. This makes clear the mutually dependent effects that are exerted between the scientific publication system and the reputation system. Individual media, such as journals, book series, and publishing house programmes within a discipline hold a greater or lesser reputation that has its basis in the reputation of the authors published and in the papers that they produce [22] (p. 13). The gaining of reputation is important for publishing houses and academic researchers alike. The reputation of the researchers is, however, also created via recognition received from specialist colleagues. Academic research disciplines differ in terms of choice of preferred publication medium. In the STM field, publication in journals is more likely because the focus is on putting out new findings first [13] (p. 658), [23] (p. 305). In the humanities and social sciences, it is frequently the case that the quality of research papers (...) can only be appropriately evaluated by specialist colleagues who are not merely investigating the same object of research, but who also share the same theoretical and methodological premises [13] (p. 658). In order to make it clear that the same theoretical and methodological premises are being shared, the humanities and social sciences tend to use the monograph as a publication medium for the dissemination of research results [13] (p. 659), [26] (p. 31). The economisation of knowledge described and the journal crisis are focused on academic journals that are of importance in the field of STM. Monographs and other publications that do not necessarily appear periodically are affected to a significantly lesser degree. Accordingly, the assumption must be that pressure to act is stronger in the STM area and that Open Access is considerably more attractive as a publication model than in the humanities and social sciences.

Publishing in prestigious specialist journals has a further purpose in terms of scientific communication and the publication system. The increasing number of publications is contrasted by a limited capacity of perception on the part of researchers. Taubert and Weingart, with reference to Luhmann, assume that the increased volume of scientific publications calls for procedures or mechanisms that reduce complexity. Luhmann describes this process as an orientation towards symptoms instead of the matter itself, which is the meant object. According to Luhmann, "reputation itself is drawn from symptoms and serves as a symptom of truth" [25] (p. 237), [22] (p. 171). To put it more simply, the scientific system needs reduction procedures, such as peer review and the attribution of reputation to a publisher and a published journal. The reputation of the journal is partly based on the reputation of the scientists who publish in it. Based on the reputation of the journal reviewed, a reviewed journal article is considered to be highly relevant, and the quality of the scientific work itself is thus no longer questioned by the readers. Instead, the journal's reputation is trusted. Experts, alongside the Impact Factor Journals, are perceived by young scientists as gate keepers. It is questionable as to whether these quality assurance systems actually function in the manner that is assumed (for the debate see, for example [27–31]). Publishing in OA journals does not differ from subscribed journals in terms of quality assurance. Here, too, peer review is often used; a list of peer-reviewed OA journals is available on the Directory of Open Access Journals (DOAJ) platform.

4. Issues Leading the Research and Methodological Approach

Analysis of the literature listed indicates that technical and structural, policy-related, and normative and inherent academic research conditions may exert an influence on the acceptance, dissemination, and use of OA. Table 1 summarises the findings from the literature. The terms acceptance, dissemination and use of OA are understood by the authors, as follows. Acceptance signifies that the authors understand, endorse, and support the OA model by publishing with Open Access. Use signifies that the authors use Open Access publications for their own scientific work (even if their stance on OA is in fact a critical one). By dissemination we mean the different models for making Open Access publications accessible (green open access road, gold open access road).

Technical and structural conditions include factors that affect the storage, archiving, distribution, and findability of OA publications. The operation of repositories to serve as a location for the systematic storage of documents is one example in this regard. The financing of OA publications, e.g., by means of a publication fund, represents a further aspect.

Policy-related and normative conditions mainly relate to the statutory foundations of OA. These range from Article 5 (1) of the Basic Law of the Federal Republic of Germany and its implications for transparency and the democratic decision-making process to regulations contained within the German Freedom of Information Act (IFG) and extend to encompass provisions from the Copyright Act (UrhG), such as the right to secondary publication (§ 38 (4) UrhG) and further limitations on copyright (§§ 44a–63a UrhG) [17] (p. 4) [32]. Consideration also needs to be accorded to the new regulations that are promulgated in the Gesetz zur Angleichung des Urheberrechts an die aktuellen Erfordernisse der Wissensgesellschaft (UrhWissG) [Copyright Law Knowledge Society Act].

Legal certainty regarding the use of OA publications that are created by the application of alternative licensing models such as Creative Commons Licences is a further aspect. These assure users that the author has the right to issue the publication, as well as showing them whether and how they may reuse such publications.

Conditions inherent within the academic research system include quality assurance procedures, such as "peer review" and the reputation system. Our assumption is that quality assurance in the OA publication model is a crucial factor for the acceptance, dissemination and use of OA publications. Against the background of the prevailing pressure to publish that exists in the field of research ("publish or perish"), we need to look at how quality and this publication pressure relate to each other with regard to Open Access, and thus constitute the acceptance and use of OA. This also gives rise to the question as to the significance accorded to OA in VET research from the point of view of the academic researchers themselves, particularly with respect to status and career issues.

The following matrix summarises possible conditions relating to the acceptance, dissemination, and use of OA.

The aspects and questions summarised in the RLTW Matrix show the complexity of the object of research. It will help us to structure our findings during the different steps of the analysis during the research process.

To answer the research question we will carry out an empirical analysis, which will follow a Sequential Mixed Design [33] (p. 21). It will combine a chronologically occurring qualitative strand and a quantitative strand.

Focus Group [34] is the research method chosen for the qualitative strand. It allows for the topic of Open Access to be explored and hypotheses to be generated. By conducting Focus Group, we aim to establish a picture of relevant technical and structural, policy-related, and normative and inherent academic research conditions that exert an influence on the acceptance, dissemination, and use of Open Access in vocational education and training research.

Table 1. RLTW [1] Matrix on possible conditions for the acceptance, dissemination and use of Open Access in vocational education and training research.

Matrix of the Possible Feature Space	Perspective of the Authors		
	Acceptance of OA	Dissemination of OA	Use of OA
Technical and structural conditions	Which technical and structural conditions influence the acceptance of OA? e.g., proofreading for quality assurance/impact measurement procedures/IT structures of long-term archiving	Which technical and structural conditions influence the dissemination of OA? e.g., publication and financing models	Which technical and structural conditions influence the possible uses of OA? e.g., access/research opportunities, usefulness, reliability, quality
Policy-related and normative conditions	Which policy-related and normative conditions influence the acceptance of OA? e.g., support for (IT) infrastructure and academic research career opportunities	Which policy-related and normative conditions influence the dissemination of OA? e.g., copyright, limitations on copyright, funding conditions	Which policy-related and normative conditions influence the use of OA? e.g., legal certainty via alternative licensing models, financial support
Conditions inherent within the academic research system	Which conditions inherent within the academic research system influence the acceptance of OA? e.g., structuring of science communication/peer review procedures for quality assurance	Which conditions inherent within the academic research system influence the dissemination of OA? e.g., change in communication opportunities	Which conditions inherent within the academic research system influence the use of OA? e.g., acceptance of academic research, reputation

[1] The matrix is named after the authors of the application, and the abbreviation comprises the initial letters of their surnames.

The research concept presents two to three Focus Groups with five to eight participants who are professionals in the field of vocational education and training research. Characteristics, such as scientific status and professional position, the academic degrees they hold, age, and gender will vary between the participants of each group. This course of action will enrich the discussion with different opinions and experiences concerning (acceptance and use of) Open Access, as well as mechanisms of the scientific community (e.g., ways to gain reputation and develop an academic career). Personal contacts to researchers in the field of VET will lead to participants from VET research institutions and universities fulfilling the described requirements. The Focus Groups will take place in different locations in Germany near to these institutions and universities.

Each Focus Group will start with a stimulus to introduce the topic of Open Access. The following phase of discussion with low moderator involvement will allow for the participants to focus on aspects that are of high relevance from their point of view. Interaction will show differences in valuation. A second phase of discussion with substantial involvement of the moderator will follow in order to refer to research results and public strategies of Open Access. Questions and assertions from the moderator will provoke comments. This phase secures results concerning aspects such as reputation via Open Access publications, financing, or quality insurance in case the first phase of discussion did not cover these.

The Focus Group discussions will be audio recorded, and a specific software for Qualitative and Mixed Methods Research (MAXQDA) will enable us to analyse the transcripts of the recording. They will undergo a Thematic Analysis, which is a special method of Qualitative Content Analysis in accordance with Mayring [35] and Schreier [36]. This method allows for the deductive and inductive coding processes to be combined in one coding system. Concept-driven, deductive categories will come from the RLTW Matrix. Data-driven, inductive (sub-)categories are filtered out from the material itself following the principles of Inductive Category Formation [35] (p. 79). An intra- and intercoder check will enhance reliability and objectivity, and, by comparing the categories with the research question, the validity of the process will be benefited.

The aim of the Thematic Analysis is to allocate each category and subcategory to one of the nine fields of the RLTW Matrix. The vertical assignment shows if it deals with acceptance, dissemination, and/or use of Open Access. The addressed conditions—echnical and structural, policy-related, and normative or conditions that are inherent within the academic research system—indicate the row. The analysis will show which conditions are more important to the researchers and if it is acceptance, dissemination, or use of Open Access that concerns them most.

The results of the Thematic Analysis will lead to hypotheses for the quantitative strand of the study. This strand consists of an online survey with a questionnaire that focuses on selected conditions of acceptance, dissemination, and use of Open Access in the field of vocational education and training research. The selection will be based on the results of the Thematic Analysis. The aim is to reduce the conditions dealt with in the questionnaire to a reasonable number as well as to focus on aspects of relevance for the VET researchers participating in the survey. We regard all academic persons who are scientifically dealing in one way or another with VET topics as 'researchers in the field of VET'.

A large-scale internet search will lead to email addresses of VET researchers in Germany, as well as additional information e.g., name, academic status, institution, academic discipline/field, research focus, and publication experience. We assume that there are at least 1000 researchers in the field of VET. Nevertheless, the number of VET researchers in Germany is still unknown and it will be revealed as a by-product of the research project.

We plan to encourage all researchers in the field of VET in Germany to participate in this online survey. They will receive a personal link to open the questionnaire. The information that is gained from the internet search helps us to assess the representability of the sample that answered the questionnaire. Statistical analysis of the closed-ended questions using a Likert-type scale will be carried out with a specific software (e.g., SPSS). However, details are determined through the first strand of the study and they will evolve during the research process.

All research will be conducted in the spirit of an "Open Science" project. This means that all texts, methods, (raw) data, evaluations, questionnaires, etc. will be published on a project homepage insofar as this is compatible with the stipulations of the Data Protection Act. Interactive tools (such as a commentary function) will be made available via this homepage in order to permit networking to take place with those members of the general public who are interested.

5. Conclusions

As described, OA is a well-established publication model in the field of science, technology, and medicine. In the humanities and social sciences, which include vocational education and training research, there is greater restraint. The reason for this is assumed to be the low level of knowledge about OA and its possibilities and advantages. Currently, only a few research results on OA as a publication model in the humanities and social sciences are available. The intention of the research project is to investigate this desideratum of research and to reveal VET researchers attitudes toward OA.

Author Contributions: Conceptualization, K.L., B.R., K.T. and M.W.; Methodology, M.W.; Resources, K.L., B.R., K.T. and M.W.; Writing-Original Draft Preparation, B.R.; Project Administration, B.R.

Funding: This research received no external funding.

Acknowledgments: Language Service of the Federal Institute for Vocational Education and Training (BIBB).

Conflicts of Interest: The authors declare no conflict of interest.

References

1. Suber, P. *Open Access*; The MIT Press: London, UK, 2012; ISBN 978-0-262-51763-8.

2. Dilthey, W. *Einleitung in die Geisteswissenschaft: Versuch einer Grundlegung für das Studium der Gesellschaft und ihrer Geschichte [Introduction to Humanities—An Attempt to Lay Basic Principles for the Study of Society and Its History]*; CreateSpace Independent Publishing Platform: Berlin, Germany, 2017; ISBN 978-1484030967.

3. Reuß, R. Unsere Kultur ist in Gefahr [Our Culture Is in Jeopardy]. Available online: http://www.faz.net/aktuell/feuilleton/buecher/urheberrecht-unsere-kultur-ist-in-gefahr-1771956.html (accessed on 25 April 2017).

4. Johnston, D.J. Open Access Policies and Academic Freedom: Understanding and Addressing Conflicts. *J. Librariansh. Sch. Commun.* **2017**, *5*, eP2104. Available online: https://jlsc-pub.org/articles/abstract/10.7710/2162-3309.2104/ (accessed on 30 June 2017). [CrossRef]

5. Herb, U. *Open Science in der Soziologie [Open Science in Sociology]*; Hülsbusch: Glückstadt, Germany, 2015; ISBN 978-3-86488-083-4. [CrossRef]

6. Bambey, D. *Fachliche Publikationskulturen und Open Access. Fächerübergreifende Entwicklungstendenzen und Spezifika der Erziehungswissenschaft und Bildungsforschung [Specialist Publication Cultures and Open Access. Cross-Disciplinary Tendencies and Specific Characteristics of the Educational Sciences and Education Research]*; Technische Universität Darmstadt: Darmstadt, Germany, 2016; urn:nbn:de:tuda-tuprints-56032.

7. Helmholtz Gemeinschaft [Heimholtz Association] Open Science. Available online: https://www.helmholtz.de/forschung/open_science/ (accessed on 30 June 2017).

8. Herb, U. Sozialwissenschaften [Social sciences]. In *Praxishandbuch Open Access [Practical Handbook of Open Access]*; Söllner, K., Mittermaier, B., Eds.; Walter de Gruyter: Berlin, Germany, 2017; pp. 254–260. ISBN 978-3-11-049203-3.

9. Open Knowledge Foundation. The Open Definition. Available online: http://opendefinition.org/ (accessed on 14 June 2017).

10. Dallmeier-Tiessen, S.; Darby, R.; Goerner, B.; Hyppoelae, J.; Igo-Kemenes, P.; Kahn, D.; Lambert, S.; Lengenfelder, A.; Leonard, C.; Mele, S.; et al. Highlights from the SOAP Project Survey. What Scientists Think about Open Access Publishing. Available online: https://arxiv.org/abs/1101.5260 (accessed on 25 April 2017).

11. Sloane, P. Berufsbildungsforschung [Vocational education and training research]. In *Handbuch der Berufsbildung [Handbook of Vocational Education and Training]*, 2nd ed.; Arnold, R., Lipsmeier, A., Eds.; VS Verlag für Sozialwissenschaften: Wiesbaden, Germany, 2006; pp. 610–627. ISBN 978-3-531-15162-5.

12. Weiß, R. Nach der Evaluation ist vor der Evaluation. Zur Berufsbildungsforschung im BIBB [Evaluation is always followed by another evaluation. On vocational education and training research at BIBB]. In *Neue Forschungsverständnisse in den Sozialwissenschaften. Konsequenzen für die Berufsbildungsforschung im Bundesinstitut für Berufsbildung [New Research Understandings in the Social Sciences. Consequences for Vocational Education and Training Research at the Federal Institute for Vocational Education and Training]*; Euler, D., Howaldt, G., Reinmann, G., Weiß, R., Eds.; Bundesinstitut für Berufsbildung: Bonn, Germany, 2008; pp. 75–93. ISBN 078-3-88555-825-5. Available online: http://www.bibb.de/dokumente/pdf/WDP_94_Screen.pdf (accessed on 25 April 2017).

13. Taubert, N.C. Eine Frage der Fächerkultur? Akzeptanz, Rahmenbedingungen und Adaption von Open Access in den Disziplinen [A question of the specialist culture? Acceptance, general conditions and adaption of Open Access in the disciplines]. *Forschung Lehre [Res. Teach.]* **2009**, *16*, 657–659.

14. Willke, H. *Systemisches Wissensmanagement [Systematic Knowledge Management]*; UTB: Stuttgart, Germany, 1998; ISBN 978-3-825220471.

15. Lyotard, J.-F. *Das Postmoderne Wissen. Ein Bericht [Post-Modern Knowledge. A Report]*, 6th ed.; Passagen-Verlag: Vienna, Austrich, 2009; ISBN 978-3-851659023.
16. Stehr, N. *Wissen und Wirtschaften. Die Gesellschaftlichen Grundlagen der Modernen Ökonomie [Knowledge and Economies. The Basic Societal Principles of the Modern Economy]*; Suhrkamp: Frankfurt a.M., Germany, 2001; ISBN 978-3-518-29107-8.
17. Rödel, B. *Open Access in der Berufsbildungsforschung. Status quo und Perspektiven [Open Access in Vocational Education and Training Research. Status quo and Perspectives]*; Bundesinstitut für Berufsbildung: Bonn, Germany, 2017; urn:nbn:de:0035-0651-9.
18. Taubert, N.C.; Weingart, P. Wandel des wissenschaftlichen Publizierens—Eine Heuristik zur Analyse rezenter Wandlungsprozesse [Shift in academic research publishing—A heuristic for the analysis of recent change processes]. In *Wissenschaftliches Publizieren [Academic Research Publishing]*; Weingart, P., Taubert, N., Eds.; De Gruyter Akademie Forschung: Berlin, Germany, 2016; pp. 3–38. ISBN 978-3-11-044810-8. urn:nbn:de:kobv:b4-opus4-26627.
19. Beall, J. Predatory publishers are corrupting open access. *Nature* **2012**, *489*, 179. [CrossRef] [PubMed]
20. Pampel, H.; Bertelmann, R.; Hübner, A. Aktionsfeld Open Access. Rahmenbedingungen und Handlungsoptionen [Action field of Open Access. General conditions and options]. In Wissenschaftsmanagement. *Z. Innov. [Acad. Res. Manag. J. Innov.]* **2009**, *15*, 11–17.
21. Berlin Declaration on Open Access to Knowledge in the Sciences and Humanities. Berlin, Germany, 2003. Available online: https://openaccess.mpg.de/67605/berlin_declaration_engl.pdf (accessed on 03 July 2018).
22. Taubert, N.C.; Weingart, P. "Open Access"—Wandel des wissenschaftlichen Publikationssystems ["Open Access"—change in the academic research publication system]. In *Medienwandel als Wandel von Interaktionsformen [Media Shift as a Change of Forms of Interaction]*; Sutter, T., Mehler, A., Eds.; VS Verlag für Sozialwissenschaften: Wiesbaden, Germany, 2010; pp. 159–181. ISBN 978-3-531-15642-2.
23. Schäffler, H. Open Access—Ansätze und Perspektiven in den Geistes- und Kulturwissenschaften [Open Access—Approaches and perspectives in the humanities and cultural studies]. *Bibliothek Forschung und Praxis [Libr. Res. Pract.]* **2012**, *36*, 305–311. Available online: https://www.degruyter.com/view/j/bfup.2012.36.issue-3/bfp-2012-0040/bfp-2012-0040.pdf (accessed on 25 April 2017).
24. Blasetti, A.; Droß, P.; Fräßdorf, M.; Naujoks, J. Digital ist teilbar. Potenziale und Erfolgsbedingungen von Open Access und Open Data [Digital is divisible. Areas of potentials and conditions for the success of Open Access and Open Data]. *WSI-Mitteilungen* **2017**, *155*, 34–37.
25. Luhmann, N. (Ed.) Selbststeuerung der Wissenschaft [Self-direction of academic research]. In *Soziologische Aufklärung. Aufsätze zur Theorie sozialer Systeme [Sociological Enlightenment. Essays on the Theory of Social Systems]*, 2nd ed.; Westdeutscher Verlag: Opladen, Germany, 1971; pp. 232–252. ISBN 978-3-531110769.
26. Doß, B.; Janello, C.; Thiessen, P. Open Access und Geisteswissenschaften. Widerspruch oder Zukunft? [Open Access and Humanities. A Contradiction or the Future?]. *Bibliotheksforum Bayern* **2014**, *8*, 30–33. Available online: https://www.bibliotheksforum-bayern.de/fileadmin/archiv/2014-1/PDF-Einzelbeitraege/BFB_0114_10_Janello_V03.pdf (accessed on 12 April 2017).
27. Roberts, R.J. Bibliometrics: An obituary for the impact factor. *Nature* **2017**, *546*, 600. [CrossRef] [PubMed]
28. Schekman, R. How Journals Like Nature, Cell and Science Are Damaging Science. Available online: https://www.theguardian.com/commentisfree/2013/dec/09/how-journals-nature-science-cell-damage-science (accessed on 13 January 2017).
29. Callaway, E. Beat it, impact factor! Publishing elite turns against controversial metric. *Nature* **2016**, *535*, 210–211. [CrossRef] [PubMed]
30. Fanelli, D. Negative results are disappearing from most disciplines and countries. *Scientometrics* **2012**, *90*, 891–904. [CrossRef]
31. Ioannidis, J. Why Most Published Research Findings Are False. *PLoS Med.* **2005**, *2*, e124. [CrossRef] [PubMed]
32. Linten, M.; Rödel, B.; Taufenbach, K.; Woll, C. *Wissenschaftliches Publizieren in Zeitschriften der Berufsbildungsforschung [Academic Research Publishing in Vocational Education and Training Research Journals]*; Bundesinstitut für Berufsbildung: Bonn, Germany, 2017; ISBN 978-3-96208-006-8. urn:nbn:de:0035-0682-2.
33. Teddlie, C.; Tshakkori, A. A General Typology of Research Designs Featuring Mixed Methods. *Res. Sch.* **2006**, *13*, 12–28.
34. Kruger, R.A.; Casey, M.A. *Focus Groups. A Practical Guide for Applied Research*, 5th ed.; Sage: London, UK, 2014; ISBN 978-1483365244.

35. Mayring, P. Qualitative Content Analysis: Theoretical Foundation, Basic Procedures and Software Solution. Klagenfurt, Austria. 2014. Available online: http://nbn-resolving.de/urn:nbn:de:0168-ssoar-395173 (accessed on 9 May 2018).
36. Schreier, M. Varianten qualitativer Inhaltsanalyse: Ein Wegweiser im Dickicht der Begrifflichkeiten. [Ways of Doing Qualitative Content Analysis: Disentangling Terms and Terminologies]. *Forum Qual. Sozialforschung [Forum Qual. Soc. Res.]* **2014**, *15*, 18. Available online: http://nbn-resolving.de/urn:nbn:de:0114-fqs1401185 (accessed on 9 May 2018).

Review

Opening the Heart of Science: A Review of the Changing Roles of Research Libraries

Jorge Revez [ID]

Alameda da Universidade, Centro de Estudos Clássicos, Faculdade de Letras, Universidade de Lisboa, 1600-214 Lisboa, Portugal; jrevez@campus.ul.pt

Received: 30 January 2018; Accepted: 5 March 2018; Published: 7 March 2018

Abstract: In a world of information overload and data deluge, is opening science a research library's duty? Or is the openness of science deeply changing libraries, ultimately converting them into something else? The purpose of the review is to highlight the challenging issues stemming from the relationship between research and libraries. A broad literature analysis was performed focused on the intersection of three different perspectives: (1) the future of research libraries, (2) the emerging new roles, and (3) the ongoing openness of science. Libraries are still at the heart of science but challenged by several stakeholders within the complexity of present science production and communication. Research support services, research data management, or research information management are emerging roles, among others, sustaining an open path where libraries thrive to be more collaborative while looking forward to establishing new partnerships.

Keywords: research libraries; open science; research support services

1. Introduction

The impact of digital technology on libraries has brought significant changes. However, their core business remained essentially the same: managing the information that can satisfy the information needs, adding competitive value. In 1933, five types of services provided by libraries to researchers were identified: the accumulation of materials, their availability, personalized help to researchers, publication support and research assistance through international cooperation [1] (p. 128).

Many other services were then added, being the main change systemic, or rather eco-systemic. The new services are but a reaction to competition in an increasingly competitive information environment, as it is no longer just the library system that is at stake, but the relationships that different systems establish between them within a given environment [2].

There is an essential relationship between the science that is produced and the sharing and communication of its results [3]. "Science is, in this sense, always open because knowledge is only effective when it is communicated: Much of the remarkable growth of scientific understanding in recent centuries is due to open practices; open communication and deliberation sit at the heart of scientific practice" [4] (p. 13).

Open science, as a new culture in science, is increasingly known in media and society. This movement towards greater openness grew apace with the development of digital networks and, therefore, it can be said that science is now more "open": "Scientists share results almost immediately and with a very wide audience. Strictly speaking, since the first scientific revolution, science has been open. Through the Internet and Web 2.0 science can become 'more Open Science', meaning that researchers share results, ideas, and data much earlier and much more extensively to the public than they do at the moment." [5] (pp. 10, 11). Among the various possible definitions of open science, let us consider the following threefold perspective: "Open science is defined here as open data (available, intelligible, assessable and useable data) combined with open access to scientific publications and effective communication of their contents" [4] (p. 16).

Recognizing, however, that the library is the heart of the university, the review was organized around three research questions: (1) can we still consider the research library as the heart of institutions dedicated to the construction of science? (2) Is "open science" changing the relationship between libraries and researchers? And (3), to what extent do these libraries contribute to scientific development and to the opening of these institutions to society? If libraries are at the heart of science, their position has undergone profound reconfigurations in a complex process of change that will now be addressed. The new roles, their position in the research lifecycle and their ability to change science itself are some of the aspects that will be analyzed.

2. Literature Search

Intensive research started in September 2016, although the initial exploratory information retrieval began a year earlier and naturally continued after that period, due to the correlation between the different references analyzed. Searches were conducted in the Web of Science databases (for the most relevant literature), Library and Information Sciences & Technology Abstracts (for information science literature), Google Scholar (to perform support searches and to receive daily alerts of new entries), being various sources consulted, available on social networks, such as Facebook, Twitter, Academia.edu, ResearchGate and professional newsletters, among others. The information retrieval here presented is part of an ongoing case study about the relationship between academic/research libraries and researchers in Portugal.

The focus of information retrieval and content analysis is on the intersection of three perspectives: the future of research libraries, the emerging new roles, and the ongoing openness of science. It was included all documents fitting that intersection, with a special attention to those most cited by authors and published after 2010. It was also mentioned some exceptions due to their relevance. A full-text database was built on Google Drive cloud platform and all the references were managed with Zotero (version 5.0.34).

3. What Is (Really) Changing?

One key element in the theoretical framework of the relationship between libraries and scientific research is the definition of "changing environment". The idea that these systems are conditioned and immersed in changes caused by the speed of digital technologies evolution is present today in the scientific discourse on the academic and research libraries. However, "the transformations we are witnessing today are more of a structural nature than essentially oriented by digital technology, that is, the main change is the breakdown of communication linearity, replaced by an interactive network model" [6] (p. 182, in our translation). It is also necessary to understand whether technologies modify the theoretical dimensions that make possible and justify the different forms of action of the libraries or whether the changes are the result of merely superficial variations in the working nature within the science institutions.

According to The Royal Society's 2012 report, this dilemma remains largely unresolved: "A particular dilemma for universities is to determine the role of their science libraries in a digital age. (. . .) The traditional role of the library has been as a repository of data, information and knowledge and a source of expertise in helping scholars access them. That role remains, but in a digital age, the processes and the skills that are required to fulfil the same function are fundamentally different. They should be those for a world in which science literature is online, all the data is online, where the two interoperate, and where scholars and researchers are supported to work efficiently in it." [4] (p. 163)

The change is thus present in the different perspectives from which the research libraries can be observed. It is not, however, a permanent state of change, as if it were an intrinsic and observable characteristic in the phenomenon [7] (p. 1). The key issue is that the environment in which libraries are embedded is deeply affected by the technology issue [8], with all its sociopolitical implications, and the amount of change does indeed promote what could appear to be a permanent state of change.

Brown describes the impact of digital technologies with the image of a S-curve in which the eighteenth, nineteenth, and twentieth centuries corresponded to an era of relative stability, where skills acquired by professionals were lifelong, careers were linear and institutional architectures seemed to last forever [9]. But in the last 50 years of the twentieth century there has been an acceleration, going through increasingly shorter steps, driven by the exponential growth of computing, which does not allow any stabilization in the short term.

Dempsey draws attention—writing on the problem of collections in higher education and research libraries—to the two long transitions that mark this process: the path from physical to digital, and the evolution of the local design of the collections (and ultimately services) to a global, networked experience that results in numerous organizational and behavioral changes [10]. The question of library collections is essential because it deals with the tensions of the so-called "archive of science" defined as "the set of publications (. . .) which is the most perennial testimony of the affirmation of the intellectual priority of scientific discovery. (. . .) It constitutes the formal communication channel of science (. . .) and should be accessible, and therefore preserved. It is on it that the current proposals for the opening of science are focused." [6] (pp. 183, 184, in our translation)

In this new ecosystem, structured by the practice of networks, two paths lie ahead. The first is a response to the reorganization of researchers' work in the digital environment. Dempsey calls it "the inside-out library". Libraries are increasingly supportive of creation, curation and discoverability of institutional outputs (research data, preprints, academic profiles, digitized special collections, etc.) because the creation of knowledge now takes place in the digital environment [10] (p. 339). The university wants to share these materials with the rest of the world, and the library participates in this endeavor. This is a complementary position to the "outside-in" library, whose traditional roles were focused on the selection and acquisition of materials produced outside the institution that were later acquired [11] (p. 5).

The second path is a response to the network reorganization of the information space, being called the "facilitated collection": increasingly, the library does not build collections for local use, it facilitates instead access to a combination of local, external and collaborative services, available in the network and gathered around user needs [10] (p. 339). Immersion in the digital environment and in the networks' fabric is transforming research libraries and the way we look at them [12]. According to Dempsey, the user ceases to be in the life of the library; it is the library that is now in the life of the user [10]. This shift in focus carries libraries into the research lifecycle, and should this cycle be in an opening process, the library can or will have to participate as well.

The two transitions—physical/digital and local/global—are also reiterated in the recent perspective of the MIT Libraries: "We believe that this transformation—from libraries where knowledge is accessed individually through analog and digital means into ones where creation and access to knowledge are dynamically networked—will affect all aspects of the research library." [13] (p. 4).

Hoffman draws a parallel between the iterative nature of the research process and the exploratory culture that libraries should take up to improve user services. She makes essentially reference to the repeated alignment of this development with the satisfaction of information needs. This apparent routine coexists with a creative dimension which is put into practice by librarians: "In order for our constituents to see research libraries as dynamic spaces where research happens, we must cultivate our own interests and explore new things." In this environment, risk is something positive and failure can't be a defeat but an opportunity: "That's what research is, trying something with an uncertain outcome—whether the results are positive or negative, they deserve to be discussed and utilized. Nothing can be learned without making some mistakes." [14] (p. XV).

In summary, this exploratory culture is essential for libraries remain relevant in their institutions. The profound changes brought by a digital, global and networked environment are deeply challenging research libraries. First, print collections and long-term digitization projects are questioned, particularly outside social science and the humanities; second, local literature selection and acquisition is overridden by commercial offers and major publishers' decision; third, networks are the workspace of science and where libraries will have inevitably to be.

4. The Future Is Now: RLUK, ARL and LIBER

Looking at the most recent strategic documents of the three main professional institutions in the field of research libraries, it is interesting to note not only the identity dimension, that is, what is understood as a research library in each of them, but also the dynamics of change that these documents reveal.

RLUK (Research Libraries UK), designation adopted since 2008, was established in 1983 under the name CURL (Consortium of Research Libraries). It is a network of 37 research libraries from the UK and Ireland. Its strategic document for the years 2014–2017 is titled "Powering Scholarship". It makes reference to the place or role that research libraries are expected to play within academia: the focus on library development is intended to drive research and innovation across disciplines by acting in the duality of changes in the landscape of information and by permanent valuation of heritage (collections of books, manuscripts and rare archives), a combination of modernity and tradition [15]. The identity presented by RLUK anticipates that libraries can contribute to the knowledge economy on a large scale through innovative projects and services that add value and impact to the process of research and training of researchers.

The five pillars of RLUK's strategy for 2014–2017 suggest such ongoing reconfiguration as well. First, the reformulation of the modern collection of research libraries; followed by the opening of the science communication cycle, including the editing and management of research data. Thirdly, the exhibition and exploitation of library collections, revealing above all what seems to be still hidden from the eyes of researchers and the public. Fourth, another strategic objective is mapping the landscape of changing research, the role of libraries in research and training of researchers, especially assisting library managers to identify the areas where they can add value. Finally, the goal is to set up a creative community by developing leadership and innovation, both by thinking about good practices and encouraging libraries to measure and demonstrate their value to scholarly communities [15] (p. 5).

The ARL (Association of Research Libraries) brings together 125 libraries from the United States of America and Canada. Having been established in 1932, it is one of the most important and oldest library associations. The strategic vision presented in 2014, in view of the year 2033, was the result of a study of the professionals, as well as the analysis of the strategic documents of the various institutions that make up the association. The current change is clearly expressed in this formula: "In 2033, the research library will have shifted from its role as a knowledge service provider within the university to become a collaborative partner within a rich and diverse learning and research ecosystem. [16] (p. 17) This transition from "suppliers" to "collaborators" presents research libraries with more complex challenges, inherent to an era of constant imbalance.

One of these challenges consists in a change of attitude on the part of the information professionals themselves. In the prologue to the update of ARL's strategic document, Brown reports a dialogue that is paradigmatic. A colleague, who had asked Brown about the long-term significance of Google Glass, was laughing about the future of research libraries, having Brown replied that libraries had the opportunity to become the center of learning in the ubiquitous information world, because they complement and structure all the new ways in which we learn from each other [17]. The awareness that librarians can take on this educational mission as trainers and facilitators is a radical step towards breaking the ties with the prejudice that libraries are dispensable vis-à-vis the generalized supply of information provided by the WWW.

Participants in the strategic reconfiguration process promoted by ARL have also recognized three key changes that will occur over the next twenty years: (1) the library has shifted its focus from service provider within a single university to becoming a partner and actively collaborate within a broader higher education ecosystem; (2) libraries will be even more committed to supporting the lifecycle and range of knowledge discovery, use and preservation activities, as well as curating and sharing in various contexts of the mission of the university and society; (3) the ARL—the organization—will enable libraries to articulate both individually and collectively with one another to promote learning, research and social impact [17] (pp. 19, 20).

LIBER (Ligue des Bibliothèques Européennes de Recherche—Association of European Research Libraries) was established in 1971 and brings together over 420 national libraries, higher education and research libraries. The strategic document for 2018–2022 focuses on the role of libraries in the sustainability of knowledge in the digital age, particularly how libraries will enhance it. The foreseen changes are multiple: open access is the predominant form of publication; the research data are FAIR (Findable, Accessible, Interoperable and Reusable); digital skills support a more open and transparent research lifecycle; research infrastructures are adapted and bring together the various disciplines of knowledge; the cultural heritage of the future is built into the digital information of the present. Against this background, LIBER sets out three strategic directions. Research libraries in 2022 should be: innovative science communication platforms, service and digital competencies centers, and partners in the interoperable, scalable and interdisciplinary research infrastructure [18].

The three strategic documents recognize that the ongoing changes place the research library as an active participant in the transition between tradition and modernity. Their role as creative agents and promoters of innovation is a horizon that could allow libraries to continue to deliver value-added services and products. Likewise, the collaborative dimension is corroborated in the three documents, particularly the role of the research library as a learning center. This educational mission and the sustainability dimension of information flows will be essential bases for science production and dissemination. Libraries' intervention in the research lifecycle is seen by the three associations as the new place that libraries should occupy.

5. The Changing Roles of Research Libraries

Based on the work of Wendy Lougee it is possible to begin the mapping of ideas about the changing roles of research libraries. For this author, in the 1990s, the two key components with which libraries were debated were distributed technologies and open paradigms. To conceptualize this new standing, Lougee proposes the concept of diffuse libraries, in which it is recognized that the universe of information is more distributed and that the library is no longer the center of this universe. At the same time, the conceptions surrounding the idea of "openness" (open access, open source, etc.) also emerge, emphasizing the collaborative and sharing dimension, disruptive elements towards a central position, and ultimately isolated one, occupied by the research library. A new set of functions is thus proposed:

With the incorporation of distributed technologies and more open models, the library has the potential to become more involved at all stages, and in all contexts, of knowledge creation, dissemination, and use. Rather than being defined by its collections or the services that support them, the library can become a diffuse agent within the scholarly community (. . .) we see the library becoming more deeply engaged in the fundamental mission of the academic institution—i.e., the creation and dissemination of knowledge—in ways that represent the library's contributions more broadly and that intertwine the library with the other stakeholders in these activities. The library becomes a collaborator within the academy, yet retains its distinct identity. [19] (p. 4)

The immersion of libraries within the processes of science production and dissemination—surpassing its role as guardian of the archive of science—was thus the result of the emergence of a new culture—distributed, open, diffuse—that would later also be deeply marked by the assumption of the social web and by the new forms of sharing and collaboration that were developed. Lougee recognizes these various forces are visible in a broad set of changes in the focus of libraries: from archiving of scientific publications to participation in the whole process, including the development of an infrastructure supporting all the tasks of science; from collections' holder to the value added by the competences; from access to information provider to the creation of meaning in informational chaos; from mediation between information needs and collections to facilitation, disintermediation and development of mechanisms that favor the individual work of users; from a local library perspective to the globalization of science [20] (p. 612).

The paradigm shift seen in the roles of research libraries is, for Lougee, the result of a set of anomalies (widespread information supply, computer development, and network power) that call into question a mindset centered in collections, normalization and reactive mode of action. It is not, however, a mere transition to the digital context, since there is a deep reconfiguration of the roles of libraries [20] (p. 613). If the collection no longer occupies the center of the universe of information, a constant adaptation to changes in science is required, particularly the emergence of cyber-science or e-science [21], and digital technologies. Hence, new roles emerge such as the ability to collaborate, to render resources profitable, to simplify complex situations, to understand processes, to empower resources, as well as the ability to adapt the global science infrastructure to local needs [20] (p. 621).

From the literature review on this topic, we can see a profusion of studies (which increases in 2010) in recent years that seek to reflect on the new roles that research libraries are assuming (other reviews can be found in [22–24]). For Anglada [25], the focus of the libraries in the construction of collections was shaken by the changes in science communication [26]. This has led to a reorganization of research support services, from open access, through the development of repositories, to increasing the visibility of researchers.

Webster [27] shows that investment in libraries (percentage of university expenditure) has been declining since the 1980s, putting their traditional mission at risk. On the other hand, the scientific communication system is unsustainable, above all due to the rampant price of resources, which leads libraries to prefer acquisition models that don't guarantee ownership and long-term access. If libraries eventually reflect the problems of universities, only an articulation of collective strategies can overcome the pressure to which the system of science is subject.

Case [28] argues that research libraries should play the role of partners in the creation of knowledge. If the creation of new knowledge was previously dependent on the collection, organization, access and preservation that libraries guarantee, in the digital environment libraries now have the opportunity to integrate even more actively into the process of knowledge creation [22]. Their contribution is not only the replication of the previous roles but also the core values (access, preservation, ethics) that the professional community carries in their work. Pathways are provided that researchers can and should adopt: "By being involved in these choices, librarians can help faculty make the decisions that will increase the odds that valuable scholarship in digital form will not be lost. In fact, our goal should be to help make this scholarship easily found, readily used, and permanently preserved." [28] (p. 145)

In an essential work [29], several authors aim to understand the changes in progress. Mentioning only two examples related to changing roles of research libraries, Smith [30] insists that collection, preservation and access are essential functions perceived and received as an inheritance even though the center of gravity of information has been transferred to the internet. The management of resources will be guaranteed in the future by an entity—which may not be called a library—which must be dedicated to two concrete roles: the local function (community information needs, repository management, etc.) and network function, part of a cyberinfrastructure for local and transnational research. The library is the platform embedded in the infrastructure that researchers turn to so they can be part of the network that supports a global and distributed science.

Luce [31] stresses that the main change in the role of libraries concerns the way in which their traditional functions are extended to respond to a collaborative environment characterized by continuous and synchronous communication as well as the question of automatic description mechanisms and others that adapt to the information speed. It proposes three key roles: (1) support for the early stages of knowledge creation, i.e., greater care with the production phase, along with the dissemination of results. This implies not only active collaboration in the planning of research data management [32], but also adherence to less formal means of science communication; (2) the link between scientific communities, through the development of collaborative structures at the WWW and the information needs satisfaction in these environments; (3) the research data curation, the development of metadata standardization, and the strategic design of science participation in the semantic web.

All these aspects lead the library to a laboratory image, moving away from the idea of a warehouse or information silo (see [33]). One of the aspects that contributed decisively to the breakdown of this compartmentalization was the open access movement. Harris [34] found that although open access seems to reduce the importance of libraries in the development of institutional collections, librarians' skills remain essential for the repositories management, metadata structures that allow retrieval of information in open access and preservation mechanisms of resources. On a scale that is now more global than local, the value of libraries is measured by the quality of delivery, including the digitizing of unique collections. The future is about collaboration and sharing of resources and the main change will be the transfer of importance from the library to the librarian: «the information professional is the library of the future» [34] (p. 14).

About a decade ago, one of the most prominent leaders in the renewal of higher education and research libraries in Portugal, wrote at a meeting on research libraries in 2020: «In the coming ten years, local research libraries can and must be nodes of a global network of research information providers. This global network will be composed of different types of repositories that will store, preserve, expose and provide access to the research outputs of the communities to which they are attached» [35].

At the heart of the new ways of science manufacture we find data, but researchers only want to use them and do not spend resources on their collection, organization or preservation [36]. The role of libraries as repositories or information providers is transformed, emerging an active function in the process of scientific research [37]. This activation promotes a partnership instance [38] in which the library provides specialized skills and tools and therefore assumes itself as an integral part of the process. The experience of libraries in the field of interoperability is a guarantee of the effectiveness of this new collaboration: "Libraries have the institutional structure and many of the skills needed to maintain large data sets, make different versions available for different purposes, create metadata linkages, add provenance information, address long-term preservation and archiving, and attend to all of the tasks associated with curation and ensure accessibility on demand." [36] (p. 67).

One of the most interesting documents that has been published in recent years proposes that MIT libraries (and these as models for the world) be viewed as open and global platforms, corresponding to a vision that comprises four dimensions: (1) libraries should conceive its community as global, embracing openness, diversity, global social justice and critical thinking; (2) libraries should develop and facilitate the creation of content platforms and tools that encourage the open dissemination of research and facilitate new methods of discovery and use of information; (3) libraries should be leaders in the long-term management of information resources and in the development of collaborative models for the long-term management of science archive; (4) libraries should become a research and development center, looking for new answers to the major challenges around research libraries and science communication [13] (p. 19).

Another key study was held at Cornell University [39] on the library of the future. The design of this proposal is informed by the data collected and analyzed among the researchers, based on the premise that the traditional focus of libraries on information acquisition and research is insufficient due to the complexity of the research process. The library should thus intervene at different points in the research lifecycle: "research is about much more than finding and evaluating knowledge sources, the traditional focus of information-literacy initiatives. Research is about asking questions, about synthesizing ideas, and about creative problem solving." [40] (p. 553).

One of the main aspects is the role of technology in the research process, particularly the possibility that technology offers in terms of customization. The emergence of these idiosyncrasies forces the library to build an offer of services and products that respond to the individual preferences of researchers so that it can become an «academic hub». In the same sense, collaboration and interdisciplinarity should promote the adoption of tools and applications that allow true interoperability: "The library of the future, as we see it, lies at the juncture of customization and collaboration in support of the overlapping spheres of the research process, academic networking, and self-management." [39] (p. 40).

The main themes that lead to the vision defined by Tancheva et al. are: (1) the research is idiosyncratic and, as such, library services must, rather than organize, give meaning to information (research vs. search); (2) the investigation does not have schedules and is ubiquitous, so the services should also be; (3) notebooks are an essential part of research and are equally idiosyncratic, so services should invest in this area of academic activity; (4) information search and knowledge production systems will certainly fail at a given moment, and the specialized response of library services, personalized, flexible and portable, will be essential then; (5) research is collaborative and, therefore, libraries should support and facilitate collective work [39] (p. 40).

Acknowledging the central place of technology, libraries must respect the idiosyncratic nature of individual research practices and simultaneously link researchers to the international academic community. Therefore, the library of the future should be an academic hub and an app store—intervening in a permanent, fluid, interconnected and idiosyncratic investigative process—that allows for highly customizable research [39] (p. 41) [see also 40]. An excellent example of the development of these ideas has been the field of digital humanities, in which libraries have reinvented their custodial role, enabling the technological transformation of research and the creation of new perspectives and interpretations [41–43].

RIM (Research Information Management) or CRIS (Current Research Information System), in the European nomenclature, are a typology of tools that aim at the aggregation, curation and use of information about research, with a close relationship with the library. RIM «intersects with many aspects of traditional library services in discovery, acquisition, dissemination, and analysis of scholarly activities, and does so through the nexus with institutional data systems, faculty workflows, and institutional partners» [44] (p. 5). It is data about research rather than data generated by research: and "represents institutional curation of the institutional scholarly record" [44] (p. 8).

Libraries, while seeking to align their activities with the strategic plans of the institutions to which they belong, extend their range of services to support institutional objectives in an essentially digital environment, preserving information produced locally and interconnecting it with the network, as Dempsey had also proposed with the concept of the inside-out library [10]. However, in general, institutions don't recognize libraries as partners in the management of information of this type. Bryant et al. propose that this support can be provided in four dimensions, using the capital of experience and knowledge accumulated by libraries over the years, corresponding to four roles of libraries in research information management (RIM): (1) specialized support in the field of scholarly publications and science communication; (2) the ability to discover and exploit the different levels of network accessibility, including open access; (3) end-user training and support; (4) institutional records curation [44] (p. 13).

Given that there is a problem of visibility, which is not exclusive to research libraries but affects other information services, the concept of the intelligent library: " … an 'intelligent library' is not simply one that has the most up-to-date technology. It is a library that uses technology to respond in a timely and effective way to changes that are taking place in its university." [45] (p. 219) There are three characteristics that libraries must demonstrate: ability to transform the resources that libraries make available; collaboration to improve the way information resources are made available; visibility of the library in a context of internal competition due to the scarce resources available [45] (p. 220).

At the 2017 RLUK conference, one of the topics addressed was the role of libraries in scientific research. These systems should occupy a central place in the ecosystem of science. This requires a cultural shift from the concept of support or collaboration to the concept of partnership: "We need to be creative codevelopers working with the research community if we are to be a research library (…) We should embed library in research questions and processes. [46]" This creativity may be subversive [45] (p. 220) in the sense that one tries to develop the position out of the traditional sphere of action, but simultaneously serving the interests of the institution where one is inserted. This creativity has been applied in open science, in which libraries have sought to take on leadership roles to positively influence—for breaking and for opening—the whole cycle of scientific inquiry. Despite the loss of the monopoly of information and the ownership of the collections, it is now time to proceed with a re-appropriation of the responsibility for the preservation of the digital objects that are scattered on the servers of commercial publishers. This movement should generate not only open access, but also a shared and open collective collection.

As Lynch stresses: "There's a huge problem with public or OA materials on the web: everybody relies on them, but nobody wants to take responsibility for curating and preserving them." [47] (p. 128) In summary, "this future involves a shift away from libraries purchasing content for their local users, towards libraries curating and sharing with the rest of the world the research outputs produced at their institution." [48] (p. 2).

A study carried out in the United Kingdom with experts and information professionals revealed that these have identified five sets of trends in higher education libraries: (1) scientific research is increasingly being supported by large data sets and digital artifacts involving intelligent, open and networked systems; (2) new pedagogies are being supported by flexible and technology-based learning; (3) libraries are changing the emphasis of their collection-centric strategy for service development; (4) the boundaries between professional groups and services are blurring and their identities changing with greater collaboration and training in new skills; (5) the enormous pressure that higher education and libraries are being subject in order to respond to new situations [11] (p. 16).

Although the alignment of the libraries with the institutions is considered essential by the participants, three styles have been detected that can be found to a greater or lesser degree, depending on the context of each organization: the style of service provider, in line with the requests of the institution; the users partner style and other services within projects or embedded work; finally, the leader style, in which the library assumes a role of innovation, strategy, and vision [11] (p. 36). The authors also considered several paradigms or thought models that help anticipate the future of libraries. From the ones already identified in the literature such as the hybrid library or "library in the life of the user", the service-oriented library or globalized library were added, among others [11] (p. 50).

6. An Open Identity

One of the great challenges is to understand whether the collaborative dynamics between services and researchers don't lead to a process of identity erosion of the libraries themselves [11] (p. 56). The ability to perceive change within the scope of social sciences usually requires the use of tools capable of working large data sets. A recent example is the ongoing international study on the discovery and access to scientific information by early-career researchers, led by David Nicholas (CIBER Research Group). Preliminary results show that the problem of library support for research has to be observed in conjunction with other elements of the science ecosystem (such as publishers), and given the massive supply of information, which has increased with improvement of the WWW services (mainly the Google platforms, but also the social networks of researchers), or with the increasing availability of resources in open access [49].

However, Nicholas states that the observation of this group does not bring good news for the libraries: "The picture is more worrying for libraries, as their scholarly services seem to have lost all visibility. Many early-career researchers have not set foot in their library for years, and consider them mainly as places for undergraduates to work. As with publisher platforms, Google has supplanted their discovery systems. To make matters worse, institutional repositories are not popular, either." [50] (p. 8).

Libraries are facilitators of access to information, mainly through the acquisition of resources—when there is awareness of who acquires the information—but they don't support the capacity for discovery, which is a relevant fact if we consider that young researchers will be the researchers of the future and the trainers of future researchers.

In any case, the science network includes libraries, which are part of the R & D system. They participate in several projects and are considered in some decisions. Among other things, they are an essential tool for the archive of science management. As Bush noted in his famous report, calling for a firm investment in information services: each new finding depends on the previous ones, and the scientist must master the additions to the "knowledge warehouse". The magnitude of the task of keeping all this knowledge available to the community requires that all possible aids be provided to libraries [51].

Today, libraries support scientific research in a wide range of services: managing publications repositories, providing data required by international rankings or local and national evaluators, supporting research data management, supporting publication processes (books, journals), training of researchers in information skills, support in obtaining scholarships and contracts, among others [52]. These services can be embedded in a model that accompanies the entire research lifecycle, and also serves to promote the offer of libraries vis-à-vis the lack of knowledge of researchers: «it is clear that researchers simply do not know the scope of what librarians can do for them» [53] (p. 313). Another model was proposed in a pyramid with different levels of service, aiming to lead libraries to the development of sustainable and scalable services in order to reach the largest number of researchers [54] (p. 32).

The multiple presence of libraries in the organization of science is also confirmed in the model presented by Björk, who considers them to be relevant stakeholders, particularly in the communication process. This author understands them as crucial in the construction of the archive of science and in the provision of access to publications, although in the diagrams that form its model libraries perform other functions that go beyond this apparently smaller vision [55].

It has therefore been increasingly clear, for information professionals, one must exit the comfort zone of the so-called traditional attitude, turned inwards. Embedded librarians represent a profound conceptual shift as they are intended to take an active stance towards the communities and organizations they serve [56]. It is required today to redefine the professional profiles and training, and professional recognition of these new skills and roles that derive from traditional profile [57].

A new form of identity emerges that promotes a relocation and separation between professionals and institutions, which is cause for some discomfort for librarians such as Plutchak: "I understand the angst that many in the profession feel about making sure the library stays 'relevant'. But frankly, it sets my teeth on edge when I hear someone argue that we need to develop RDM services or institutional repositories to stay 'relevant'! It's an entirely backward way of looking at the issue." [58] (p. 5).

Anderson notes that libraries and librarians who support research today live in a culture of silent war between a local perspective (as soldiers fighting for the mission of their institution and the needs of their community) and a global perspective (as revolutionaries who want to improve the world of science communication). The conflict arises from the dispute of resources that are scarce and originates from the multidimensional complex generated from the change of the analogical information to the digital era. However, this war may have a relatively simple solution, since funding, being mainly local, will require more soldiers and less revolutionaries [59].

7. Conclusions

Libraries are still at the heart of science, but are challenged by several stakeholders within the complexity of present science production and communication. The literature shows that research libraries are trying to find a place that is not necessarily new, but which is now in an environment with new features. Libraries are and have been responsible for a very important part of the archive of science. This role makes them essential elements for the transition from the "old" processes of science production and dissemination to an environment deeply marked by digital technologies, globalization and the importance of networks. Research support services, research data management, or research information management are emerging roles, among others, sustaining an open path where libraries thrive to be more collaborative looking forward to establishing new partnerships.

The literature also reveals that research libraries contribute to scientific development and to the opening of science institutions to society, although some of the researchers and research leaders don't acknowledge it. Libraries need to remain visible and claim a central position, not based on an information «monopoly», but on an advanced expertise, strong values and willingness to help the research endeavor as they have always done. Their educational mission and their role as a learning center is essential to ensure new partnerships, which is quite clear in the embedded librarianship experiences reported on the literature. This shift in focus—providers to active promoters—transports libraries to the research lifecycle, and if this cycle is in an opening process, libraries can or will have to participate.

Networks, globalization, partnership, cultural shift, enhanced skills, discoverability are keywords in research libraries vocabulary and passwords to cooperate in the opening of science, to fulfil society's strong expectations towards public and private investment.

Acknowledgments: This research had no funding but as part of an ongoing Ph.D. study, I want to show gratitude to my thesis supervisors for all their support: Maria Manuel Borges (University of Coimbra, Portugal) and Carlos Guardado da Silva (University of Lisbon, Portugal). I also acknowledge Carla Esteves who helped me with the English version and the peer-reviewers.

Conflicts of Interest: The author declares no conflicts of interest.

References

1. Wilson, L.R. The Service of Libraries in Promoting Scholarship and Research. *Libr. Q. Inf. Community Policy* **1933**, *3*, 127–145. [CrossRef]
2. Vandegrift, M. Designing Digital Scholarship Ecologies. *LIS Scholarsh. Arch. Prepr.* **2018**. [CrossRef]
3. Garvey, W.D. *Communication: The Essence of Science: Facilitating Information Exchange among Librarians, Scientists, Engineers and Students*; Pergamon Press: Oxford, UK, 1979; ISBN 0-08-022254-4.
4. The Royal Society. *Science as an Open Enterprise*; The Royal Society Science Policy Centre Report; The Royal Society: London, UK, 2012; ISBN 978-0-85403-962-3.
5. Bartling, S.; Friesike, S. (Eds.) *Opening Science: The Evolving Guide on How the Internet is Changing Research, Collaboration and Scholarly Publishing*; Springer: Cham, Switzerland, 2014; ISBN 978-3-319-00026-8.
6. Borges, M.M. Reflexos da Tecnologia Digital no Processo de Comunicação da Ciência. In *Una Mirada a la Ciencia de la Información Desde los Nuevos Contextos Paradigmáticos de la Posmodernidad*; Oficina Universitária: Marília, Brazil, 2017; pp. 179–196, ISBN 978-85-7983-904-7.
7. Dewey, B.I. *Transforming Research Libraries for the Global Knowledge Society*; Chandos: Oxford, UK, 2010; ISBN 978-1-84334-594-7.
8. Earnshaw, R.; Vince, J. (Eds.) *Digital Convergence—Libraries of the Future Rae Earnshaw and John Vince*; Springer: London, UK, 2008; ISBN 978-1-84628-903-3.
9. Brown, J.S. Changing How We Think About and Lead Change. In *Library Workforce for 21st Century Research Libraries*; Association of Research Libraries: Washington, DC, USA, 2012.
10. Dempsey, L. Library Collections in the Life of the User: Two Directions. *Liber Q.* **2017**, *26*, 338–359. [CrossRef]
11. Pinfield, S.; Cox, A.M.; Rutter, S. *Mapping the Future of Academic Libraries: A Report for SCONUL*; Society of College, National & University Libraries: London, UK, 2017.
12. Dempsey, L. *The Network Reshapes the Library: Lorcan Dempsey on Libraries, Services, and Networks*; ALA: Chicago, IL, USA, 2014; ISBN 978-0-8389-1997-2.
13. Institute-wide Task Force on the Future of Libraries. *Preliminary Report*; Massachusetts Institute of Technology: Boston, MA, USA, 2016.
14. Hoffman, S. *Dynamic Research Support for Academic Libraries*; Facet: London, UK, 2016; ISBN 978-1-78330-049-5.
15. Research Libraries UK. *Powering Scholarship: RLUK Strategy 2014-17*; Research Libraries UK: London, UK, 2014.
16. Association of Research Libraries. *Report of the Association of Research Libraries Strategic Thinking and Design Initiative*; Association of Research Libraries: Washington, DC, USA, 2014.

17. Association of Research Libraries. *Strategic Thinking and Design Initiative: Extended and Updated Report*; Association of Research Libraries: Washington, DC, USA, 2016.

18. LIBER. *Research Libraries Powering Sustainable Knowledge in the Digital Age: LIBER Europe Strategy 2018–2022*; LIBER: The Hague, The Netherlands, 2017.

19. Lougee, W.P. *Diffuse Libraries: Emergent Roles for the Research Library in the Digital Age*; Council on Library and Information Resources: Washington, DC, USA, 2002; ISBN 1-887334-93-9.

20. Lougee, W.P. The diffuse library revisited: Aligning the library as strategic asset. *Libr. Hi Tech* **2009**, *27*, 610–623. [CrossRef]

21. Marcum, D.B.; George, G. (Eds.) *The Data Deluge: Can Libraries Cope with e-Science?* Libraries Unlimited: Santa Barbara, CA, USA, 2010; ISBN 978-1-59158-887-0.

22. Lincoln, Y.S. Research Libraries in the Twenty-First Century. In *Higher Education: Handbook of Theory and Research*; Springer: Dordrecht, The Netherlands, 2010; Volume 25, pp. 425–448. ISBN 978-90-481-8598-6.

23. Koltay, T. Are you ready? Tasks and roles for academic libraries in supporting Research 2.0. *New Libr. World* **2016**, *117*, 94–104. [CrossRef]

24. Cox, J. Communicating New Library Roles to Enable Digital Scholarship: A Review Article. *New Rev. Acad. Librariansh.* **2016**, *22*, 132–147. [CrossRef]

25. Anglada, L. ¿Son las bibliotecas sostenibles en un mundo de información libre, digital y en red? *Prof. Inf.* **2014**, *23*, 603–611.

26. Borgman, C.L. *Scholarship in the Digital Age: Information, Infrastructure, and the Internet*; The MIT Press: Cambridge, MA, USA, 2007; ISBN 978-0-262-02619-2.

27. Webster, D. Strategic Challenges Facing Research Libraries. In *Report and Proceedings of a Seminar on Managing University Libraries, Held on 26–27 August 2002 at the OECD Headquarters in Paris*; OECD: Paris, France, 2002.

28. Case, M.M. Partners in Knowledge Creation: An Expanded Role for Research Libraries in the Digital Future. *J. Libr. Adm.* **2008**, *48*, 141–156. [CrossRef]

29. *No Brief Candle: Reconceiving Research Libraries for the 21st Century*; Council on Library and Information Resources: Washington, DC, USA, 2008; ISBN 978-1-932326-30-7.

30. Smith, A. The Research Library in the 21st Century: Collecting, Preserving, and Making Accessible Resources for Scholarship. In *No Brief Candle: Reconceiving Research Libraries for the 21st Century*; Council on Library and Information Resources: Washington, DC, USA; 2008; pp. 13–20. ISBN 978-1-932326-30-7.

31. Luce, R.E. A New Value Equation Challenge: The Emergence of eResearch and Roles for Research Libraries. In *No Brief Candle: Reconceiving Research Libraries for the 21st Century*; Council on Library and Information Resources: Washington, DC, USA, 2008; pp. 42–50. ISBN 978-1-932326-30-7.

32. Heidorn, P.B. The Emerging Role of Libraries in Data Curation and E-science. *J. Libr. Adm.* **2011**, *51*, 662–672. [CrossRef]

33. Gold, A. Cyberinfrastructure, Data, and Libraries, Part 2: Libraries and the Data Challenge: Roles and Actions for Libraries. *D-Lib Mag.* **2007**, *13*. [CrossRef]

34. Harris, S. *Moving Towards an Open Access Future: The Role of Academic Libraries*; Sage: Thousand Oaks, CA, USA, 2012.

35. Rodrigues, E. GRL2020 Position Paper. In *Paving the Way for a Collaborative Global Research Environment: Outcomes of GRL2020 Europe*; GRL2020: Pisa, Italy, 2008.

36. Griffin, S. New Roles for Libraries in Supporting Data-Intensive Research and Advancing Scholarly Communication. *IJHAC* **2013**, *7*, 59–71. [CrossRef]

37. 2nd Global Research Library 2020. *Paving the Way for a Collaborative Global Research Environment: Outcomes of GRL2020 Europe*; GRL2020: Pisa, Italy, 2008.

38. Corrall, S. Designing Libraries for Research Collaboration in the Network World: An Exploratory Study. *Liber Q.* **2014**, *24*, 17–48. [CrossRef]

39. Tancheva, K.; Gessner, G.C.; Tang, N.; Eldermire, E.; Furnas, H.; Branchini, D.; Steinhart, G. *A Day in the Life of a (Serious) Researcher: Envisioning the Future of the Research Library*; ITHAKA and Cornell University Library: New York, NY, USA, 2016.

40. Gessner, G.C.; Eldermire, E.; Tang, N.; Tancheva, K. The Research Lifecycle and the Future of Research Libraries: A Library of Apps. In *At the Helm: Leading Transformation: The Proceedings of the ACRL 2017 Conference*; ACRL: Chicago, IL, USA, 2017; pp. 533–543.

41. Hartsell-Gundy, A.; Braunstein, L.; Golomb, L. (Eds.) *Digital Humanities in the Library: Challenges and Opportunities for Subject Specialists*; The Association of College & Research Libraries: Chicago, IL, USA, 2015; ISBN 978-0-8389-8768-1.

42. White, J.W.; Gilbert, H. (Eds.) *Laying the Foundation: Digital Humanities in Academic Libraries*; Charleston Insights in Library, Archival, and Information Sciences; Purdue University Press: West Lafayette, IN, USA, 2016; ISBN 978-1-55753-739-3.

43. Kamposiori, C. *The Role of Research Libraries in the Creation, Archiving, Curation, and Preservation of Tools for the Digital Humanities*; RLUK Report; RLUK: London, UK, 2017.

44. Bryant, R.; Clements, A.; Feltes, C.; Groenewegen, D.; Huggard, S.; Mercer, H.; Missingham, R.; Oxnam, M.; Rauh, A.; Wright, J. *Research Information Management: Defining RIM and the Library's Role*; OCLC: Dublin, OH, USA, 2017; ISBN 978-1-55653-031-9.

45. Johnson, I.M. The intelligent university library: Developing a more comprehensive option for the researcher. *Inf. Dev.* **2017**, *33*, 219–223. [CrossRef]

46. Kingsley, D. "Become Part of the Research Process"—Observations from RLUK2017. Available online: https://unlockingresearch-blog.lib.cam.ac.uk/?p=1384 (accessed on 7 March 2018).

47. Lynch, C. Updating the Agenda for Academic Libraries and Scholarly Communications. *Coll. Res. Libr.* **2017**, *78*, 126–130. [CrossRef]

48. Confederation of Open Access Repositories. *Next Generation Repositories: Behaviours and Technical Recommendations of the COAR Next Generation Repositories Working Group*; COAR: Göttingen, Germany, 2017.

49. Nicholas, D.; Boukacem-Zeghmouri, C.; Rodríguez-Bravo, B.; Xu, J.; Watkinson, A.; Abrizah, A.; Herman, E.; Świgoń, M. Where and how early career researchers find scholarly information. *Learn. Publ.* **2017**, 1–11. [CrossRef]

50. Nicholas, D. Publish or perish thwarts young researchers' urge to innovate. *Res. Eur.* **2016**, *440*, 7–8.

51. Bush, V. *Science: The Endless Frontier*; National Science Foundation: Washington, DC, USA, 1945.

52. Research Information Network. *The Value of Libraries for Research and Researchers: A RIN and RLUK Report*; RIN: London, UK, 2011.

53. Vaughan, K.T.L.; Hayes, B.E.; Lerner, R.C.; McElfresh, K.R.; Pavlech, L.; Romito, D.; Reeves, L.H.; Morris, E.N. Development of the research lifecycle model for library services. *J. Med. Libr. Assoc.* **2013**, *101*, 310–314. [CrossRef] [PubMed]

54. Vinopal, J.; McCormick, M. Supporting Digital Scholarship in Research Libraries: Scalability and Sustainability. *J. Libr. Adm.* **2013**, *53*, 27–42. [CrossRef]

55. Björk, B.-C. A model of scientific communication as a global distributed information system. *Inf. Res.* **2007**, *12*, 307.

56. Carlson, J.; Kneale, R. Embedded librarianship in the research context: Navigating new waters. *Coll. Res. Libr. News* **2011**, *72*, 167–170. [CrossRef]

57. Brewerton, A. Re-Skilling for Research: Investigating the Needs of Researchers and How Library Staff Can Best Support Them. *New Rev. Acad. Librariansh.* **2012**, *18*, 96–110. [CrossRef]

58. Plutchak, T.S. A Librarian out of the Library. *J. eSci. Librariansh.* **2016**, *5*, 1–5. [CrossRef]

59. Anderson, R. A quiet culture war in research libraries—and what it means for librarians, researchers and publishers. *Insights* **2015**, *28*, 21–27. [CrossRef]

MDPI

St. Alban-Anlage 66

4052 Basel

Switzerland

Tel. +41 61 683 77 34

Fax +41 61 302 89 18

www.mdpi.com

Publications Editorial Office

E-mail: publications@mdpi.com

www.mdpi.com/journal/publications

CPSIA information can be obtained
at www.ICGtesting.com
Printed in the USA
BVHW022310160419
545763BV00016B/455/P